GREGG SHORTHAND 1

LOUIS A. LESLIE
CHARLES E. ZOUBEK
HENRY J. BOER

Shorthand written by CHARLES RADER

Diamond Jubilee Edition

Gregg Adult Education Series

ROBERT FINCH, Consulting Editor
Director of Continuing Education
Cincinnati Public Schools
Cincinnati, Ohio

GREGG DIVISION McGraw-Hill Book Company

New York Chicago Dallas San Francisco Toronto London Sydney

GREGG SHORTHAND 1

16 17 WCWC 0 9 8 7

ISBN 07-037225-X

To the Student

Gregg Shorthand, the Universal System

Millions of people have learned Gregg Shorthand and use it every day. You will find it in business offices, in courtrooms, in government offices, at committee meetings —wherever it is desirable to have a record of the spoken word. At this moment hundreds of thousands of people like yourself all over the world are learning Gregg Shorthand — in high schools, in business and secretarial schools, in colleges, in continuing education classes, and in individual study. Gregg Shorthand is truly the universal system.

The reason that Gregg Shorthand is the most popular system in the world (nearly all schools that offer shorthand instruction offer Gregg) is that it is easy to learn, easy to write, and easy to read. Once it is learned, Gregg Shorthand is fun to write. Aside from its practical value, Gregg Shorthand offers many people an artistic satisfaction. It is graceful and it seems to flow from the pen.

You *can* learn Gregg Shorthand; you *will* learn Gregg Shorthand if you follow the suggestions given in this text and practice faithfully. When you are able to write Gregg Shorthand, you will have acquired a job-assurance policy that money cannot buy. In addition, you will have a personal tool that will be of value to you throughout your lifetime.

Your Gregg Text-Kit — Gregg Shorthand 1

Your Gregg Text-Kit contains the following materials:

A Textbook *(This is it, of course!)*
A Pad of Self-Checks *(tests)*
The Transcript of Shorthand
Dictation Records *(6 discs)*

A good deal of your practice will be done in the textbook itself. However, you will use your notebook when you take dictation in class and from the records, as well as when you copy the shorthand sentences and letters that appear throughout your text.

You will need a fountain pen or a good ball-point pen with which to write (a lead pencil is not recommended for writing shorthand).

Organization of the Textbook

Gregg Shorthand 1 is divided into two parts. Part One, containing 30 sections, presents all the principles of the system. When you have completed Part One, you will be able to construct a legible shorthand outline for any word in the English language.

Part Two contains 10 review and reinforcement sections. Its purpose is to strengthen your grasp of the major word-building principles of the system and to develop your ability to construct shorthand outlines for new words under the stress of dictation.

Today's Secretary

Today's Secretary is a magazine for professional secretaries that provides information on the newest and best in office procedures, skills, and equipment. It makes the shorthand writer aware of the opportunities in the business world and challenges him to go beyond the confines of his desk – both as an employee and as an individual engaged in useful work.

Today's Secretary helps him to do a better job, for each issue contains skill-building materials, such as typing and transcribing speed tests, shorthand reading and writing exercises, spelling, punctuation, and grammar.

For complete information about Today's Secretary, write to Gregg/Community College Division, McGraw-Hill Book Company, 1221 Avenue of the Americas, New York, New York 10020.

Gregg Shorthand 2

When you have completed Gregg Shorthand 1, you will have an excellent foundation for the next phase of your shorthand study – the building of shorthand speed.

Gregg Shorthand 2 – A Gregg Kit in Continuing Education picks up where Gregg Shorthand 1 leaves off. It is designed to help you gain dictation skill and to develop further your mastery of the system. Gregg Shorthand 2 contains shorthand vocabulary drills, Reading and Self-Dictation exercises, as well as step-by-step instructions on how to practice.

Part One

The Principles of
GREGG SHORTHAND

Diamond Jubilee Edition

Your Practice Program

Each of the first 30 sections presents a number of shorthand strokes or word-building principles of the system. In addition, it contains a number of Reading and Self-Dictation Practice exercises, in shorthand, that will help build your shorthand vocabulary. Some of these Reading and Self-Dictation Practice exercises are recorded on your dictation records. Following are suggestions for study and practice.

Principles

Read the explanation of each stroke or word-building principle; then practice the illustrative list of examples in this way:

1. With the key exposed, pronounce and spell, aloud if possible, the shorthand strokes in each outline in the list, thus: *say, s-a; ace, a-s; safe, s-a-f.* By reading aloud, you will be sure that you are concentrating on each word as you study it. Repeat this procedure with all the words in the list until you feel you can read the shorthand outlines without referring to the key.

2. Cover up the key with a card or slip of paper. Then spell and pronounce each word aloud, thus: *s-a, say; a-s, ace; s-a-f, safe.* If you cannot read an outline after a few seconds, move the card or slip of paper aside and refer to the key. *Do not lose time trying to decipher an outline.* Practice reading in this way until you can read all the shorthand outlines without referring to the key.

NOTE: In reading brief forms and phrases, it is not necessary to spell the shorthand strokes in the outline.

3. In the space provided next to each shorthand outline, write each outline just

An effective way to practice is to place a card or slip of paper over the type and spell and read the shorthand words aloud.

Write each outline once; then go back and write each outline twice; finally, fill the space that is remaining.

once, using the shorthand outline in the book as your model. Be sure to say each word aloud as you write it.

4. Then, go back and write each outline *twice*, next to your first attempt, again spelling and pronouncing as you write.

5. Write each outline as many more times as you can in the space remaining.

CAUTION: Don't fill the practice line completely at your first writing. Too much repetition of an outline does little good; it may even deter your progress.

6. Finally, read the Quick Check as a further test of your mastery.

Reading and Self-Dictation Practice

The Reading and Self-Dictation exercises, written in shorthand, contain many illustrations of the strokes and principles presented in the section. They also provide a continuing, automatic review of all the strokes and principles you studied in previous sections. In order to derive the greatest benefit from these exercises, practice them as follows:

Reading

First, read the Reading and Self-Dictation Practice, aloud if possible (reading aloud will help to fix the shorthand characters firmly in your mind).

1. Place your Transcript, which contains the key to the shorthand, conveniently at the right of your textbook. Open it to the page and paragraph that contains the key to the Reading and Self-Dictation Practice from which you are about to read.

2. Place your *left* index finger under the shorthand outline you are about to read.

3. Place your *right* index finger on the key to that shorthand outline.

4. Read the shorthand aloud until you come to an outline that you cannot read. Spell the shorthand characters in the outline. If this spelling does not immediately

Refer to your Transcript whenever you cannot read an outline. Keep your left index finger anchored in the shorthand; the right index finger on the corresponding place in the Transcript.

When copying, read a convenient group of words aloud and then write that group in your notebook. Keep your place in the shorthand as you copy.

give you the meaning, anchor your left index finger on that outline and refer to the Transcript, where your right index finger rests.

IMPORTANT: Do not spend more than a few seconds trying to decipher any outline.

5. Determine the meaning of the outline, and then place your right index finger just below the word in the Transcript.

6. Return to the paragraph in your textbook from which you are reading, where your left index finger has kept your place, and continue reading.

7. If time permits, read the material a second time – perhaps even a third time. The additional readings will impress the outlines on your mind more forcefully.

Copying

After you have read the Reading and Self-Dictation Practice, make a shorthand copy of it in your notebook.

1. Read a convenient group of words, aloud if possible; then write that group in your notebook.

2. Keep your place in the shorthand with your *left* index finger if you are right-handed; with your *right* index finger if you are left-handed.

3. After you have made one complete copy of the exercise, make a second copy if time permits. You will find that this second writing will go much more smoothly than the first.

Your early writing efforts, quite naturally, may not be very fluent, and your outlines may not be as exact as those in your book. As you practice from day to day, however, you will become so proud of your shorthand notes that you will be impatient with any longhand writing that you must do!

Self-Checks

At the end of each section you will be instructed to fill out the appropriate Self-Check in your pad of Self-Checks. The Self-Check will enable you to determine how well you have mastered the strokes and principles presented in a section. Strive to achieve the time and accuracy goals suggested at the head of each Self-Check. When you have completed the Self-Check, compare your work with the key in the Transcript.

Recorded Dictation

Beginning with Section 3, some of the Reading and Self-Dictation exercises are dictated on your dictation records. Instructions on how to get the most out of your records are given in Section 3.

SECTION 1

GREGG SHORTHAND BASED ON LONGHAND

Anyone who has learned to read and write longhand can learn to read and write Gregg Shorthand; it is as simple as that! The strokes you will write in Gregg Shorthand are those that you are accustomed to writing in longhand. In fact, many of the strokes in the Gregg Shorthand alphabet are derived directly from the longhand forms.

In many ways Gregg Shorthand is easier to learn than longhand. In Gregg Shorthand you will have to learn only *one* way to represent a letter; in longhand you had to learn many different ways to represent each letter. Take, for example, the letter *f*. Here are five different ways to write *f* in longhand—and no doubt you can think of other ways:

In Gregg Shorthand there is only *one* way to write *f*, as you will discover later in this lesson.

S-Z

1. S. The first shorthand character you will learn is the stroke for *s*, which is perhaps the most frequently used consonant in the English language. In shorthand, *s* is a very small *downward* curve resembling the longhand comma. Notice how it is derived from the longhand form of *s*.

S 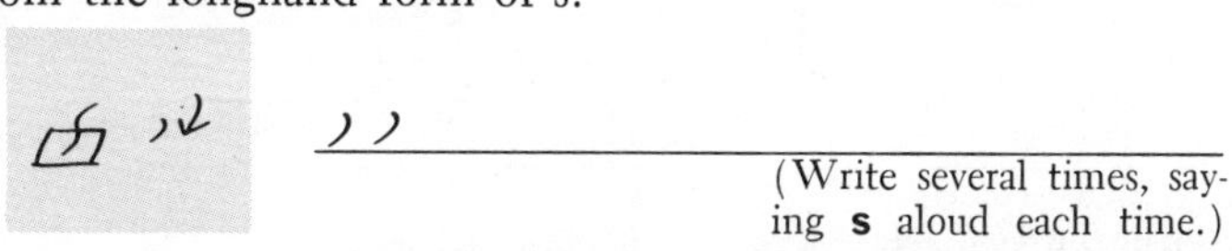

(Write several times, saying **s** aloud each time.)

Often the sound of *z* is represented by *s* in longhand, as in the word *saves*; therefore, in shorthand the *s* stroke is also used to represent the sound of *z*.

A

2. A. The shorthand *a* is a large circle. Notice how it resembles the longhand *a* with its tail cut off.

A 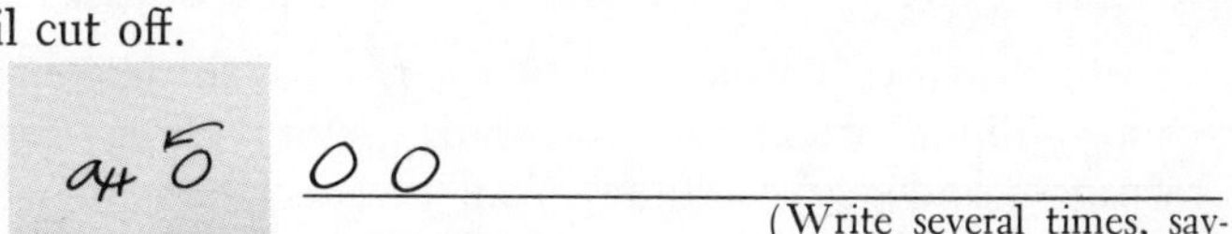

(Write several times, saying **a** aloud each time.)

3. Silent Letters Omitted. In the English language, many words contain letters that are not pronounced. In shorthand, these silent letters are omitted; only the sounds that are actually pronounced in a word are written. In the word *say*, for example, only two letters are pronounced—*s* and *a*; the *y* would not be written in shorthand because it is not pronounced. The word *face* would be written *f-a-s;* the *e* would be omitted because it is not pronounced, and the *c* would be represented by the shorthand *s* because it has the sound of *s*.

An excellent illustration of the time and effort that is saved by writing only the sounds that are pronounced is the word *neighbor*. In longhand, that word requires eight longhand letters; in shorthand, it requires only four—*n-a-b-r*.

In the following words, cross out the letters that would not be written in shorthand because they are not pronounced.

same	**tea**	**train**	**stay**
mean	**save**	**steam**	**snow**
main	**gay**	**stain**	**toe**

4. S-A Words. With the letters *s* and *a*, you can form two words. Write each word several times, spelling each word aloud as you write it, thus: *s-a, say; a-s, ace.*

say, *s-a* 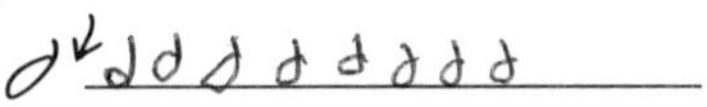 **ace,** *a-s* 

Note: the *c* in *ace* is represented by the shorthand *s* because it has the *s* sound.

F

5. F. The shorthand character for *f* is the same shape as the shorthand *s*, except that it is about three times as big. It, too, is written *downward*.

F 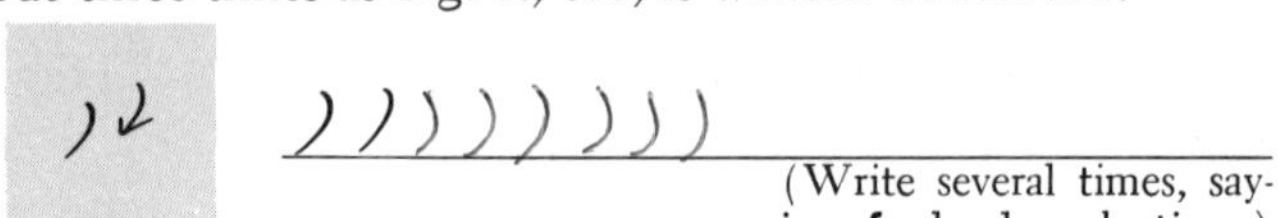

(Write several times, saying **f** aloud each time.)

V

6. V. The shorthand character for *v* is the same shape as *f*, but about twice as big as *f*. Note that it, too, is written *downward*.

V 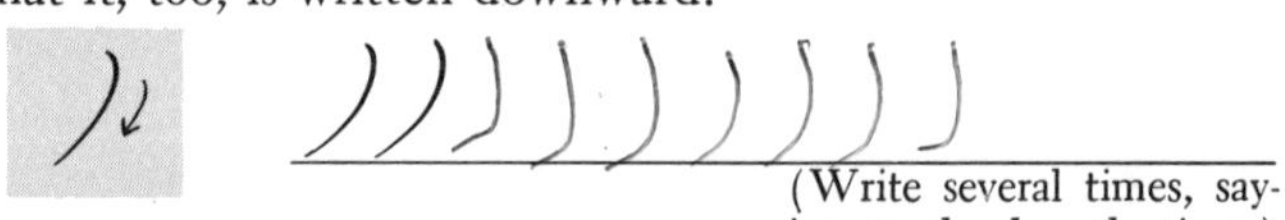

(Write several times, saying **v** aloud each time.)

Observe the difference in the size of the strokes for *s, f, v.*

S F V

(Write this group several times, saying each stroke aloud as you write.)

F-V Words. With the three consonant strokes *s, f, v* and the circle vowel *a*, you can form shorthand outlines for a number of words. Before writing these outlines, however, turn to page 6 and read carefully "Your Practice Program – Principles." Use the procedures suggested there in practicing the following words.

face,
f-a-s
safe,
s-a-f
safes,
s-a-f-s

vase,
v-a-s
save,
s-a-v
saves,
s-a-v-s

Note: The c in *face* has the *s* sound and is, therefore, represented by the *s* stroke.

QUICK CHECK *(Read)*

E

7. E. The shorthand stroke for e is a *small* circle. Notice how it is derived from the longhand e.

E 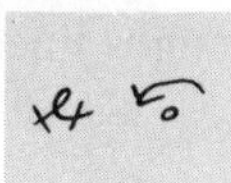

(Write several times, saying **e** aloud each time.)

Here are some words combining the e circle with the s and f strokes. Write each word once. Then go back and write each word twice. Finally, fill in the remaining space.

see,
s-e
sees,
s-e-s
fee,
f-e

fees,
f-e-s
ease,
e-s
easy,
e-s-e

Note: The y in the word easy is pronounced e—it is, therefore, represented by the e circle.

QUICK CHECK *(Read)*

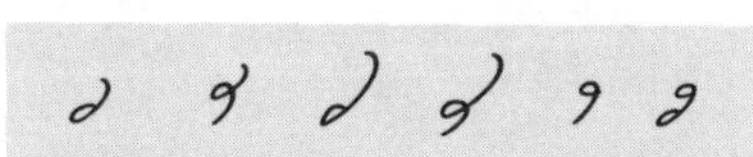

N

8. N. The shorthand character for *n* is a very short forward straight line, written horizontally.

N 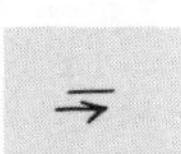

(Write several times, saying **n** aloud each time.)

Note: When you write on ruled paper, place the *n* stroke *slightly* above the line so that it will not be obscured by the printed line.

Practice these words, following the suggestions given on page 6.

see, ______ s-e	**say,** ______ s-a
seen, ______ s-e-n	**sane,** ______ s-a-n
knee, ______ n-e	**vain** ______ v-a-n

Note: The *k* in *knee* is not written because it is not pronounced.

QUICK CHECK *(Read)*

M

9. M. The shorthand character for *m* is a longer forward straight line; it is about three times as long as *n*.

M 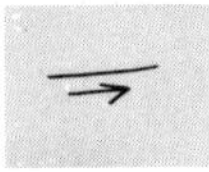 ______ (Write several times, saying **m** aloud each time.)

COMPARE: — N —— M ______ (Write **n-m** alternately a few times.)

Practice these words, following the procedures suggested on page 6.

me, ______ m-e	**seem,** ______ s-e-m
may, ______ m-a	**same,** ______ s-a-m
name, ______ n-a-m	**mean,** ______ m-e-n

QUICK CHECK *(Read)*

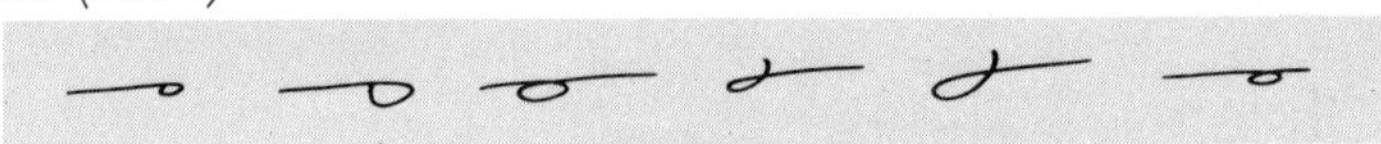

10. Capitalization. In shorthand, capitalization is indicated by two short upward strokes written underneath the word to be capitalized.

Amy **Fay** **May**

11. Punctuation. These special marks of punctuation are used in shorthand.

Period \ **Paragraph** > **Parentheses** ( )

Question × **Dash** ═ **Hyphen** =

12. Reading and Self-Dictation Practice. Frequent reading and writing exercises are provided throughout this textbook under the heading "Reading and Self-Dictation Practice." In the early lessons, these exercises will be partly in longhand and partly in shorthand; in the later lessons, all in shorthand.

The purpose of these exercises is to fix the shorthand forms firmly in your mind and to help you develop facility in constructing shorthand outlines for a constantly expanding vocabulary.

To derive the greatest benefit from this material, be sure to follow the practice suggestions on pages 7 and 8 for reading and copying the Reading and Self-Dictation Practice exercises.

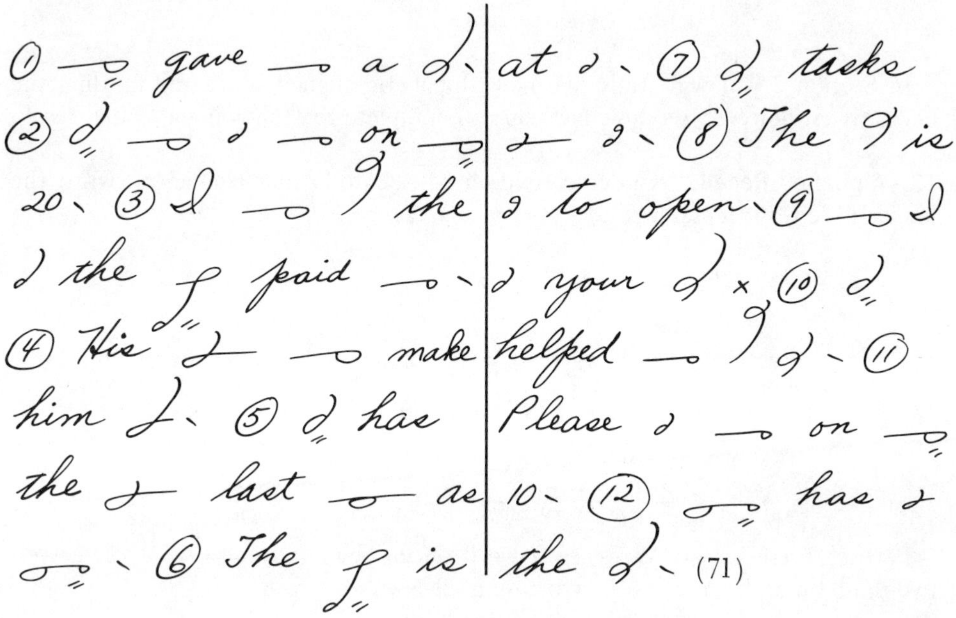

SELF-CHECK 1

To help you determine your progress from time to time, a set of short self-checks is provided in a separate pad that is included in your Text-Kit.

At this point you are ready to check your mastery of the strokes you have studied thus far. Turn to Self-Check 1 on the pad and follow this procedure:

1. Note the time at which you begin your work on the Self-Check.
2. Complete Part 1 of Self-Check 1.
3. Detach the sheet from the pad.
4. Transcribe (in longhand or on the typewriter) the sentences in Part 2 on the back of the sheet.
5. Note the time at which you complete the Self-Check.
6. Check your work against the key to Self-Check 1, which appears in your Transcript.
7. Compare your speed and accuracy achievements against the goals suggested for Self-Check 1. If you reach or surpass those goals, you may proceed to the next section with confidence; if you fall considerably short of those goals, you would be wise to review Section 1.

SECTION 2

In Section 2 you will study five new alphabetic characters. Before tackling the new strokes, however, see how fast you can complete the following alphabet recall.

13. Alphabet Recall. Underneath each of the following characters, write the longhand letter it represents.

T

14. T. The shorthand character for *t* is a very short upward straight stroke.

T  (Write several times, saying **t** aloud each time.)

Practice these words. Write each word once. Then return to write each word two more times. Finally, fill the remaining space. *Spell as you write.*

eat, *e-t*
tea, *t-e*
stay, *s-t-a*
meet, *m-e-t*
seat, *s-e-t*
team, *t-e-m*

QUICK CHECK *(Read)*

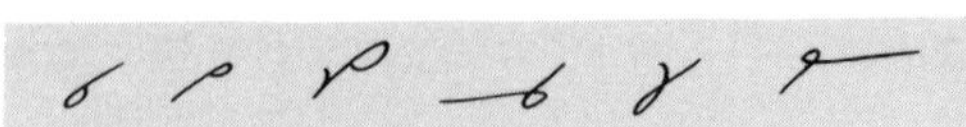

D

15. D. The shorthand character for *d* is a longer upward straight stroke, approximately three times as long.

D  (Write several times, saying **d** aloud each time.)

COMPARE: T D (Write **t-d** alternately a few times.)

Practice writing the following words, using the procedures suggested on page 7. Spell as you write.

aid, a-d	**saved,** s-a-v-d
need, n-e-d	**day,** d-a
made, m-a-d	**date,** d-a-t

QUICK CHECK *(Read)*

16. Reading and Self-Dictation Practice. Be sure to follow the suggestions for reading and copying the Reading and Self-Dictation Practice given on page 7.

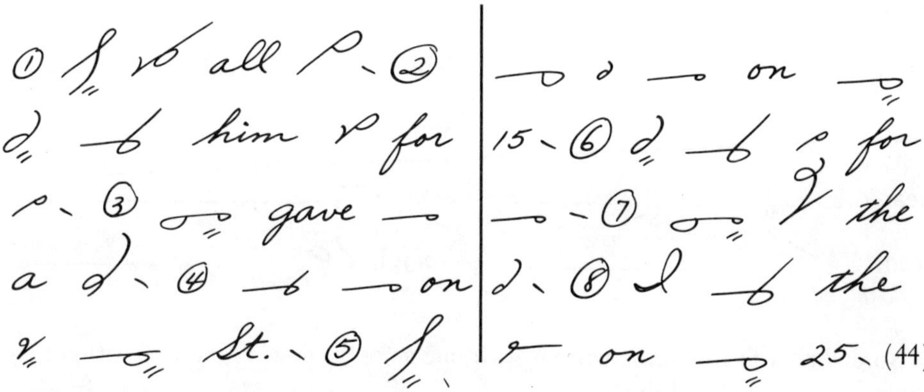

(44)

O

17. O. The shorthand character for o is a small, deep hook. Notice how it is derived from the bottom half of the longhand o.

o 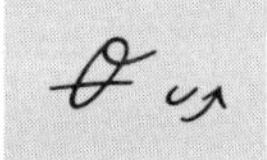 (Write several times, saying **o** aloud each time.)

Practice these words as previously instructed, spelling aloud as you write each outline.

no, n-o	**note,** n-o-t
snow, s-n-o	**own,** o-n
so, s-o	**tone,** t-o-n

phone, ______________
f-o-n

stone, ______________
s-t-o-n

Note: In *own, tone, stone,* the *o* is turned on its side. This enables us to obtain an easy, quick joining.

QUICK CHECK *(Read)*

R

18. R. The shorthand character for *r* is a short forward under curve. Notice how it, too, is derived from longhand—the final curve of the longhand *r*.

R 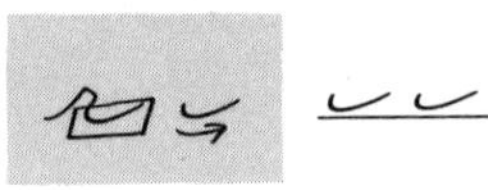 ______________ (Write several times, saying **r** aloud each time.)

Practice these words as previously instructed, spelling each word aloud as you write.

ear, ______________
e-r

dear, ______________
d-e-r

near, ______________
n-e-r

read, ______________
r-e-d

fare, ______________
f-a-r

more, ______________
m-o-r

store, ______________
s-t-o-r

freight, ______________
f-r-a-t

Note: *Fr,* as in *freight,* is written with one smooth, flowing motion, without an angle between the *f* and the *r*.

QUICK CHECK *(Read)*

L

19. L. The shorthand character for *l* is the same shape as *r*, but it is about three times as long. Notice how it is derived from the longhand form.

L 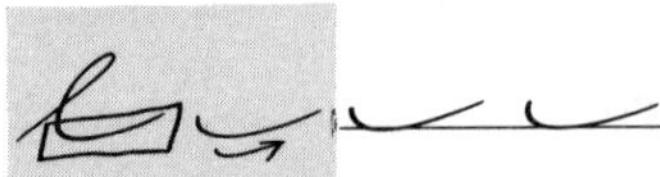 ______________ (Write several times, saying **l** aloud each time.)

COMPARE: 
R L
______________ (Write **r-l** alternately a few times.)

Practice these words. Spell as you write the outlines.

lay, ______________ l-a
late, ______________ l-a-t
ail, ______________ a-l
mail, ______________ m-a-l
deal, ______________ d-e-l
feel, ______________ f-e-l
low, ______________ l-o
floor, ______________ f-l-o-r

Note: *Fl,* as in *floor,* is written with one smooth motion, without an angle between the *f* and the *l.*

QUICK CHECK *(Read)*

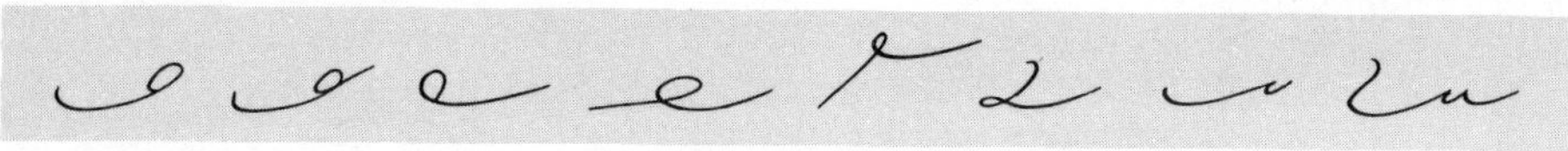

20. Reading and Self-Dictation Practice. Reread the practice suggestions given on page 7 before you begin your work on this Reading and Self-Dictation Practice.

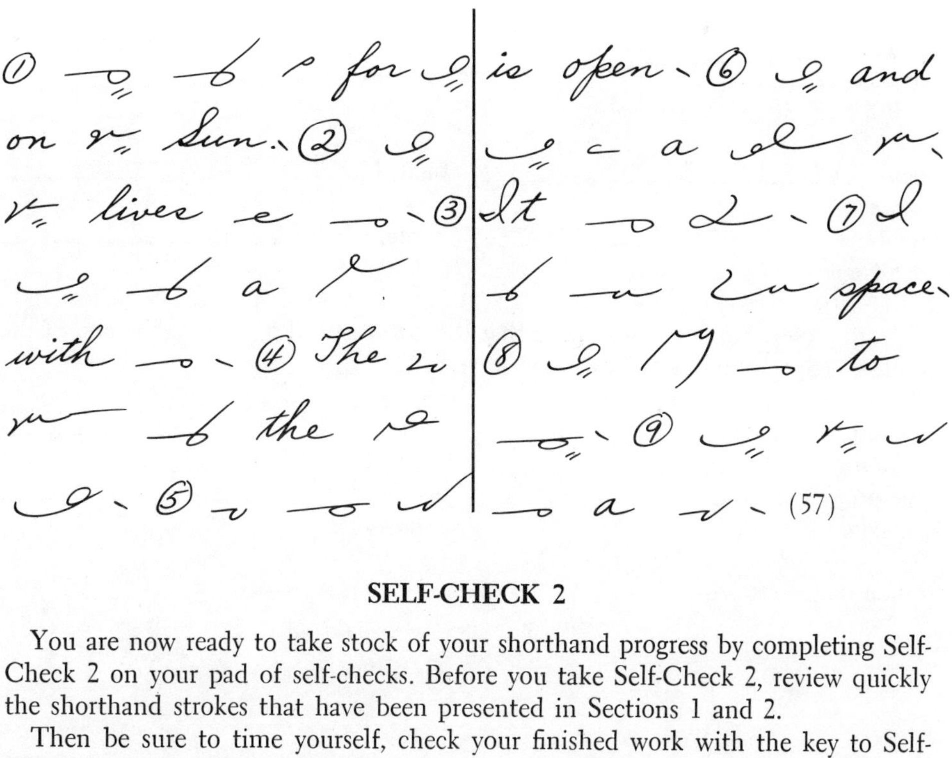

SELF-CHECK 2

You are now ready to take stock of your shorthand progress by completing Self-Check 2 on your pad of self-checks. Before you take Self-Check 2, review quickly the shorthand strokes that have been presented in Sections 1 and 2.

Then be sure to time yourself, check your finished work with the key to Self-Check 2 in your Transcript, and compare your achievements with the goals suggested for Self-Check 2.

SECTION 3

This section presents several new strokes, and two very useful, timesaving devices —brief forms for common words and phrasing.

21. Alphabet Recall. How rapidly can you identify the shorthand strokes you previously studied? Write the longhand letter below each of the following shorthand characters:

H

-ing

22. H, -ing. The letter *h* is simply a *dot* placed above the vowel. With few exceptions, *h* occurs at the beginning of a word.

The sound of *ing*, which almost always occurs at the end of a word, is also indicated by a dot.

Practice* these words:

he,  ______ *h-e*

hear,  ______ *h-e-r*

heat,  ______ *h-e-t*

home,  ______ *h-o-m*

In the following *-ing* words, note that the *dot* is placed *just below* the end of the outline. (Spell the dot as *-ing*—not as *i-n-g*.)

saying,  ______ *s-a-ing*

rowing,  ______ *r-o-ing*

seeing,  ______ *s-e-ing*

heeding, 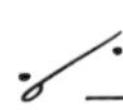 ______ *h-e-d-ing*

QUICK CHECK *(Read)*

*Hereafter when you are instructed to "practice" material in a list, follow the procedure outlined on page 6.

I

23. Long I. The shorthand stroke for the long sound of *i*, as in the word *my*, is a large broken circle.

I 

(Write several times, saying **i** aloud each time.)

Practice these words:

my, ____ *m-i*	**line,** ____ *l-i-n*
night, ____ *n-i-t*	***right,** ____ *r-i-t*
tire, ____ *t-i-r*	**drive,** ____ *d-r-i-v*
sign, ____ *s-i-n*	**side,** ____ *s-i-d*
fine, ____ *f-i-n*	***write,** ____ *r-i-t*

*Note that *right* and *write* are sounded alike; therefore, they are written alike.

QUICK CHECK *(Read)*

Minor Vowels

24. Omission of Minor Vowels. Some words contain vowels that are either not pronounced or are slurred in ordinary speech. For example, the word *even* is really pronounced *e·vn;* the word *motor* is pronounced *mot·r.* These vowels may be omitted in shorthand.

Practice these words:

even, ____ e-v-n	**total,** ____ *t-o-t-l*
hasten, ____ h-a-s-n	**reader,** ____ r-e-d-r
nearer, ____ n-e-r-r	**later,** ____ l-a-t-r
dearer, ____ d-e-r-r	**owner,** ____ o-n-r

QUICK CHECK *(Read)*

25. Reading and Self-Dictation Practice

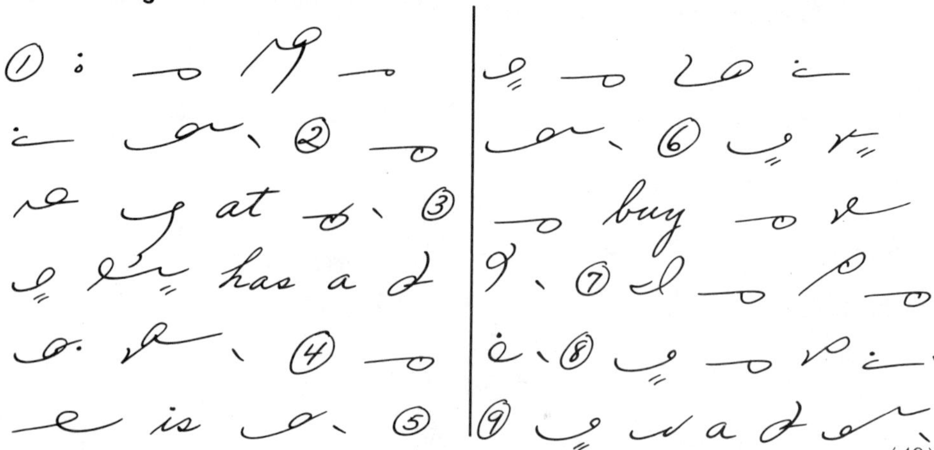

(48)

Brief Forms

26. Brief Forms. The English language contains many words that are used again and again in all writing and speaking. As an aid to rapid shorthand writing, special abbreviations, called "brief forms," are provided for some of these words; for example, the shorthand *m* represents *am;* the shorthand *v* represents *have.*

You are already familiar with the principle of abbreviation in longhand—*Mr.* for *Mister; memo* for *memorandum; Ave.* for *Avenue.*

Because these brief forms occur so frequently, you will be wise to learn them well—to master them so you can write them without a second's hesitation, automatically.

IMPORTANT: As you write the following outlines for brief forms, say each *word* aloud. DO NOT SPELL.

I	**Mr.**
have	
a, an	**will, well**
am	
it, at	**are, our, hour**
in, not	

Note: Some of the strokes represent more than one word. You will have no difficulty selecting the correct word in a sentence; the sense of the sentence will indicate the correct word.

Phrasing

27. Shorthand Phrasing. As you have just learned, we save time by using short, easily written outlines for common, frequently used words. Another device for saving time is "phrasing," the writing of two or more words together as one outline. See how easily and quickly the following phrases can be written.

WRITE AND SAY ALOUD:

I have  ____________ **he will**  ____________

I am  ____________ ____________

are not  ____________ **I will**  ____________

in our ____________ ____________

QUICK CHECK *(Read)*

Brief Forms 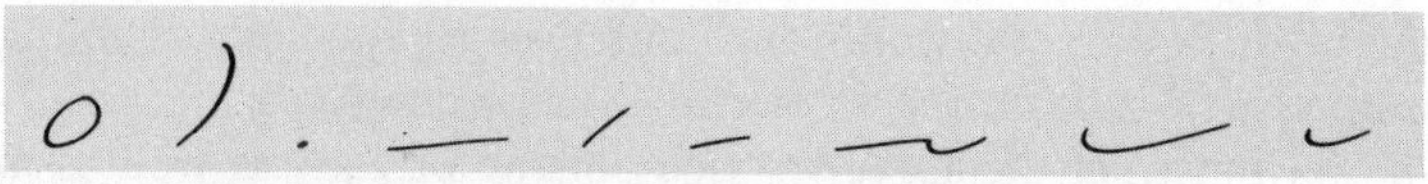

Phrases 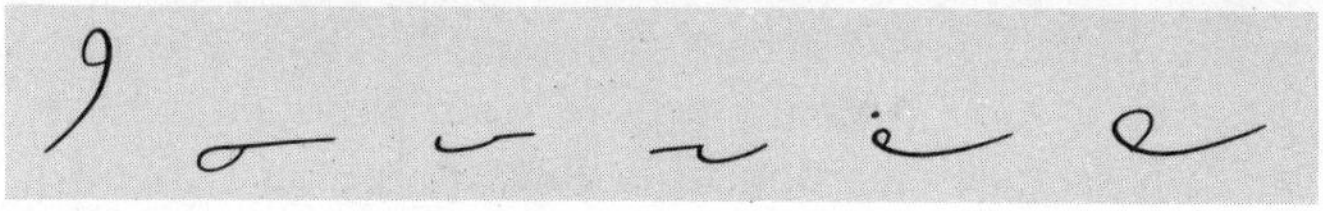

28. Reading and Self-Dictation Practice

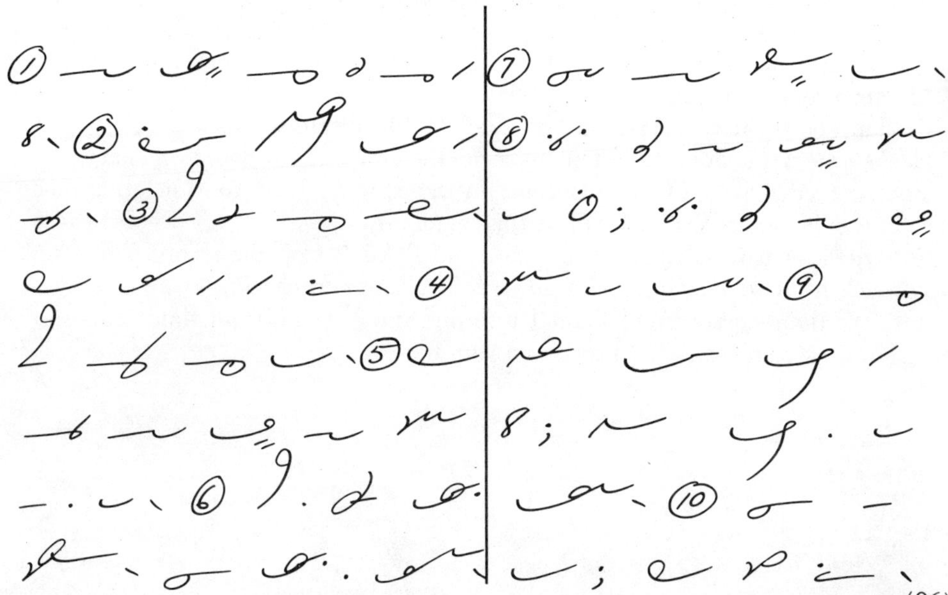

(96)

*From this point on, some of the Reading and Self-Dictation Practice exercises are recorded on the records that are part of your text-kit. The number, the side, and the band of the record on which each recorded exercise appears will be indicated as shown in Paragraph 28.

When you have completed the self-check for this section, read the suggestions on page 22 on how to derive the greatest benefit from these dictation records.

SELF-CHECK 3

At this point you are ready for Self-Check 3 on your pad of self-checks. Before you take Self-Check 3, review quickly the alphabetic strokes you studied in Sections 1, 2, and 3. This review will help you obtain the best possible score.

Strive to reach or exceed the time and accuracy goals suggested for Self-Check 3. The key to Self-Check 3 appears in your Transcript.

RECORDED DICTATION

You are now about to undertake a new phase of your shorthand instruction—recorded dictation. If you have been attending regular classes, your instructor has no doubt dictated some words and sentences to you so that you could write from hearing, as well as from seeing or copying. To develop your speed in writing shorthand, you must get dictation practice outside of class as well as in class. To help you supplement the dictation you get in class, your Text-Kit provides six dictation records. They may be used at various stages of your shorthand course.

You are now ready to take dictation from Record 1, Side 1, Band 1, which contains the material in the Reading and Self-Dictation Practice of Paragraph 28. The material is dictated at 40 words a minute. Before you place this record on your record player, however, be sure to read the directions on the inside cover of the record album in order to get the best wear from your records.

Then follow these steps:

1. Reread Paragraph 28 and, if time permits, make another shorthand copy of it.
2. Keep your book open to Paragraph 28.
3. Turn on the record player and get ready to take dictation.
4. As you write from dictation, refer to the printed shorthand whenever you cannot immediately think of an outline. In the early stages of your dictation practice, it is only natural that you will do this frequently.
5. After you have taken the dictation from Band 1, stop the record player and read back from your own notes. Use your Transcript to check.
6. Take the dictation from Band 1 a second time, even a third time. You need not, however, read back repetitions from your notes.

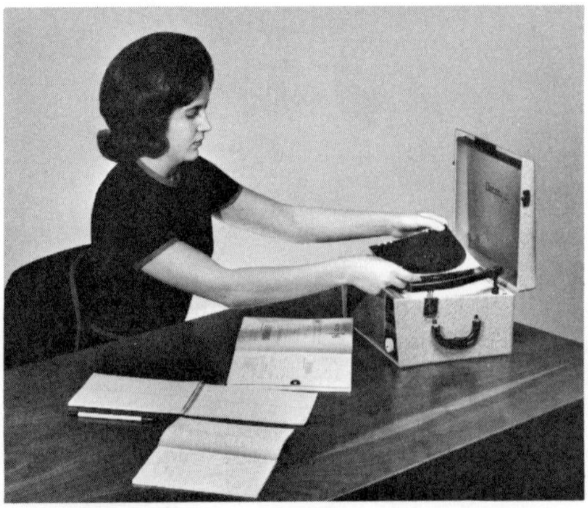

SECTION 4

In this section you will learn three new left curve strokes – *p, b,* and a second form of *s.*

As you work with this material, be sure to follow the practice procedures outlined on pages 6, 7, and 8.

29. Alphabet Recall. See how rapidly you can write the longhand letters for each of the following shorthand characters.

Left S-Z

30. Left S-Z. The first shorthand stroke you learned was the small downward curve for *s* and *z.* Because these sounds are so frequent, a second form has been provided to represent them – a *backward comma,* written downward.

S-Z  
(Write several times, saying **s-z** aloud each time.)

The use of the right and left forms of *s* and *z* makes it possible to obtain an easy joining in any combination of strokes. Use whichever *s* makes the easier joining in a word. For convenience, this stroke is called "left *s.*"

Practice these words:

days, 
d-a-s

stores, 
s-t-o-r-s

sales, 
s-a-l-s

seems, 
s-e-m-s

most, 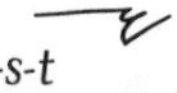
m-o-s-t

trades, 
t-r-a-d-s

QUICK CHECK *(Read)*

31. Reading and Self-Dictation Practice

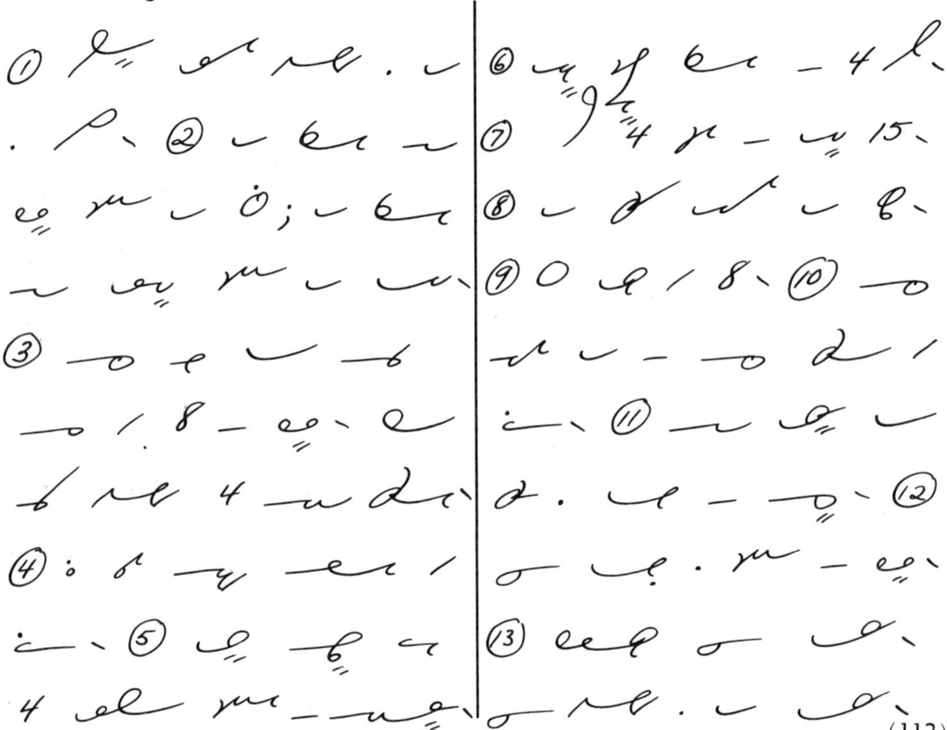

(112)

P

32. P. The shorthand character for *p* is the same shape as the left *s* except that it is about three times as long.

P 

(Write several times, saying **p** aloud each time.)

Practice the following words:

pay, ______________ p-a
spare, ______________ s-p-a-r
paid, ______________ p-a-d
praise, ______________ p-r-a-s
please, ______________ p-l-e-s
hope, ______________ h-o-p

Note: In *praise* and *please,* the *p* stroke joins to *r* and *l* with one smooth, flowing motion. There is no angle when *p* joins to *r* or *l.*

QUICK CHECK *(Read)*

33. Reading and Self-Dictation Practice

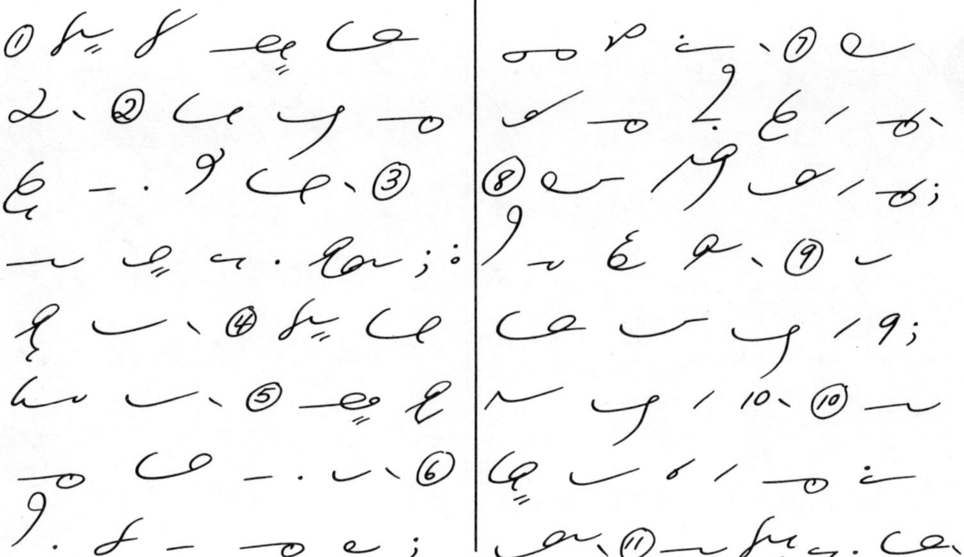

(87)

B

34. B. The shorthand character for *b* is the same shape as the stroke for *p*, but it is about twice as long.

B 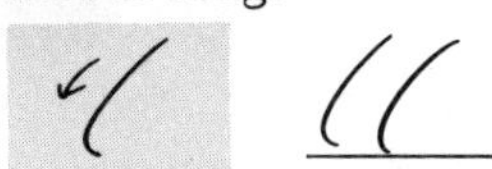

(Write several times, saying **b** aloud each time.)

COMPARE: 

Left S P B

(Write this group several times.)

Practice these words:

buy,  *b-i*

base,  *b-a-s*

boat, 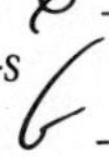 *b-o-t*

brief, 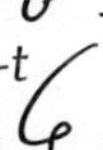 *b-r-e-f*

neighbor,  *n-a-b-r*

blame, 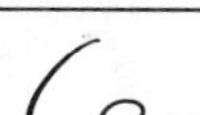 *b-l-a-m*

Note: The joinings of *b-r* and *b-l*, as in *brief, neighbor,* and *blame,* are made with one smooth motion, without an angle.

QUICK CHECK *(Read)*

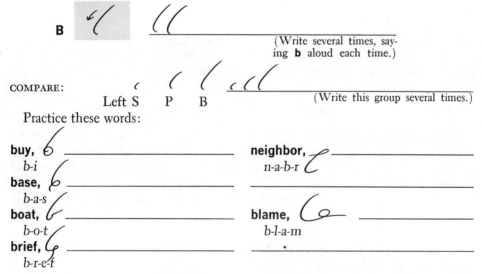

35. Reading and Self-Dictation Practice

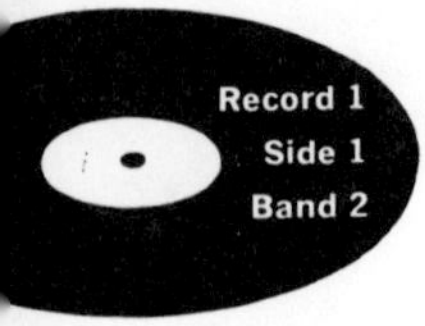

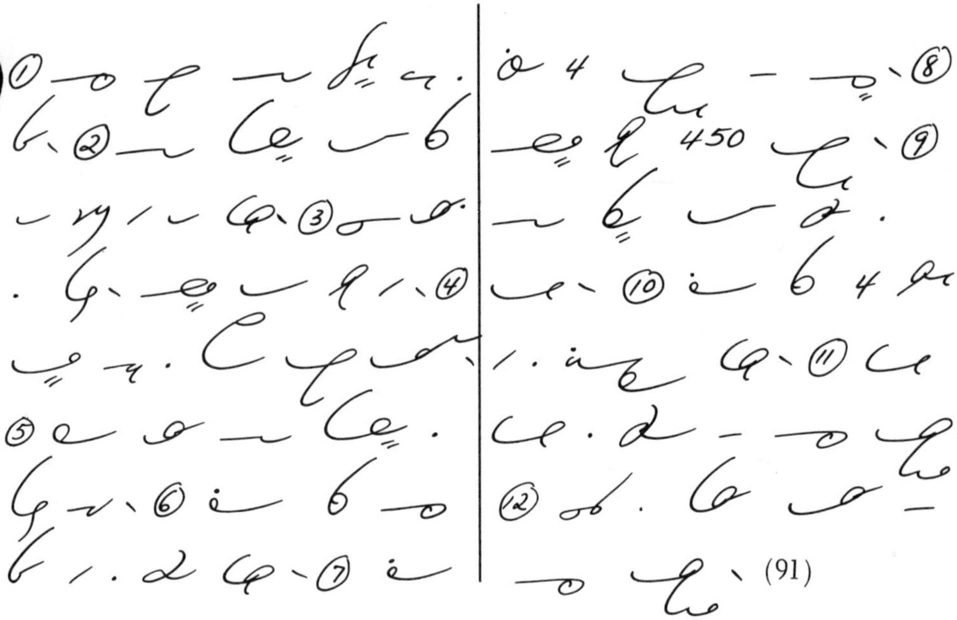

SELF-CHECK 4

Check your mastery of the shorthand principles you have studied thus far by completing Self-Check 4 on your pad of self-checks. Fill out the self-check as rapidly as you can; at the same time, strive for accuracy. Try to reach or exceed the time and accuracy goals suggested for Self-Check 4.

RECORDED DICTATION

At this point you can take from dictation the material on Record 1, Side 1, Band 2, which contains the sentences in Paragraph 35 dictated at 40 words a minute.

Procedure (a reminder): Reread Paragraph 35 and make a shorthand copy of the sentences if time permits. Then:

1. Play Record 1 from the beginning. The material on Band 1, which you have already taken from dictation, will give you a fine warm-up for writing the material on Band 2.
2. Keep your book open to Paragraph 35 and refer to it when necessary as you take dictation from Band 2.
3. After you have taken Band 2 from dictation, read it back from your own notes.
4. Take Band 2 from dictation several times. You need not read back your notes on the repeated writings.

If you find that you can't get all the recorded dictation, even after two or three repetitions, don't be discouraged. Remember that you are in the very early stages of your shorthand study. Your ability to take dictation will rapidly improve if you follow the practice procedures suggested on page 22.

SECTION 5

In this section you will study three more alphabetic strokes, represented by downward straight strokes.

36. Alphabet Recall. You should be able to identify these shorthand letters in a half minute or less. Can you? Write the longhand letters below the shorthand.

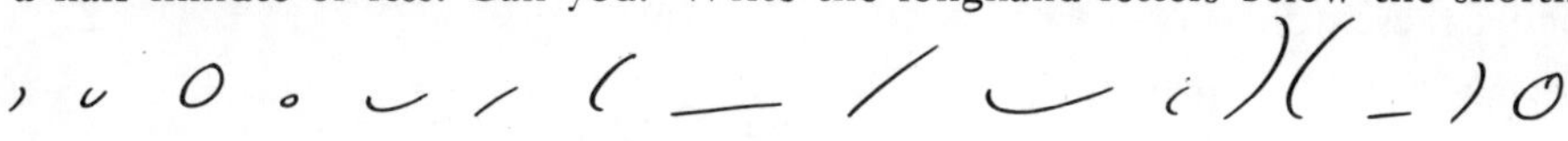

SH

37. Sh. The shorthand character for the sound of *sh,* as in *she,* is a very short downward straight line. It is called "ish."

Sh  ______________ (Write several times, saying **ish** aloud each time.)

Practice these words:

she, ______ *ish-e*	**shape,** ______ *ish-a-p*
show, ______ *ish-o*	**share,** ______ *ish-a-r*
shade, ______ *ish-a-d*	**sheep,** ______ *ish-e-p*

QUICK CHECK *(Read)*

38. Reading and Self-Dictation Practice

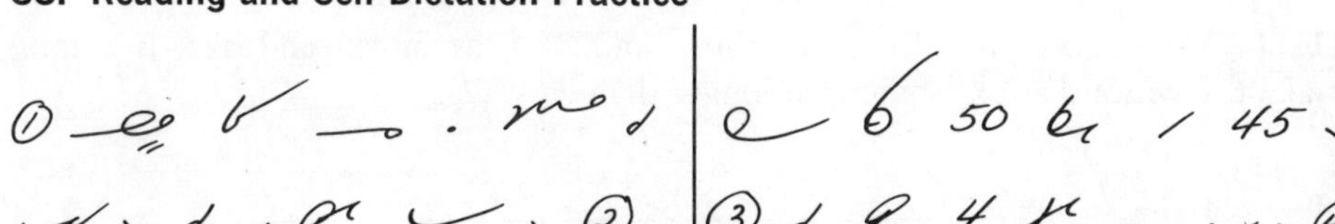

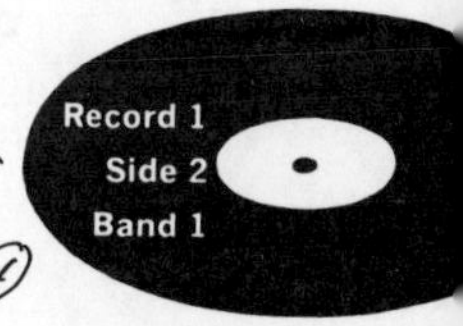

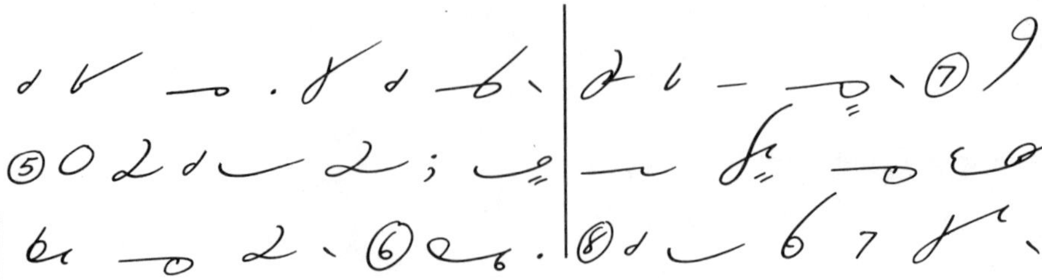
(60)

CH

39. Ch. The shorthand character for the sound of *ch*, as in *each*, is also a downward straight stroke about three times as long as the stroke for *ish*. It is called "chay."

Ch 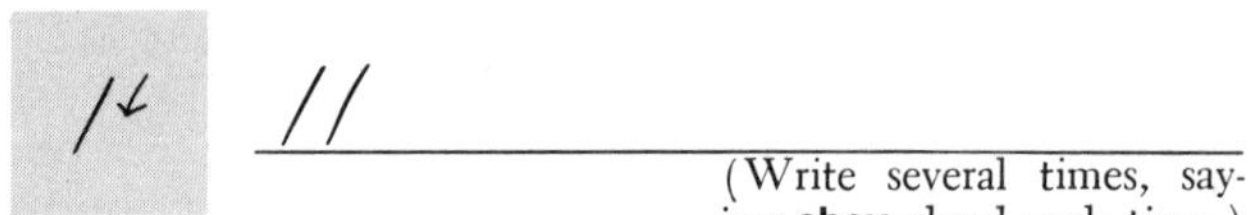

(Write several times, saying **chay** aloud each time.)

Practice these words:

each, ______ e-chay

teach, ______ t-e-chay

reach, ______ r-e-chay

chair, ______ chay-a-r

chain, ______ chay-a-n

speech, ______ s-p-e-chay

QUICK CHECK (Read)

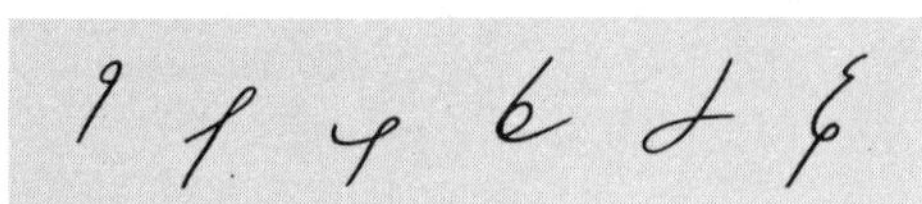

40. Reading and Self-Dictation Practice

Record 1 Side 2 Band 2

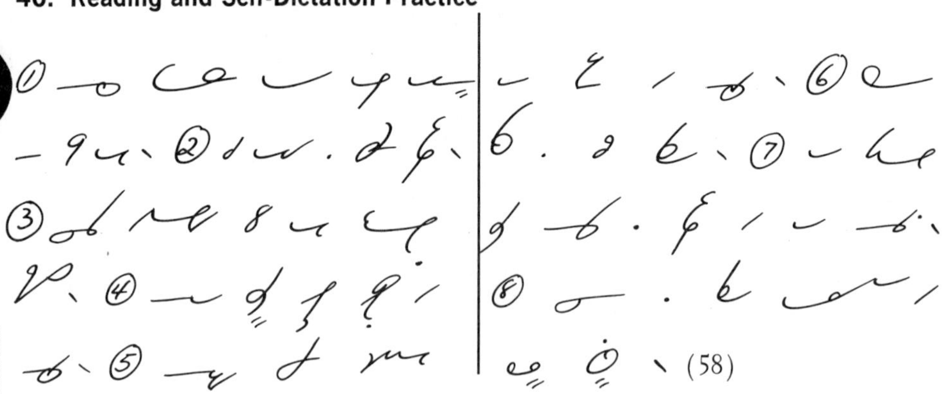
(58)

J

41. J. The shorthand stroke for the sound of *j*, as in *jail* and *age*, is a long straight downward stroke somewhat longer than *ch*.

J 

(Write several times, saying **j** aloud each time.)

COMPARE: 

sh chay j

(Write this group several times.)

Practice these words:

age,  a-j

page, 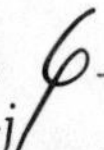 p-a-j

stage,  s-t-a-j

rage,  r-a-j

change, 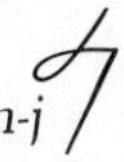 chay-a-n-j

jail,  j-a-l

QUICK CHECK *(Read)*

42. Reading and Self-Dictation Practice

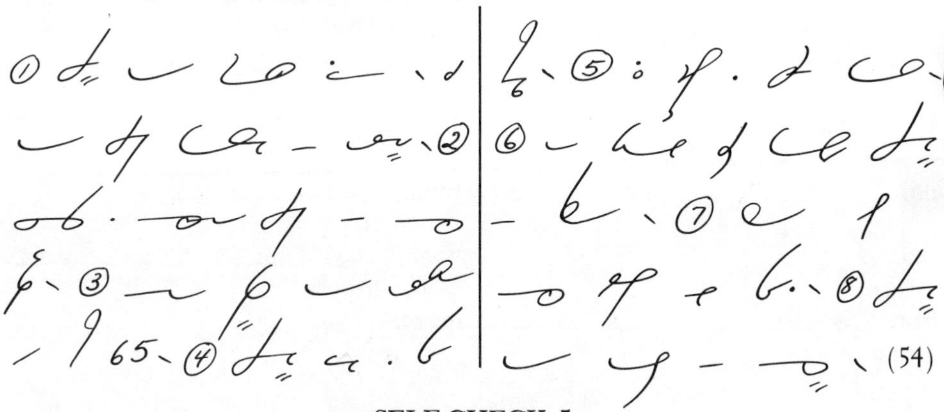

SELF-CHECK 5

You are now ready to give yourself another checkup. After completing Self-Check 5 on your pad, compare your answers with the key in your Transcript.

RECORDED DICTATION

You are now ready to take dictation from Record 1, Side 2, Bands 1, 2, and 3, which contain the sentences in Paragraphs 38, 40, and 42 dictated at 40 words a minute.

Practice the material on Record 1, Side 2, *one band at a time*. Thus:

1. Reread and copy, if time permits, Paragraph 38, which is dictated on Band 1.
2. Take Band 1 from dictation and stop the record player.
3. Read back from your own notes.
4. Take Band 1 from dictation a second time.

Follow this procedure with Band 2 (Paragraph 40) and Band 3 (Paragraph 42). Finally, take all three bands from dictation.

SECTION 6

OO

In this section you will study three new shorthand strokes and two additional sounds represented by the large *a* circle.

43. OO. The sound heard in *too* is represented by a small upward hook. It is called the *oo* hook.

OO ________________ (Write several times, saying **oo** aloud each time.)

Practice these words:

to, too, two, ________________ *t-oo*

do, ________________ *d-oo*

who, ________________ *h-oo*

fruit, ________________ *f-r-oo-t*

true, ________________ *t-r-oo*

room, ________________ *r-oo-m*

noon, ________________ *n-oo-n*

move, ________________ *m-oo-v*

Note: The *oo* hook is placed on its side in *noon, move,* and similar words. The *oo* hook joins more easily to *n* and *m* if it is placed on its side than if it were written in the normal manner.

QUICK CHECK *(Read)*

44. Reading and Self-Dictation Practice

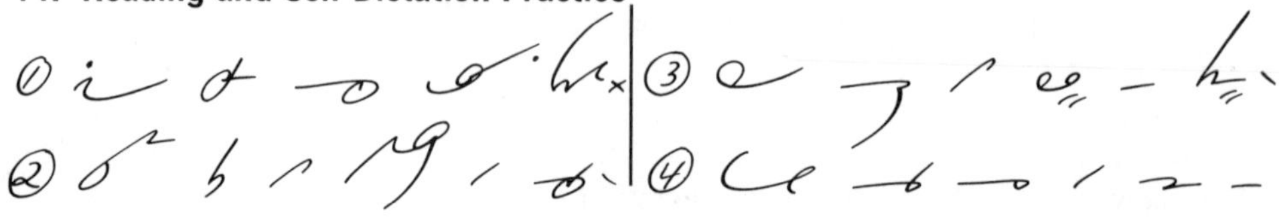

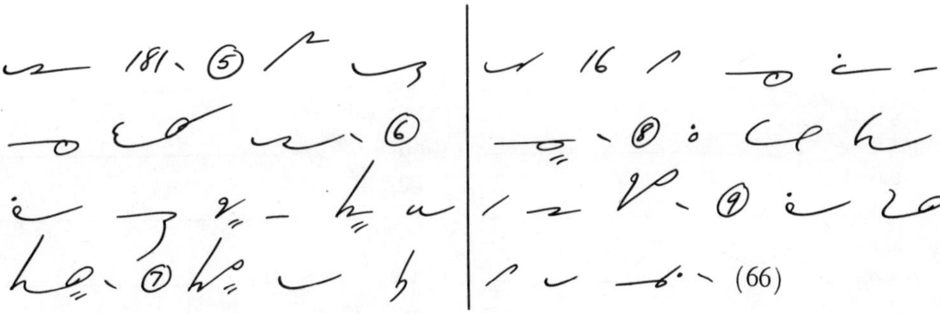

K

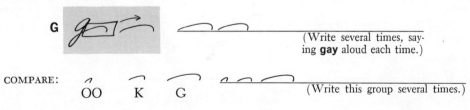

45. K. The shorthand character for *k* is a short forward curve. Notice how it is derived from the longhand form.

K 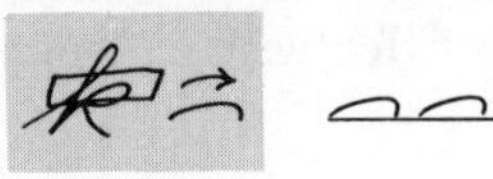

(Write several times, saying **k** aloud each time.)

Practice these words:

ache, a-k

cake, k-a-k

make, m-a-k

baker, b-a-k-r

take, t-a-k

keep, k-e-p

like, l-i-k

claim, k-l-a-m

case, k-a-s

care, k-a-r

Note: *K* and *r*, as in *baker*, join with a smooth, wavelike motion. On the other hand, *k* and *l*, as in *claim*, join with a "hump."

QUICK CHECK *(Read)*

G

46. G. The shorthand character for *g*, as in *go*, is the same shape as *k* but it is about three times as long. It is called "gay." Notice how it is derived from the longhand form.

G 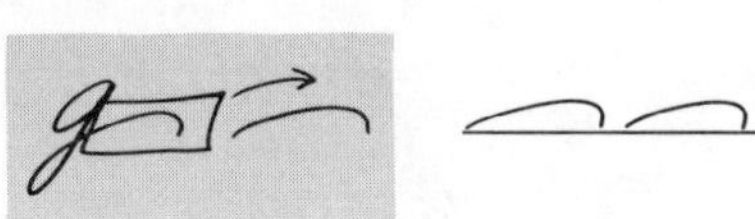

(Write several times, saying **gay** aloud each time.)

COMPARE: 

(Write this group several times.)

Practice these words:

go, gay-o ____________ **gave,** gay-a-v ____________

goal, gay-o-l ____________ **gain,** gay-a-n ____________

grade, gay-r-a-d ____________ **glare,** gay-l-a-r ____________

Note: When g joins to *l*, as in *glare*, it is written with one smooth motion; but when g joins to *r*, as in *grade*, the combination is written with a "hump" between the strokes.

QUICK CHECK *(Read)*

47. Reading and Self-Dictation Practice

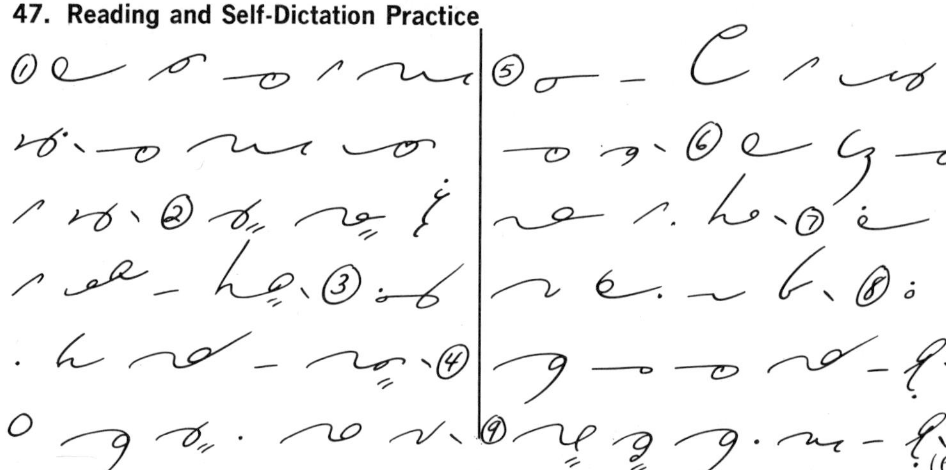

(69)

A

48. A. The large circle that represents *a*, as in *aim*, also represents the sound of *a* heard in *has*.

Practice these words:

has, h-a-s ____________ **ask,** a-s-k ____________

had, h-a-d ____________ **past,** p-a-s-t ____________

man, m-a-n ____________ **last,** l-a-s-t ____________

act, a-k-t ____________

QUICK CHECK *(Read)*

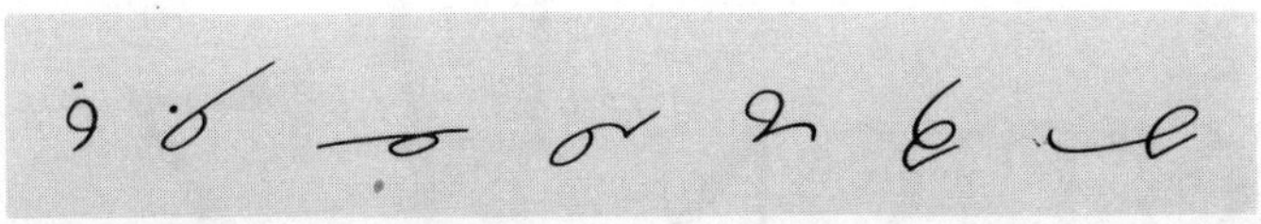

A

49. A. The large circle also represents the sound of *a* heard in *mark*. Practice these words:

mark,  ____________________
m-a-r-k

calm,  ____________________
k-a-m

large,  ____________________
l-a-r-j

arm,  ____________________
a-r-m

QUICK CHECK *(Read)*

50. Reading and Self-Dictation Practice

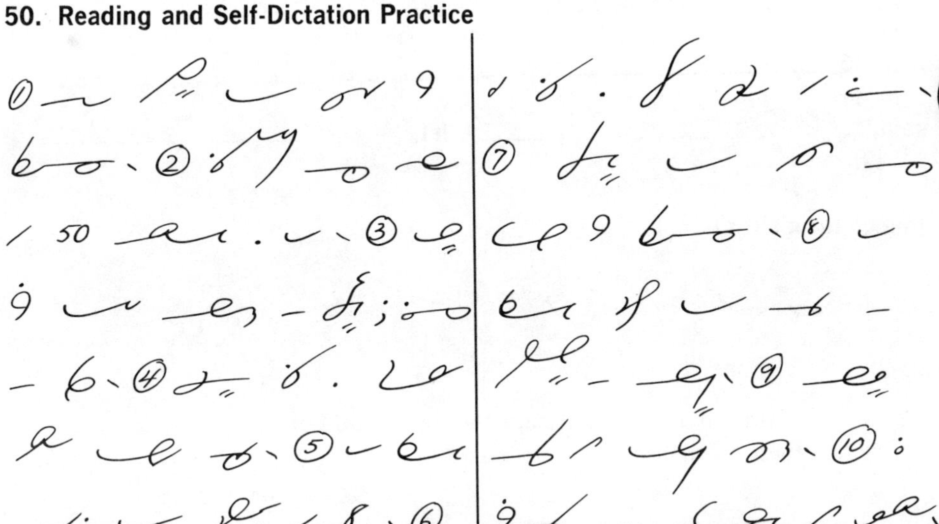

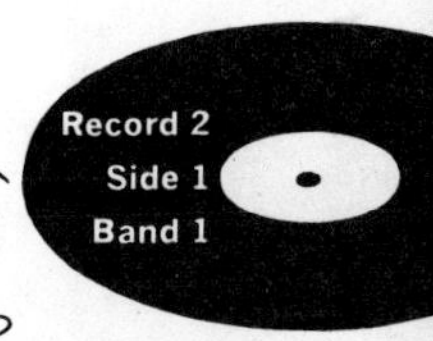

(74)

SELF-CHECK 6

You are now ready for Self-Check 6. See how rapidly and accurately you can complete it. Be sure to correct your work when you have completed the self-check.

RECORDED DICTATION

You can now take from dictation the material on Record 2, Side 1, Band 1, which consists of the sentences in Paragraph 50 dictated at 40 words a minute.

SECTION 7

In this section you will study additional sounds represented by the small e circle. You will also learn the strokes that express the sound of *th*.

E

51. E. The tiny circle that represents the long sound of e, as in *me*, also represents the sound of e heard in *rest*.

Practice these words:

rest, ________ *r-e-s-t*
test, ________ *t-e-s-t*
help, ________ *h-e-l-p*
said, ________ *s-e-d*
tell, ________ *t-e-l*
get, ________ *gay-e-t*
any, ________ *e-n-e*
let, ________ *l-e-t*

QUICK CHECK *(Read)*

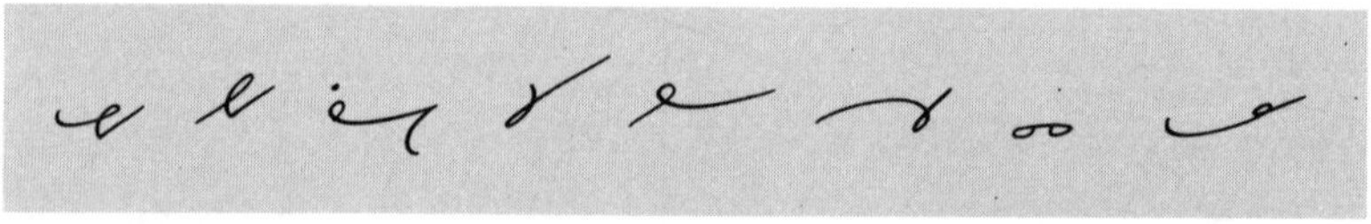

I

52. I. The tiny circle also represents the short sound of *i*, as in *if*.

Practice these words:

if, ________ *e-f*
him, ________ *h-e-m*
give, ________ *gay-e-v*
bill, ________ *b-e-l*
hit, ________ *h-e-t*
did, ________ *d-e-d*
ship, ________ *ish-e-p*
list, ________ *l-e-s-t*
still, ________ *s-t-e-l*
tip, ________ *t-e-p*

QUICK CHECK *(Read)*

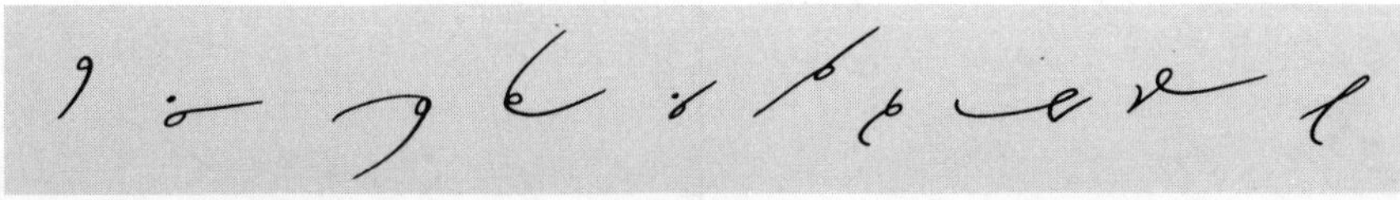

53. Reading and Self-Dictation Practice

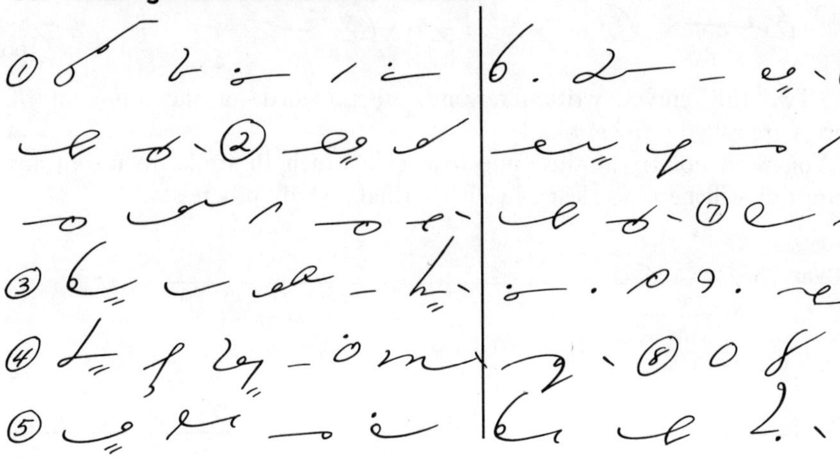

(61)

54. Obscure Vowel. The small circle also represents the obscure vowel heard in words like *her, church, firm.*

Obscure Vowel

Practice these words. (Are you following the practice procedures recommended on pages 6 and 7?)

her, ______ *h-e-r*	**urge,** ______ *e-r-j*
hurry, ______ *h-e-r-e*	**church,** ______ *chay-e-r-chay*
serve, ______ *s-e-r-v*	______
firm, ______ *f-e-r-m*	**hurt,** ______ *h-e-r-t*

QUICK CHECK *(Read)*

55. Reading and Self-Dictation Practice

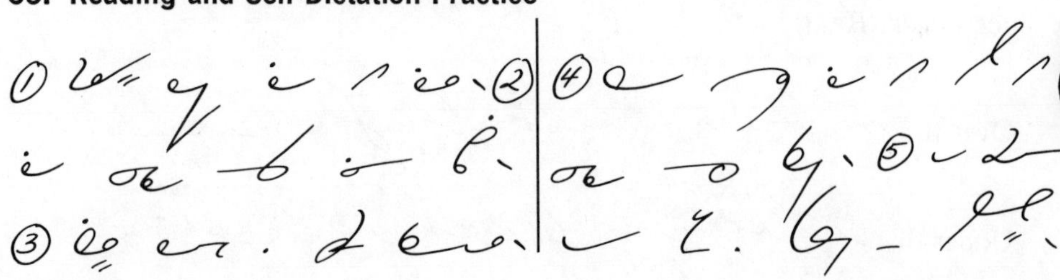

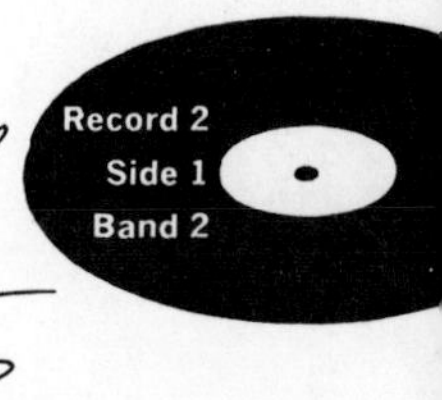

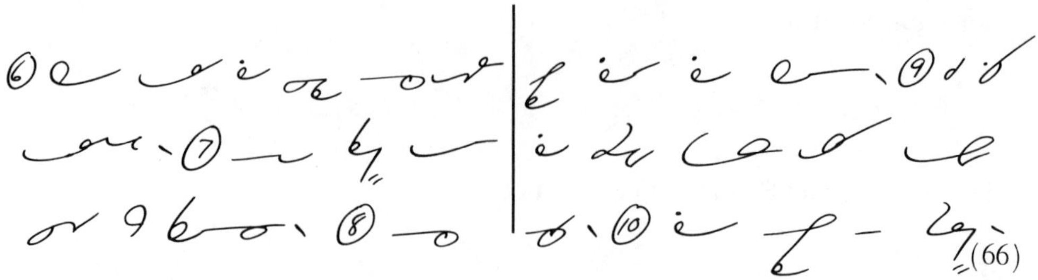

(66)

TH

56. Th. Two tiny curves, written upward, are provided for the sound of *th*. These curves are called "ith" strokes.

Note: You need not try at this time to decide which *th* stroke to use in any given word; this will become clear as your shorthand study progresses.

Over Th ______________________ (Write several times, saying **ith** aloud each time.)

Practice these words:

these, ______________________
ith-e-s
then, ______________________
ith-e-n
thick, ______________________
ith-e-k
teeth, ______________________
t-e-ith

faith, ______________________
f-a-ith
booth, ______________________
b-oo-ith
bath, ______________________
b-a-ith
smooth, ______________________
s-m-oo-ith

Under Th ______________________ (Write several times, saying **ith** aloud each time.)

though, ______________________
ith-o
throw, ______________________
ith-r-o
three, ______________________
ith-r-e
both, ______________________
b-o-ith

thorough, ______________________
ith-e-r-o
through, ______________________
ith-r-oo
health, ______________________
h-e-l-ith

QUICK CHECK *(Read)*

Over th 

Under th 

57. Reading and Self-Dictation Practice

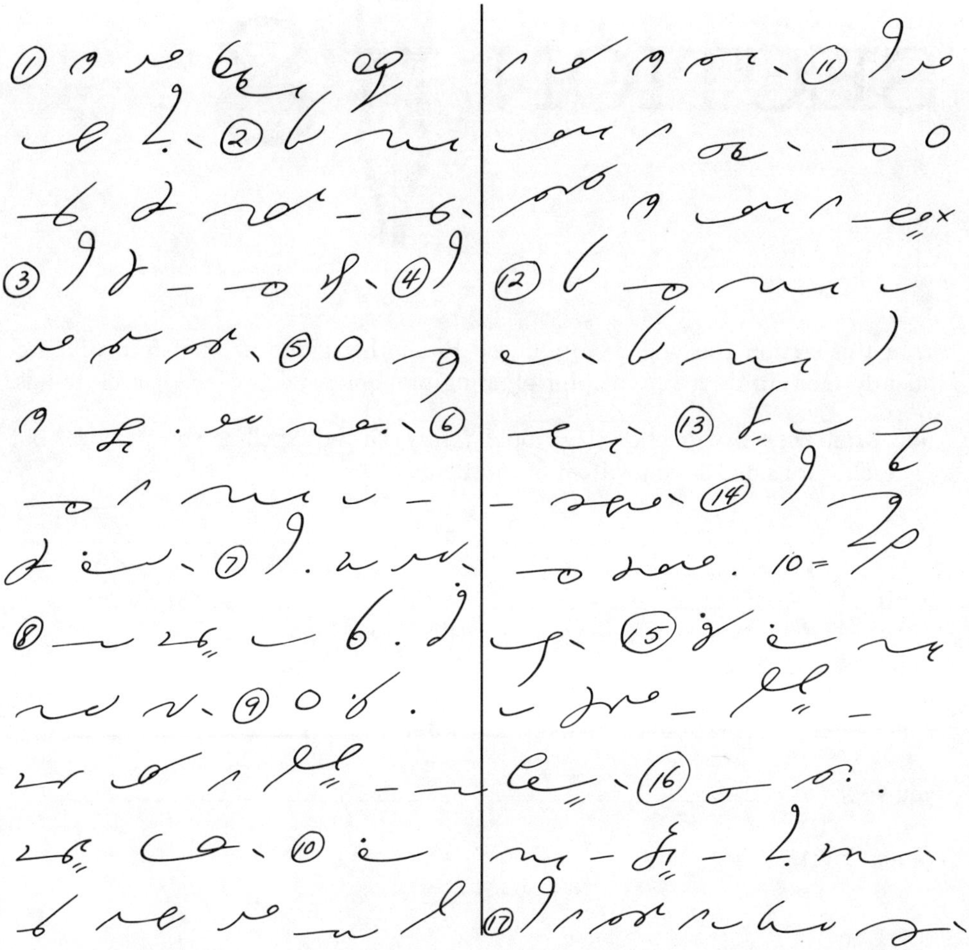

(139)

SELF-CHECK 7

Complete Self-Check 7 on your pad of self-checks and compare your work with the key in your Transcript.

Are you meeting the time and accuracy goals set for each self-check? You should be!

RECORDED DICTATION

You can now take from dictation the material on Record 2, Side 1, Band 2, which contains the sentences from Paragraph 55 dictated at 40 words a minute.

Play Record 2 from the beginning. Band 1 will provide good warm-up dictation.

If you have time, take dictation from Band 2 several times. The repetition will help develop your shorthand speed.

SECTION 8

In this section you will be introduced to another group of brief forms for frequently used words, a very helpful phrasing principle, and two new vowel sounds.

Brief Forms

58. Brief Forms. Practice these brief forms. Do not spell as you practice, but say each word aloud as you write it in shorthand.

the ______	**of** ______
is-his ______	**with** ______
that ______	**but** ______
can ______	**Mrs.** ______
you-your ______	______

QUICK CHECK *(Read)*

Phrases

59. Phrases. Here are a few of the most common business phrases. As you write them, say the phrases aloud.

Dear Sir ______	**Sincerely yours** ______
Dear Madam ______	**Yours very truly** ______
Yours truly ______	**Very truly yours** ______

QUICK CHECK *(Read)*

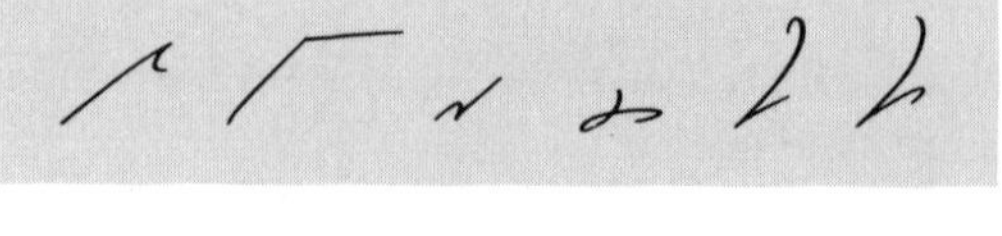

60. Reading and Self-Dictation Practice. Your mastery of the principles of Gregg Shorthand is now sufficiently advanced so that you can read business letters written completely in shorthand. (Incidentally, are you following the procedures suggested on page 7 as you work on each Reading and Self-Dictation Practice? You might be wise to take a moment or two to reread them at this time.)

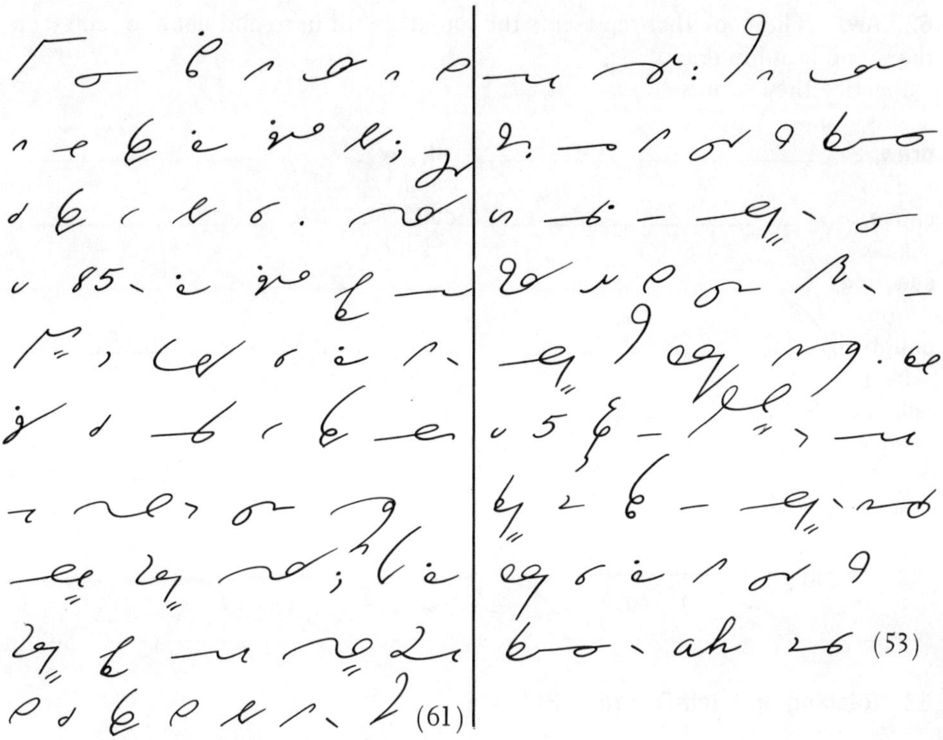

O

61. O. The small hook that represents the long sound of o, as in so, also represents the sound heard in *hot*.

Practice these words:

hot, ______
h-o-t

top, ______
t-o-p

drop, ______
d-r-o-p

job, ______
j-o-b

sorry, ______
s-o-r-e

shop, ______
ish-o-p

copy, ______
k-o-p-e

on, ______
o-n

QUICK CHECK *(Read)*

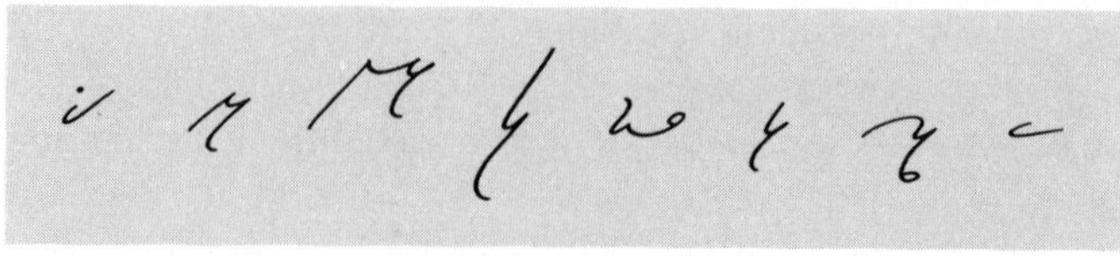

AW

62. Aw. The hook that represents the sounds heard in *so* and *hot* also represents the sound heard in *draw*.

Practice these words:

draw, *d-r-o* ____ **all,** *o-l* ____

cause, *k-o-s* ____ **call,** *k-o-l* ____

saw, *s-o* ____

bought, *b-o-t* ____ **small,** *s-m-o-l* ____

fall, *f-o-l* ____

QUICK CHECK *(Read)*

63. Reading and Self-Dictation Practice

Record 2
Side 2
Band 1

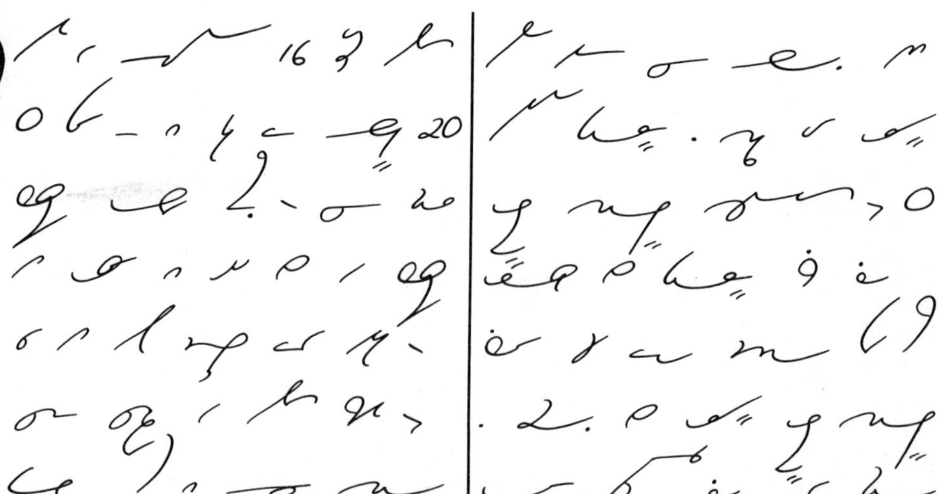

(53)

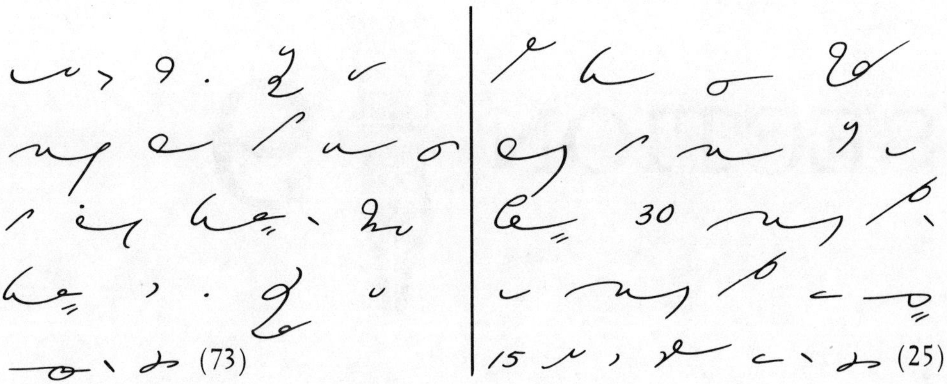

SELF-CHECK 8

Complete Self-Check 8 on your pad of self-checks; then check your work against the key in your Transcript.

RECORDED DICTATION

On Record 2, Side 2, Band 1, you will find the first letter in Paragraph 63 dictated at 40 words a minute. You will derive the greatest benefit from the dictation on the records if you follow this procedure:

1. Read the material before you take dictation from the records.
2. Keep your book open to the material being dictated and refer to it whenever you cannot immediately think of the outline.
3. Read back from your notes the first dictation of each band.

SECTION 9

In this section you will learn nine additional brief forms, three frequently used word endings, and a rapid method of expressing amounts and quantities.

Brief Forms

64. Brief Forms. Practice these brief forms. It isn't necessary to spell the brief forms as you practice them. However, say each word aloud as you write it in shorthand.

for ____________________ there, their ____________________

shall ____________________ ____________________

which ____________________ be, by ____________________

would ____________________ this ____________________

put ____________________ good ____________________

QUICK CHECK *(Read)*

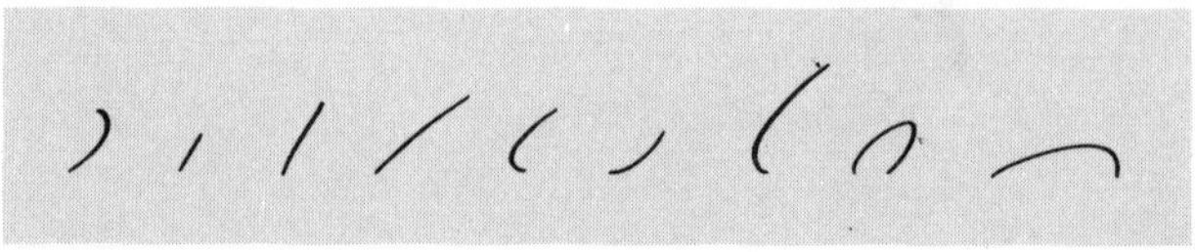

-ly

65. Word Ending -ly. The frequent word ending *-ly* is expressed by the small e circle.

Practice these words:

only ____________________ nearly ____________________

fairly ____________________ early ____________________

nicely ____________________ briefly ____________________

____________________ ____________________

sincerely ____________________ highly ____________________

QUICK CHECK *(Read)*

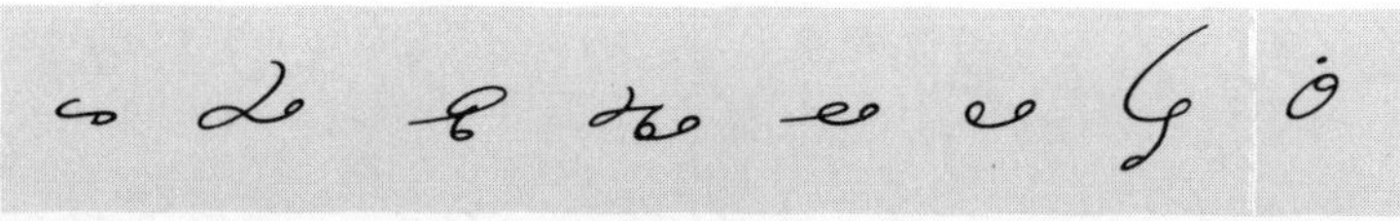

66. Reading and Self-Dictation Practice

Record 2
Side 2
Band 2

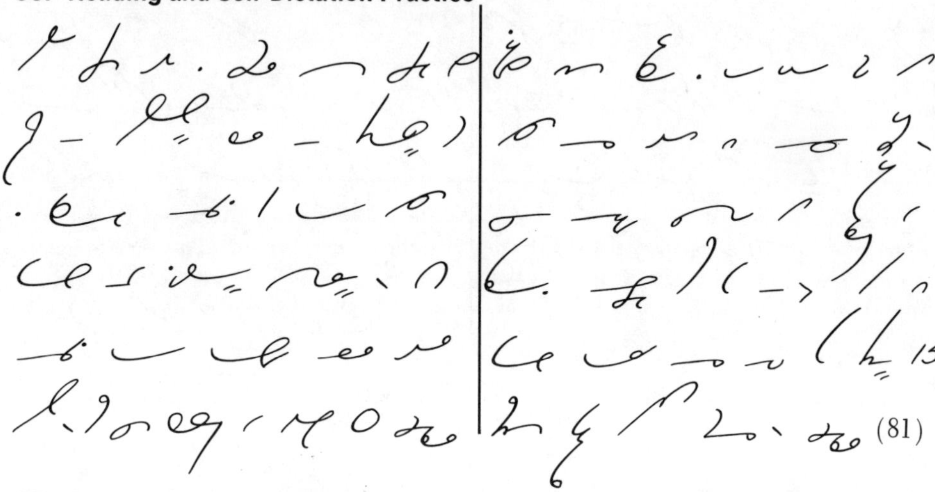

Amounts

67. Amounts and Quantities. In business letters you will frequently encounter amounts and quantities. Here are a few shortcuts that will enable you to write them rapidly.

Practice:

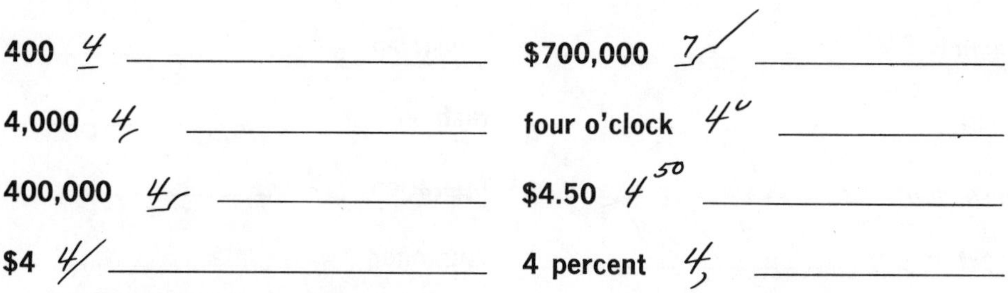

QUICK CHECK *(Read)*

68. Reading and Self-Dictation Practice

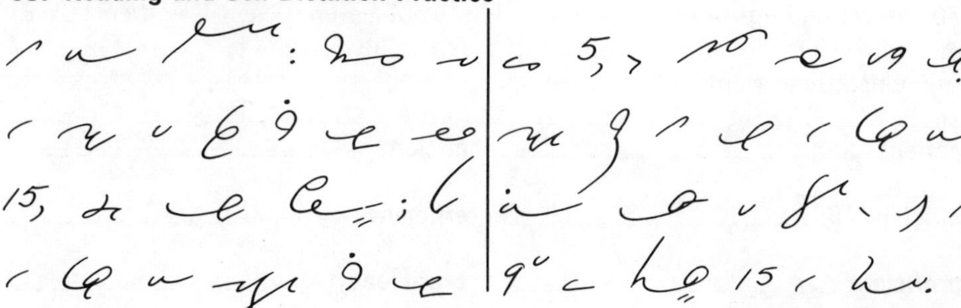

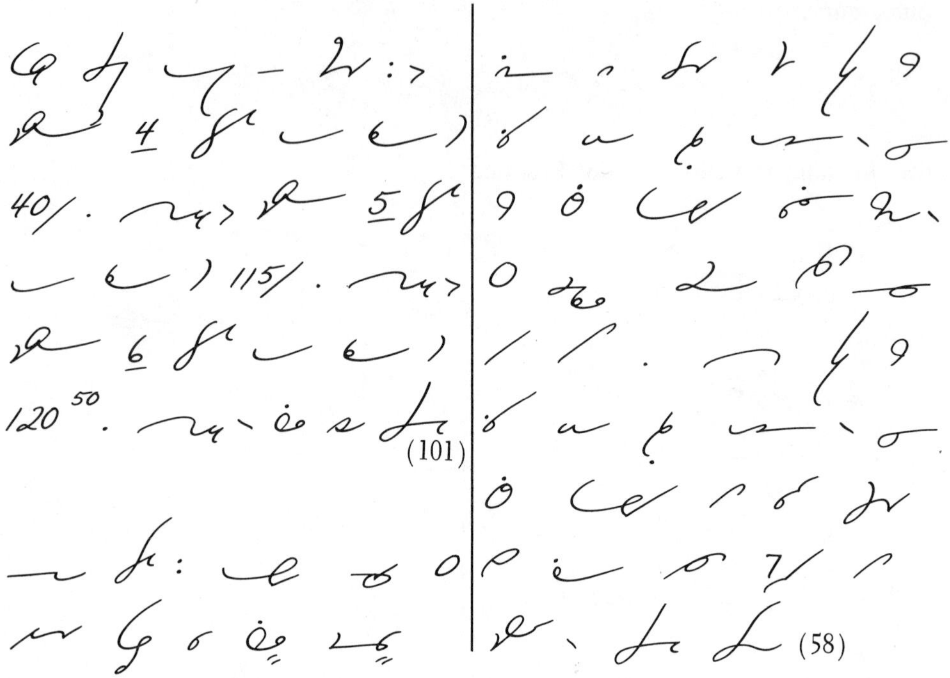

-tion

69. Word Ending -tion. The word ending *-tion* (sometimes spelled *-sion, -cian,* or *-shion*) is represented by the *sh* stroke.

Practice these words:

action ______ **physician** ______

nation ______ **fashion** ______

occasion ______ **operation** ______

section ______ **cautioned** ______

QUICK CHECK *(Read)*

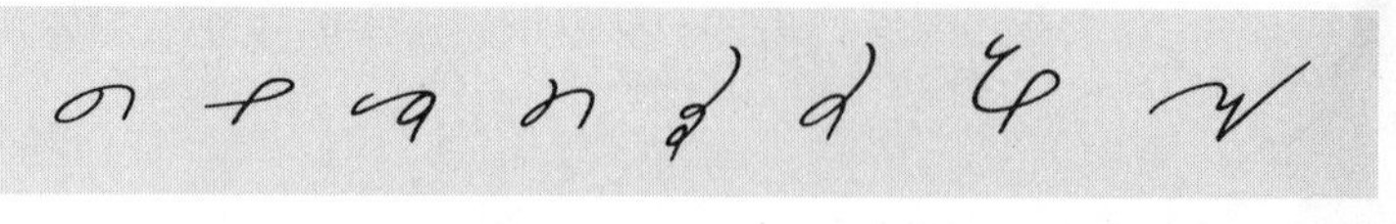

-cient

-ciency

70. Word Endings -cient, -ciency. The word ending *-cient* (or *-tient*) is expressed by *sh-t*. The word ending *-ciency* is represented by *sh-s-e*.

Practice these words:

patient ______ **ancient** ______

efficient ______ **efficiency** ______

proficient ______ **proficiency** ______

QUICK CHECK *(Read)*

71. Reading and Self-Dictation Practice

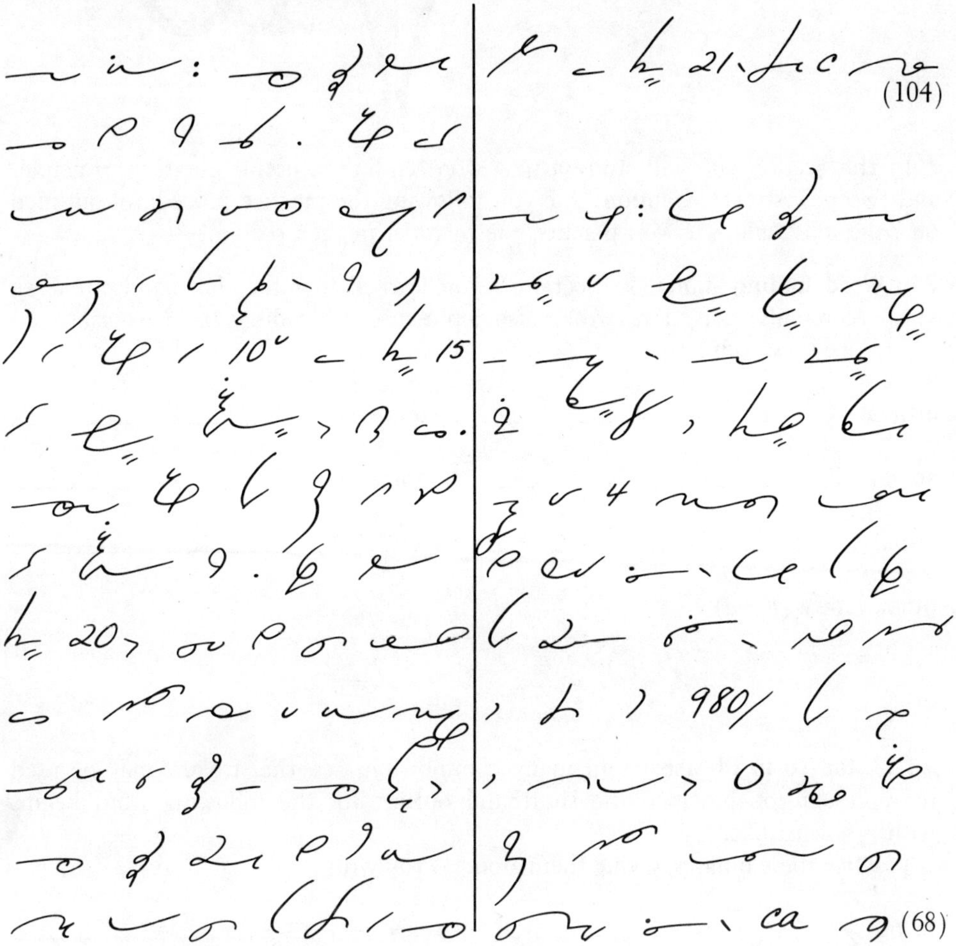

(104)

(68)

SELF-CHECK 9

Time to check yourself again. Complete Self-Check 9 on your self-check pad. After you have completed it, compare your work with the key in your Transcript.

RECORDED DICTATION

Your shorthand speed should gradually be increasing. On Record 2, Side 2, Band 2, is Paragraph 66, which is dictated at 40 words a minute. Play Record 2, Side 2, from the beginning; Band 1 will provide a good warm-up for you.

SECTION 10

In this section you will study a new word ending, a useful phrasing principle, and two new strokes. Caution: Are you following the practice procedures outlined on pages 6, 7, and 8 as you practice the material in each section?

-tial

72. Word Ending -tial. In Section 9 you learned that the shorthand stroke *sh* (ish) represents *-tion*. This stroke also represents the ending *-tial* (or *-cial*).

Practice these words:

official ________	**special** ________
social ________	**financial** ________
initial ________	**essential** ________

QUICK CHECK *(Read)*

T for To

73. T for To in Phrases. In many common phrases, the stroke *t* may be used to represent *to*—provided the shorthand outline for the following word begins with a *downstroke*.

Practice these phrases, saying them aloud as you write:

to be ________	**to say** ________
to have ________	**to put** ________
to see ________	**to which** ________
to plan ________	**to sell** ________

QUICK CHECK *(Read)*

74. Reading and Self-Dictation Practice

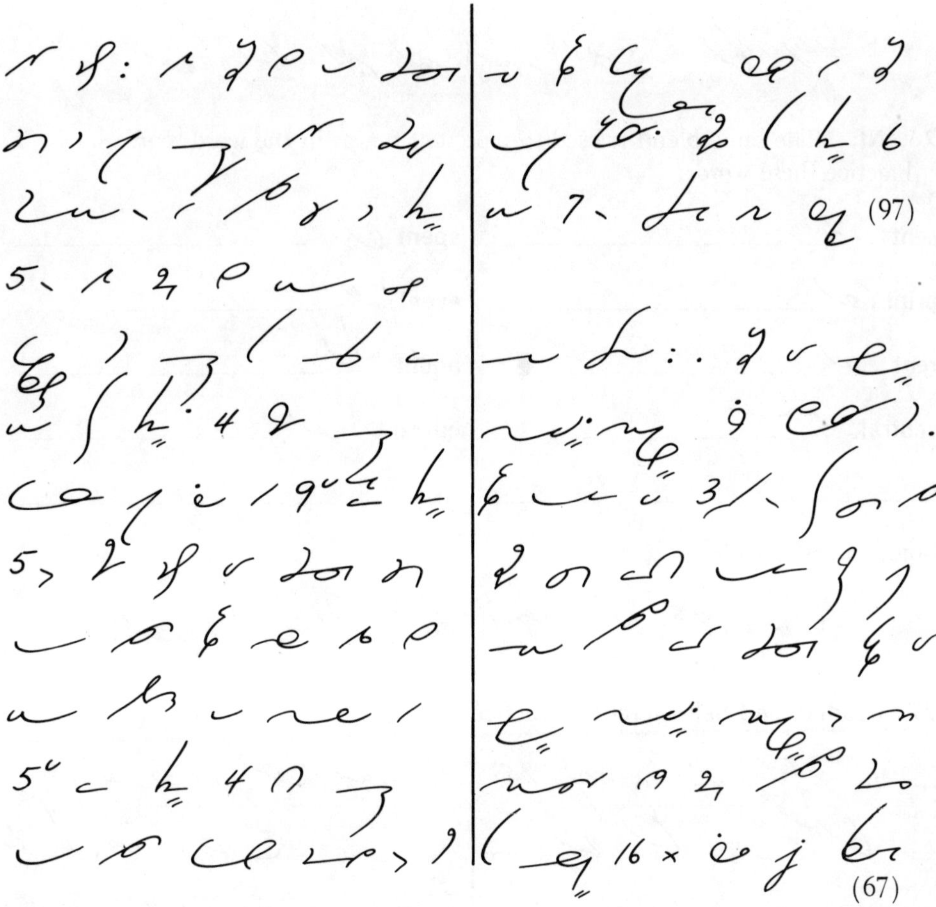

ND

75. Nd. The shorthand strokes for *n-d* are joined without an angle to form the *nd* blend, as in the word *trained.*

Nd 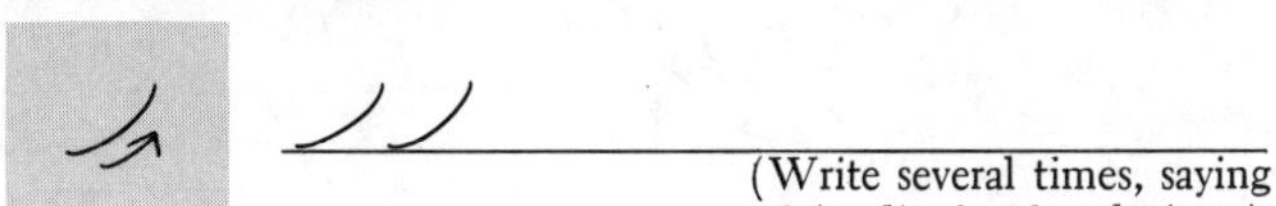

(Write several times, saying **nd** (end) **aloud** each time.)

COMPARE: train  trained 

Practice these words:

end 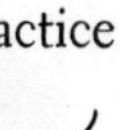 ____________ **signed**  ____________

bind  ____________ **find**  ____________

lined  ____________ **bond**  ____________

kind  ____________ **friend** 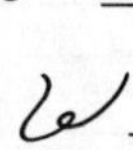 ____________

QUICK CHECK *(Read)*

NT

76. Nt. The same blend is used to represent *n-t*, as in the word *sent*. Practice these words:

sent ______	**spent** ______
print ______	**event** ______
rent ______	**agent** ______
central ______	**current** ______

QUICK CHECK *(Read)*

77. Reading and Self-Dictation Practice

Record 2
Side 2
Band 3

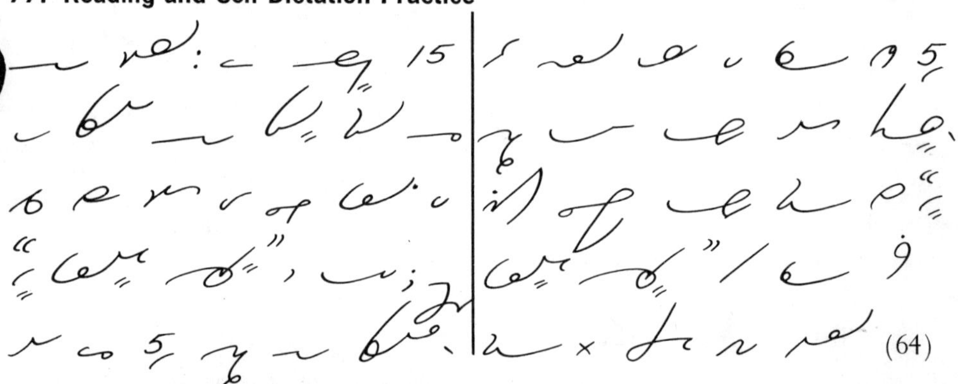

(64)

Ses

78. Ses. The sound of *ses*, as in the word *senses*, is represented by joining the two forms of *s*. The similar sounds of *sis*, as in *sister*, and *sus*, as in *versus*, are represented in the same way.

COMPARE: sense   senses

face   faces

Practice these words:

causes ______	**offices** ______
passes ______	**bases** ______

closes ____________ sister ____________

____________ versus ____________

cases ____________ necessary ____________

QUICK CHECK *(Read)*

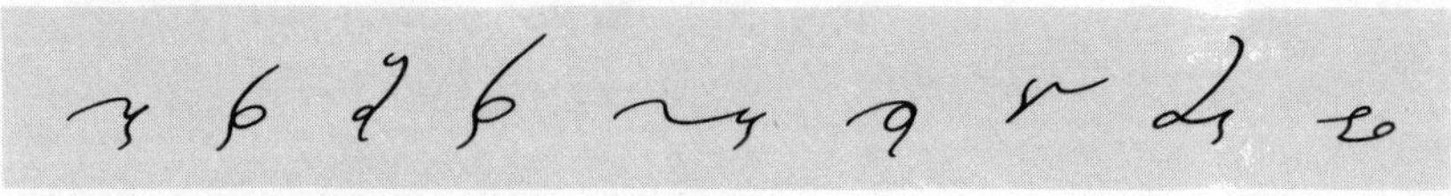

79. Reading and Self-Dictation Practice

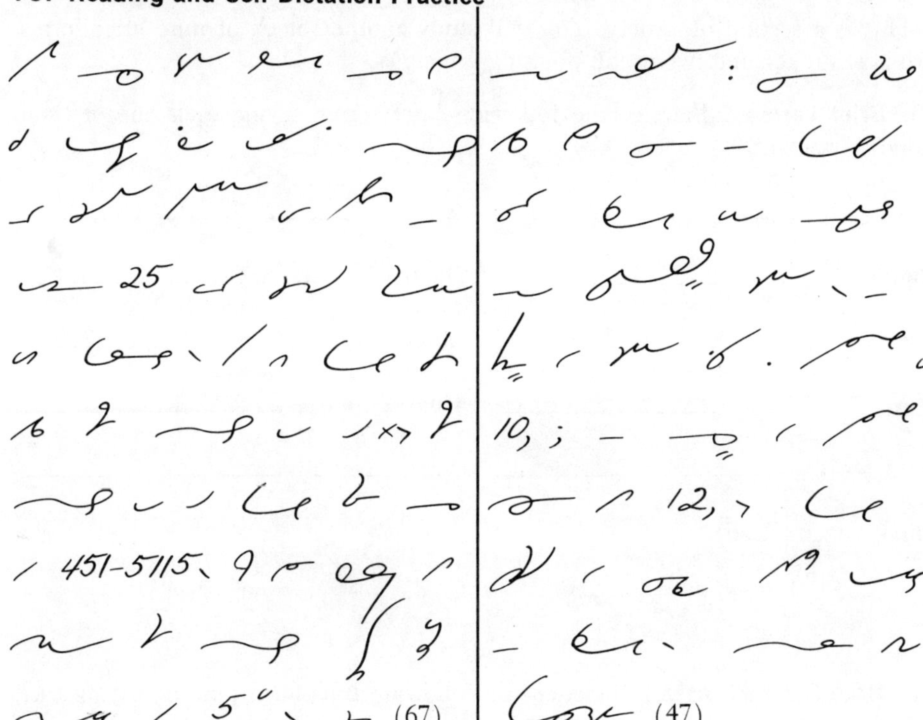

SELF-CHECK 10

At this point, complete Self-Check 10. Then compare your work with the key in your Transcript.

RECORDED DICTATION

On Record 2, Side 2, Band 3, is Paragraph 77, which you can now take from dictation. The material is dictated at 40 words a minute. Before you start the record player, however, be sure to do all the preliminary practice that has been suggested earlier.

Play the record from the beginning. If time is available, you will find that you can profitably replay Records 1 and 2 for extra dictation.

SECTION 11

This is a section of variety. You will study another block of nine brief forms, two new strokes, and two useful phrasing principles.

Brief Forms

80. Brief Forms. Practice the following brief forms, saying each one of them aloud as you write:

and	**was**
should	**them**
when	**could**
they	**from**
send	

QUICK CHECK *(Read)*

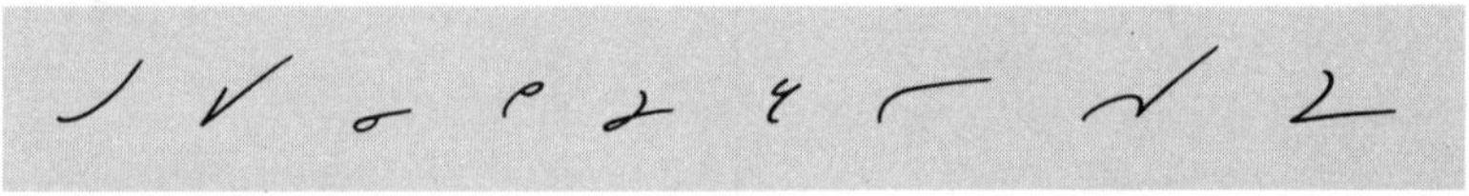

Phrases

81. Brief-Form Phrases. Practice the following brief-form phrases, saying each one aloud as you write it.

I was	**into the**
send them	**that they**
should be	**from the**

QUICK CHECK *(Read)*

82. Reading and Self-Dictation Practice

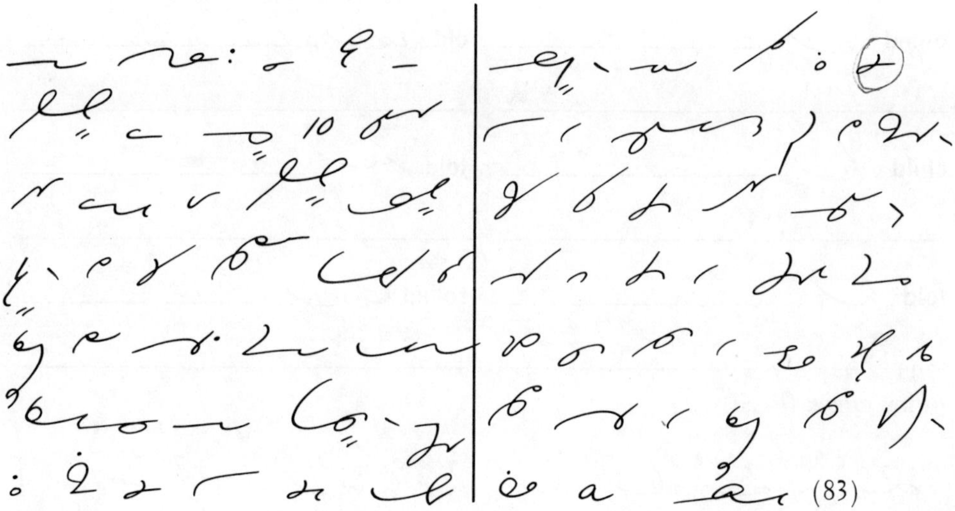

(83)

RD

83. Rd. The combination *rd* is expressed by an *r* stroke turned up at the end.

COMPARE: fear   feared

Practice these words:

stored

appeared

heard

tired

guarded

toward

record

hired

harder

QUICK CHECK *(Read)*

LD

84. Ld. The combination *ld* is expressed by an *l* stroke turned up at the end.

COMPARE: mail   mailed

Practice these outlines containing the *ld* stroke:

failed

mailed

billed ______ old ______

child ______ told ______

fold ______ rolled ______

QUICK CHECK *(Read)*

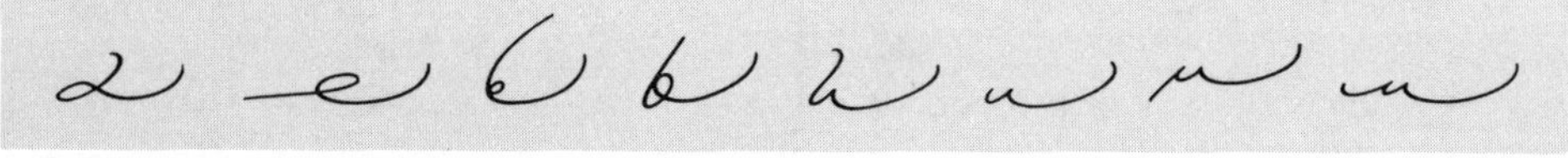

85. Reading and Self-Dictation Practice

Record 3
Side 1
Band 1

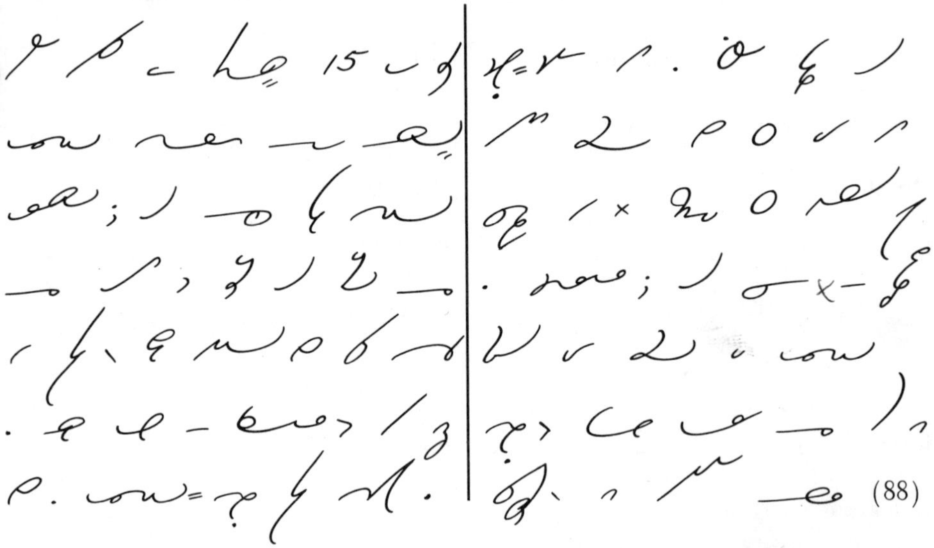

(88)

BEEN in Phrases

86. Been in Phrases. The word *been* is expressed by the *b* stroke after *have, has,* and *had.*

Practice these phrases:

had been ______ you have been ______

it has been ______ have been ______

I have not been ______ there has been ______

I have been ______ has been ______

87. Able in Phrases. The word *able* in phrases is represented by the *a* circle after *be* or *been*.

Practice these outlines, using the circle *a* for *able:*

have been able  ______ **has been able**  ______

I should be able  ______ **you have not been able** 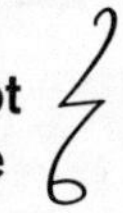 ______

to be able  ______ **had been able**  ______

QUICK CHECK *(Read)*

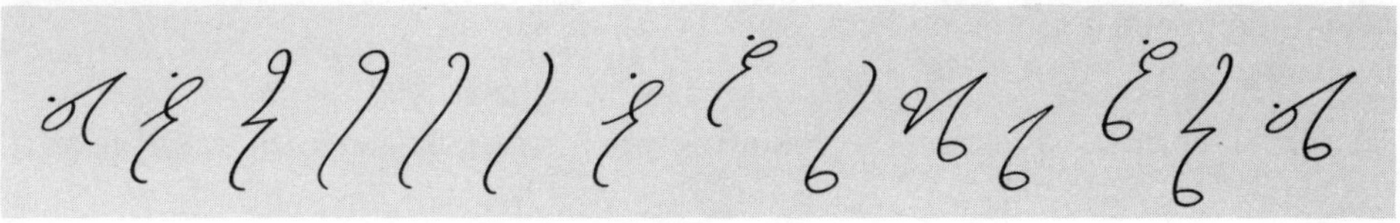

88. Reading and Self-Dictation Practice

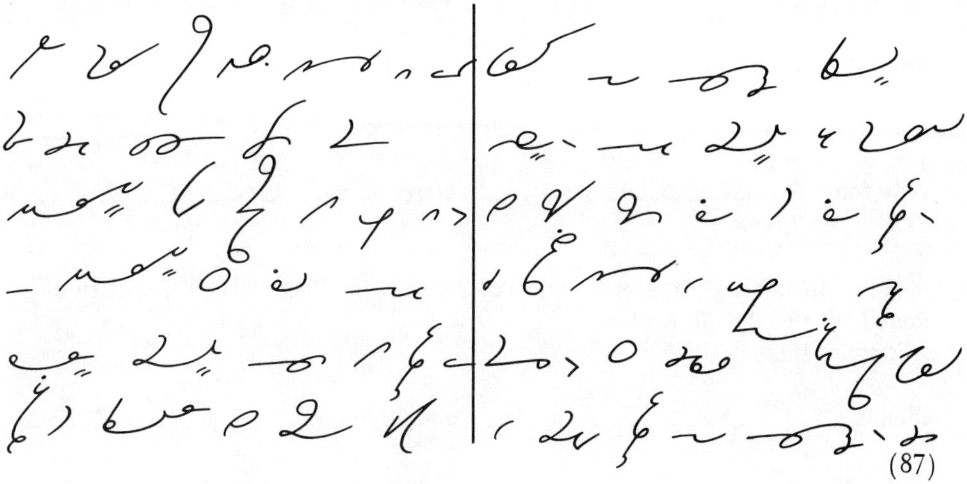

(87)

SELF-CHECK 11

Turn to Self-Check 11 in your pad of self-checks and determine how well you have mastered the material in Section 11. The key to Self-Check 11 appears in your Transcript.

RECORDED DICTATION

You are now ready to take dictation from Record 3, Side 1, Band 1, which contains the material in Paragraph 85. The dictation speed will be slightly higher – 50 words a minute.

Be sure to do the preliminary work on Paragraph 85 (reading and copying it), before you turn on the record player.

SECTION 12

In this section you will learn another block of nine brief forms, two additional sounds represented by the oo hook, and the expression of *w*.

Brief Forms

89. Brief Forms. Practice the following brief forms, saying each word aloud:

glad   **very**

work

soon   **enclose**

thank   **order**

yesterday   **were, year**

Note: In phrases, the dot is omitted from *thank*. *Thanks* is written with a disjoined left s in the dot position.

Practice these outlines:

thanks   **thank you for**

thank you   **thank you for the**

QUICK CHECK *(Read)*

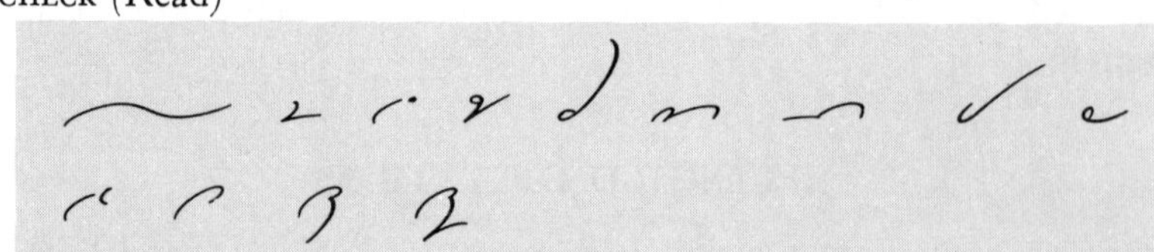

U

90. U. The *oo* hook is used to express the sound heard in *drug, does.*

Practice these words:

does   **trust**

drug ______________________ number ______________________

______________________ ______________________

enough ______________________ us ______________________

above ______________________ just ______________________

Note: The hook in *enough* and *number*, is turned on its side; *oo-s*, as in *us, just*, join without an angle.

QUICK CHECK (*Read*)

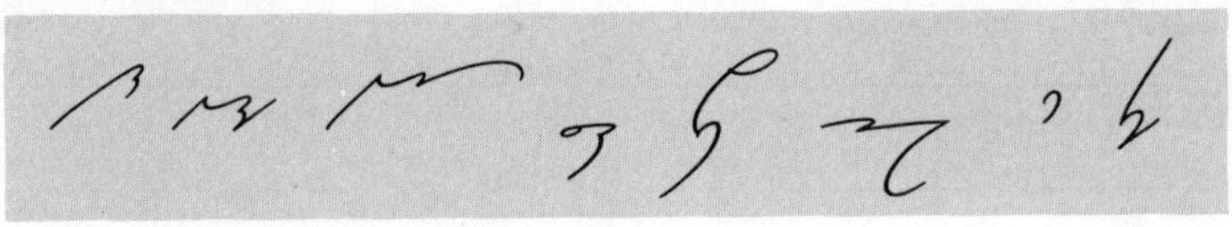

91. Reading and Self-Dictation Practice

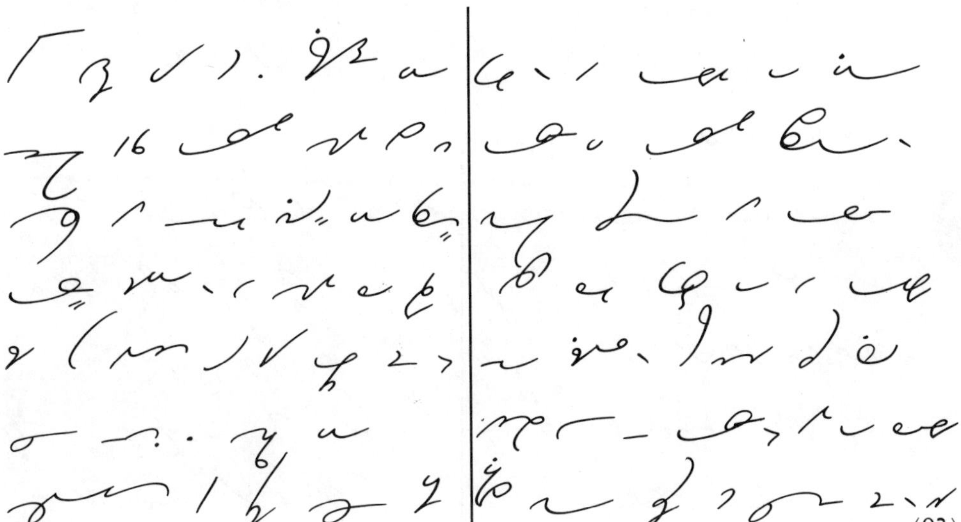

(93)

92. OO. The *oo* hook also represents the sound heard in *foot, full*.
Practice the following words:

foot ______________________ book ______________________

took ______________________ pushed ______________________

pull ______________________ stood ______________________

full ______________________ cooked ______________________

QUICK CHECK (Read)

W

Sw

93. W, Sw. At the beginning of words, the sound of *w* is represented by the oo hook; *sw* is represented by s-oo.

Practice the following words:

we ______	**wood** ______
way ______	**swim** ______
wait ______	**sweet** ______
want ______	**swear** ______

QUICK CHECK (Read)

94. Reading and Self-Dictation Practice

Record 3
Side 1
Band 2

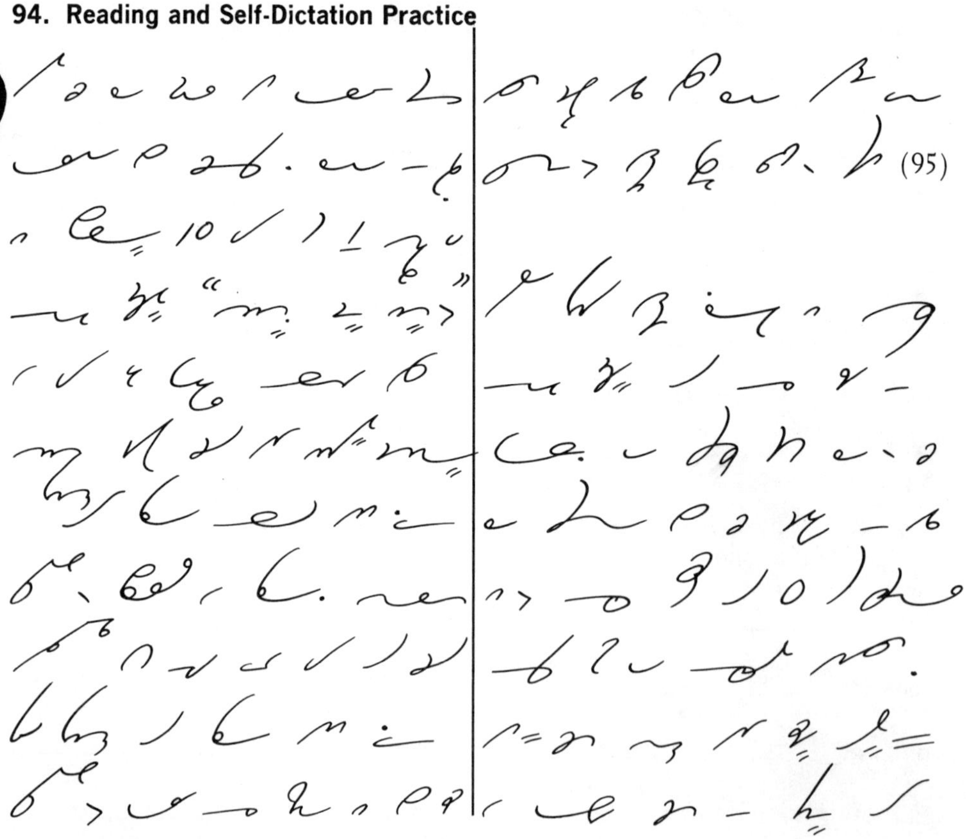

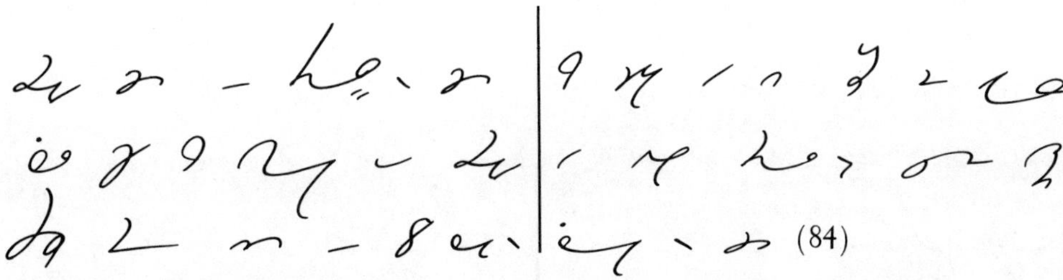

WH

95. Wh. The combination *wh*, as in *while*, is pronounced *h-w*. Therefore, it is written *h-w* in shorthand – the *h* dot is written first.

Practice writing these *wh* words:

white ______ wheat ______

whale ______ while ______

QUICK CHECK (Read)

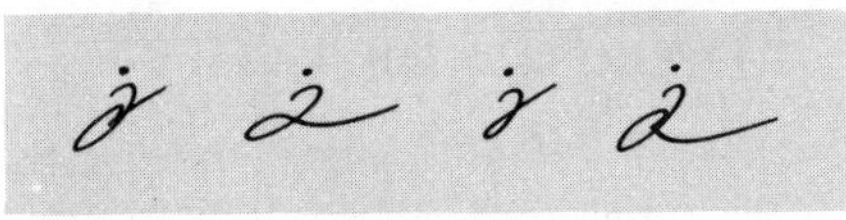

W Dash

96. W in the Body of a Word. When the sound of *w* occurs in the body of a word, as in the words *quick*, *roadway*, it is represented by a short dash underneath the vowel that follows the *w* sound. The dash is inserted after the rest of the outline has been written.

Practice these words:

quick ______ equip ______

twice ______ always ______

quite ______

quit ______ roadway ______

QUICK CHECK (Read)

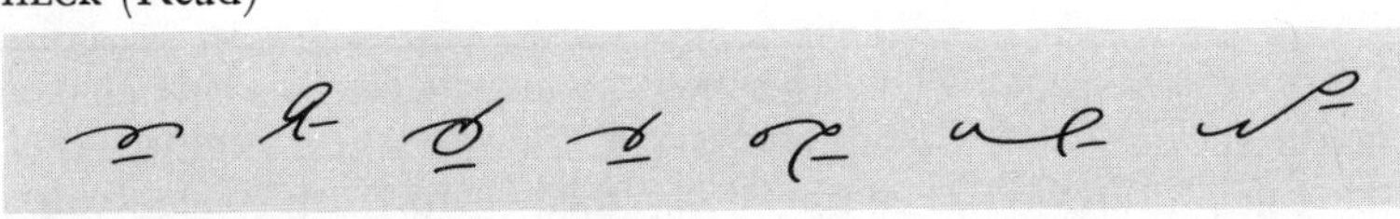

97. Reading and Self-Dictation Practice

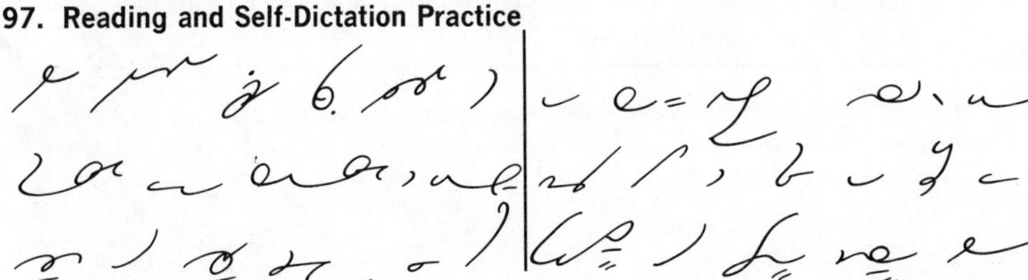

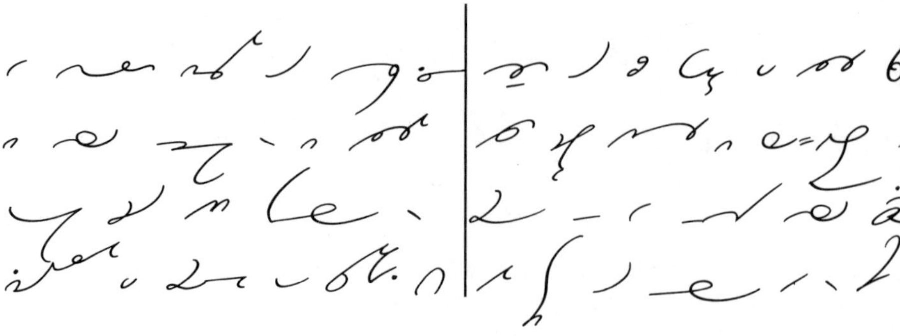

(84)

SELF-CHECK 12

Turn to Self-Check 12 on your self-check pad, complete it, and check your answers with the key in your Transcript. Strive to meet the time and accuracy goals suggested on your self-check.

RECORDED DICTATION

You can now take the dictation on Record 3, Side 1, Band 2, which contains the material in Paragraph 94 dictated at 50 words a minute. Play the record from the beginning, using Band 1 as a warm-up.

If time is available, retake from dictation Records 1 and 2. They will help you review the shorthand principles you have studied in earlier sections as well as improve your shorthand penmanship.

PRACTICE HINT: On page 175 of this book, you will find a chart that gives the brief forms in the order of their presentation. Devote a few minutes each day to reading the brief forms you have already studied. (Up to this stage you can read the first five groups.) A few minutes spent on this brief-form recall daily will do much to improve your writing speed.

SECTION 13

In this section you will study a useful shorthand blend, another block of brief forms, one common word ending, and one common word beginning.

Ted

98. Ted. The combination *ted* is represented by a very long straight upward stroke.

Ted 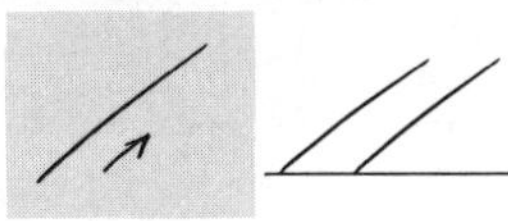

(Write several times, saying **ted** aloud each time.)

COMPARE: heat heed heated

Practice the following words:

acted ______ **dated** ______

waited ______ **tested** ______

rated ______ **today** ______

rested ______ **steady** ______

QUICK CHECK *(Read)*

Ded
Det
Dit

99. Ded, Det, Dit. The combinations *ded, det, dit* are also represented by the long upward *ted* stroke.

Practice the following words:

traded ______ **needed** ______

guided ______ **added** ______

graded ______

editor ______

______ detail ______

credit ______ deduct ______

QUICK CHECK *(Read)*

100. Reading and Self-Dictation Practice

Record 3
Side 1
Band 3

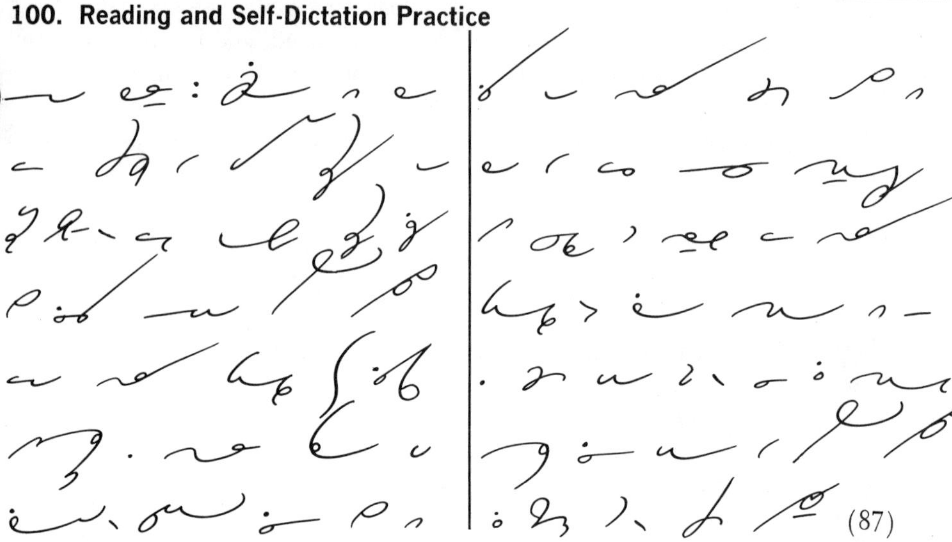

(87)

Brief Forms

101. Brief Forms. Practice the following brief forms, saying each one aloud as you write:

value ______ what ______

______ than ______

thing, think ______ why ______

about ______ great ______

______ ______

one, won ______ business ______

QUICK CHECK *(Read)*

-ble

102. Word Ending -ble. The word ending *-ble* is represented by the shorthand *b.* Practice the following words:

payable ____________ sensible ____________
tables ____________ available ____________
terrible ____________ ____________
reliable ____________ trouble ____________
____________ possible ____________

QUICK CHECK (Read)

103. Reading and Self-Dictation Practice

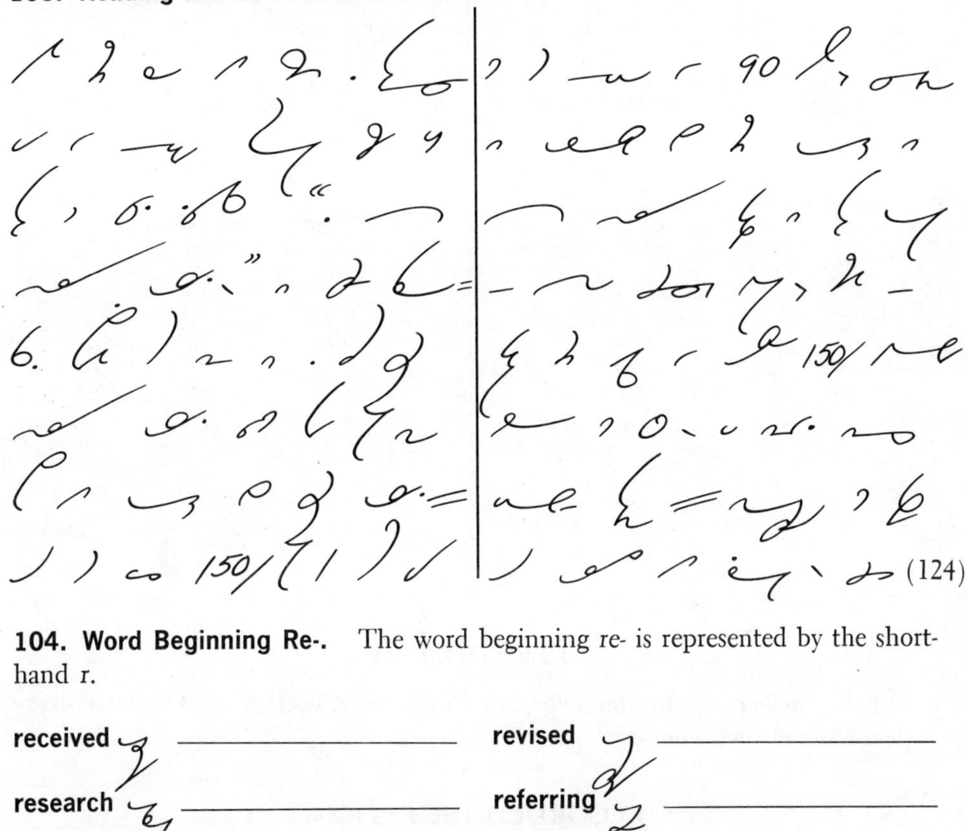

(124)

Re-

104. Word Beginning Re-. The word beginning *re-* is represented by the shorthand *r.*

received ____________ revised ____________
research ____________ referring ____________
revise ____________ repaired ____________
reappear ____________ reopen ____________

QUICK CHECK *(Read)*

105. Reading and Self-Dictation Practice

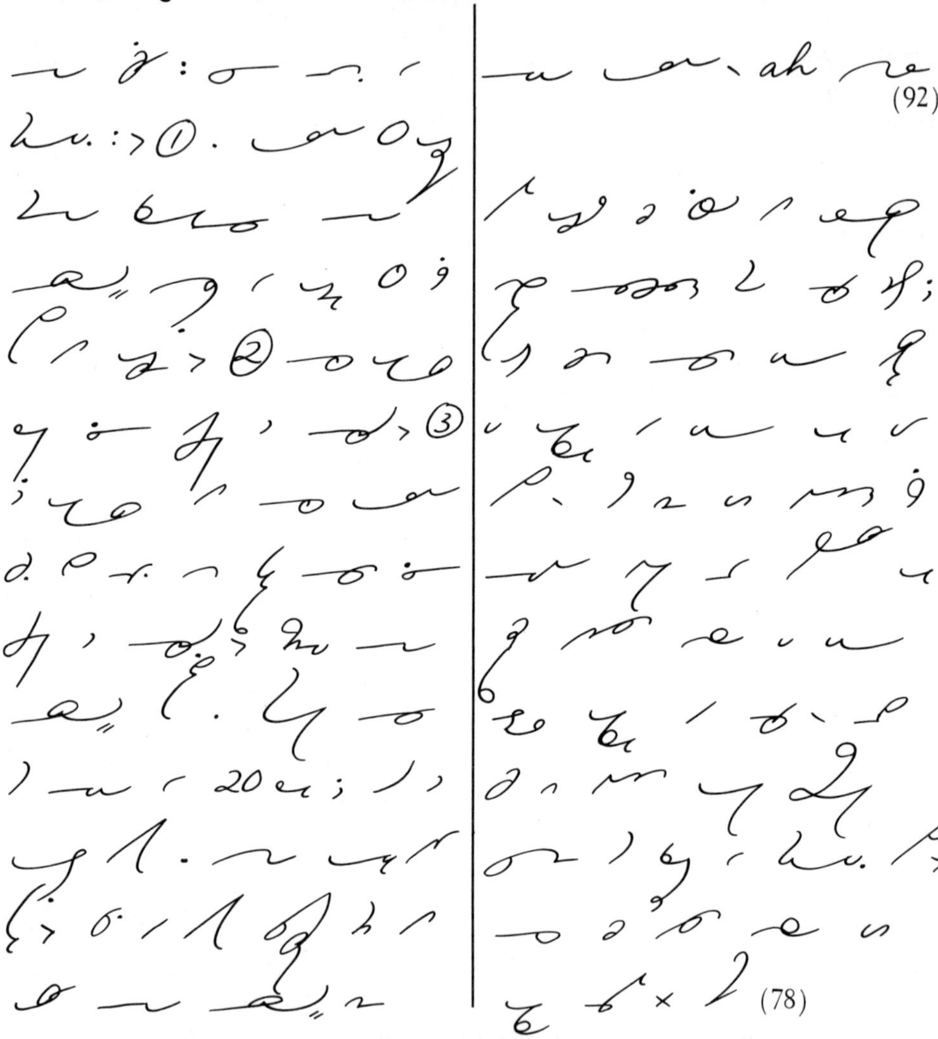

SELF-CHECK 13

You are now ready to complete Self-Check 13. Check your completed work with the key in your Transcript.

RECORDED DICTATION

You can now take Record 3, Side 1, Band 3, which dictates the material in Paragraph 100 at 50 words a minute.

Play the record from the beginning, using Bands 1 and 2 as a warm-up.

SECTION 14

In this section you will study the character representing the sound of *oi*, another shorthand blend stroke, a very common word beginning, and one more block of brief forms.

OI

106. Oi. The sound of *oi*, as in the word *toy*, is represented by combining the *o* and *e* strokes.

Oi  ______ (Write several times, saying **oi** aloud each time.)

Practice the following words:

toy ______ **boy** ______

noise ______ **oil** ______

join ______ ______

annoy ______ **appoint** ______

coin ______ **voice** ______

QUICK CHECK *(Read)*

Men

107. Men. The combination *men* is represented by joining the shorthand strokes *m* and *n* into one long stroke. The stroke is called *men*.

Men 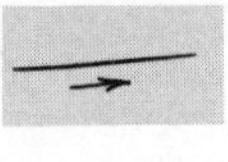 ______ (Write several times, saying **men** aloud each time.)

COMPARE: knee me many

Practice the following words:

men

meant 

mend 

mentioned 

mentally 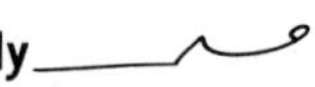

women 

QUICK CHECK *(Read)*

108. Reading and Self-Dictation Practice

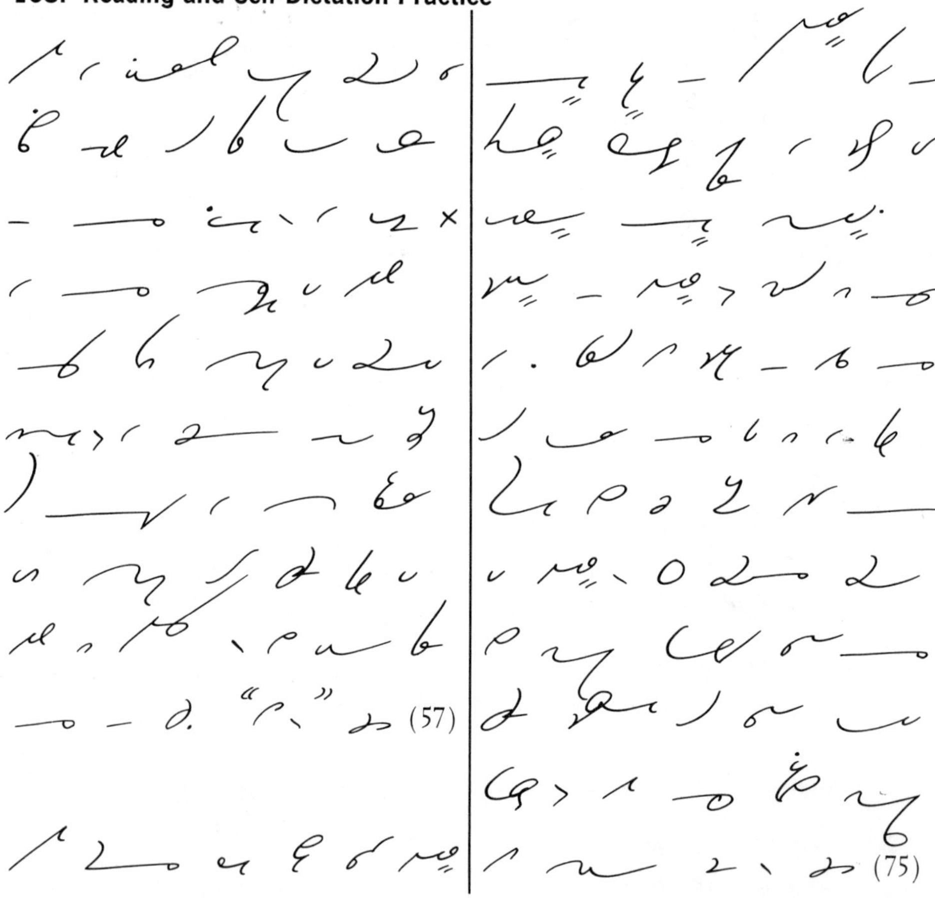

(57) (75)

Mem

109. Mem. The straight long stroke that represents *men* also represents *mem*.
Practice these words:

member ____________ **memory** ____________

remember ____________ **memorize** ____________

QUICK CHECK *(Read)*

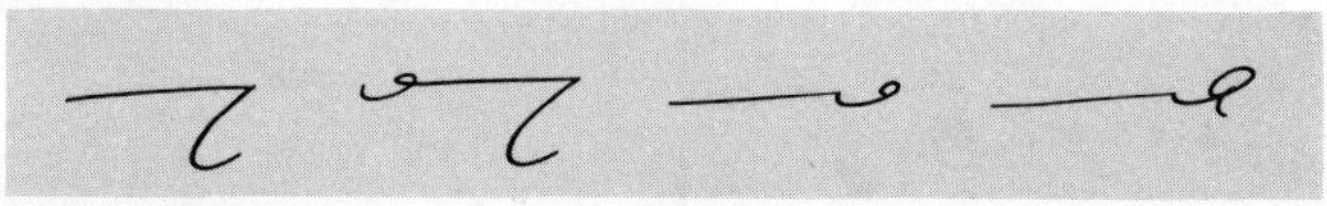

Min Mon etc.

110. Min, Mon, Mun, Man. The straight long stroke also represents *min, mon, mun,* and *man*.
Practice these words:

minute ____________ **manner** ____________

month ____________ **manage** ____________

money ____________ **managed** ____________

QUICK CHECK *(Read)*

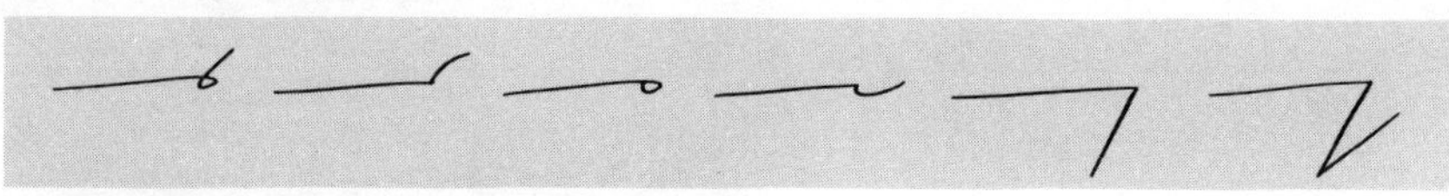

111. Reading and Self-Dictation Practice

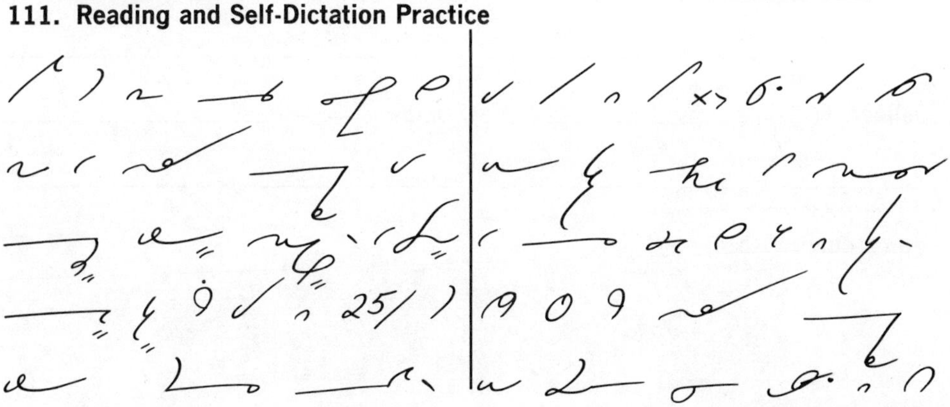

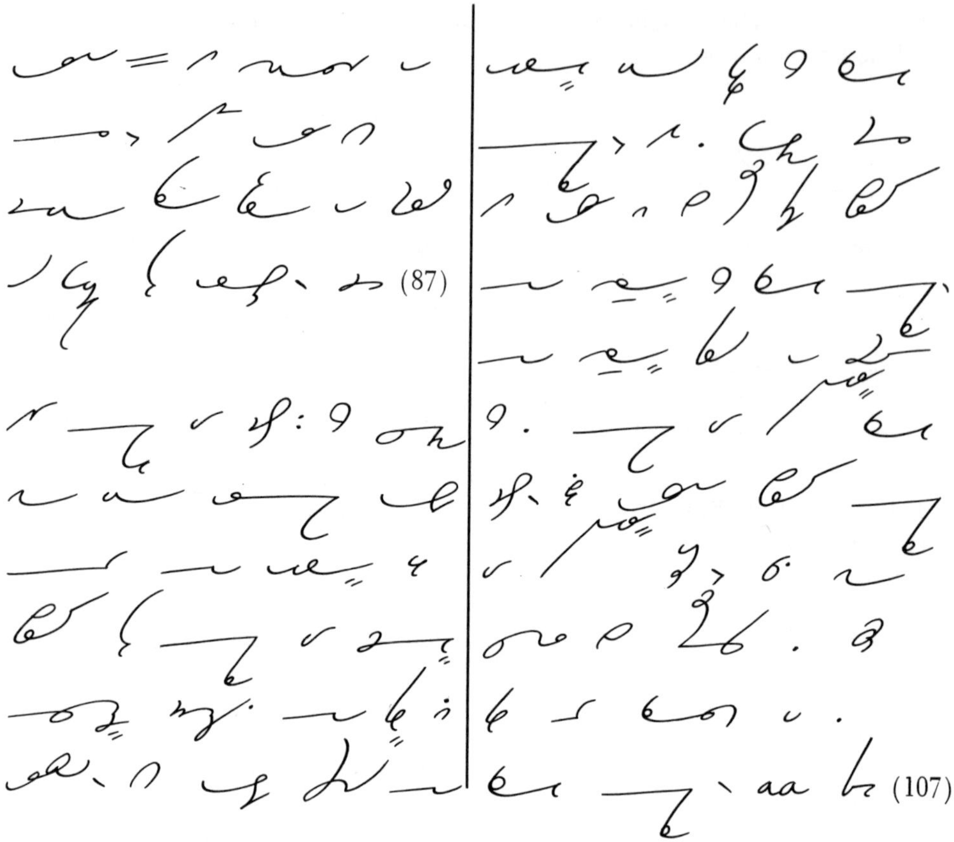

(87) (107)

Be-

112. Word Beginning Be-. The common word beginning *be-* is represented by the shorthand stroke for *b*.

Practice these words:

became  **belief** 

because  **begin** 

believe  **below** 

QUICK CHECK *(Read)*

113. Brief Forms. Practice the following brief forms:

gentlemen	**important, importance**
where	**morning**
those	**manufacture**

QUICK CHECK *(Read)*

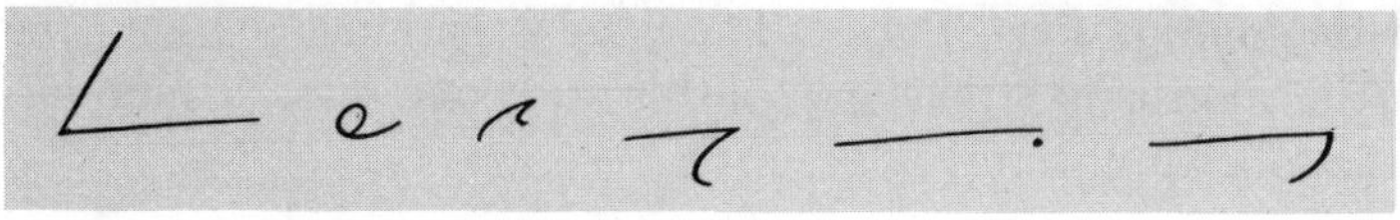

114. Reading and Self-Dictation Practice

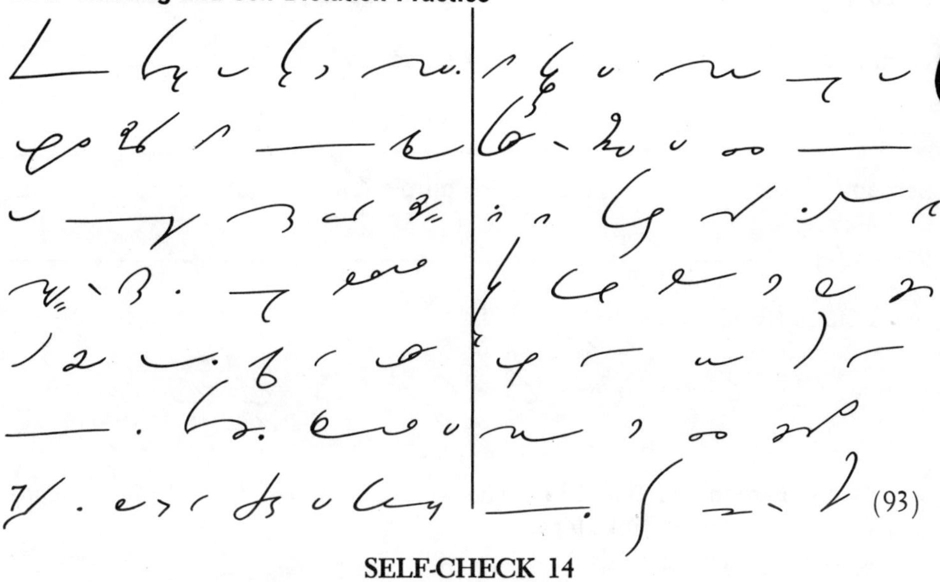

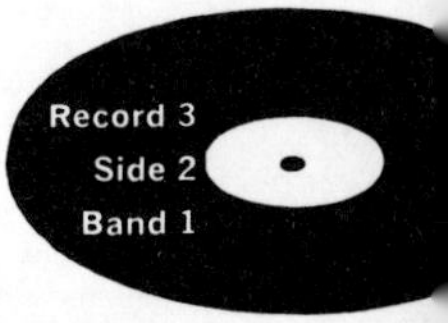

(93)

SELF-CHECK 14

You are ready for another short self-test. Turn to Self-Check 14 in your pad and complete both parts. Then check your work against the key in your Transcript.

RECORDED DICTATION

You are now ready to take Record 3, Side 2, Band 1 from dictation at 50 words a minute. This contains the material from Paragraph 114.

If you have time available, you might once again take from dictation the material on Record 3, Side 1.

SECTION 15

In this section you will study two new word beginnings, another block of brief forms, a new vowel sound, and one word ending.

Per-
Pur-

115. Word Beginnings Per-, Pur-. The word beginnings *per-* and *pur-* are represented by the shorthand strokes *p-r* written with one smooth motion.

Practice the following words:

person ____________ **persuade** ____________

permit ____________ **purse** ____________

____________ **purchase** ____________

perhaps ____________ **purple** ____________

persist ____________ ____________

QUICK CHECK *(Read)*

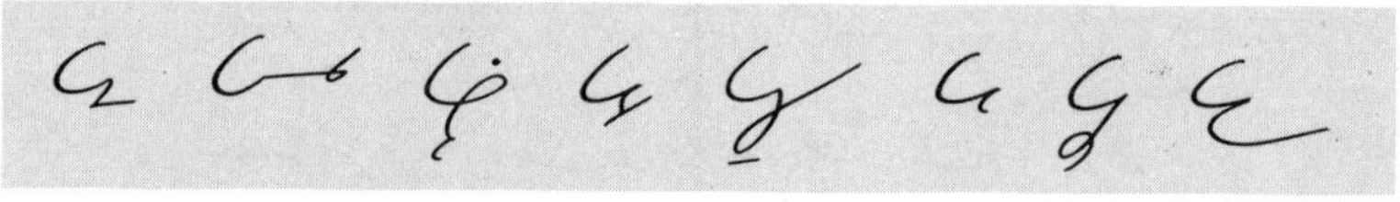

De-
Di-

116. Word Beginnings De-, Di-. The word beginnings *de-* and *di-* are represented by the shorthand stroke for *d*.

Practice the following words:

decide ____________ **direct** ____________

desire ____________ **diplomat** ____________

deserve ____________ ____________

deposit ____________ **diploma** ____________

delay ____________ ____________

QUICK CHECK (Read)

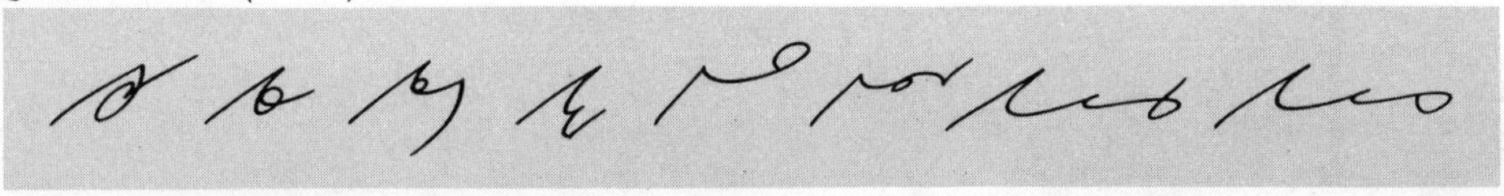

117. Reading and Self-Dictation Practice

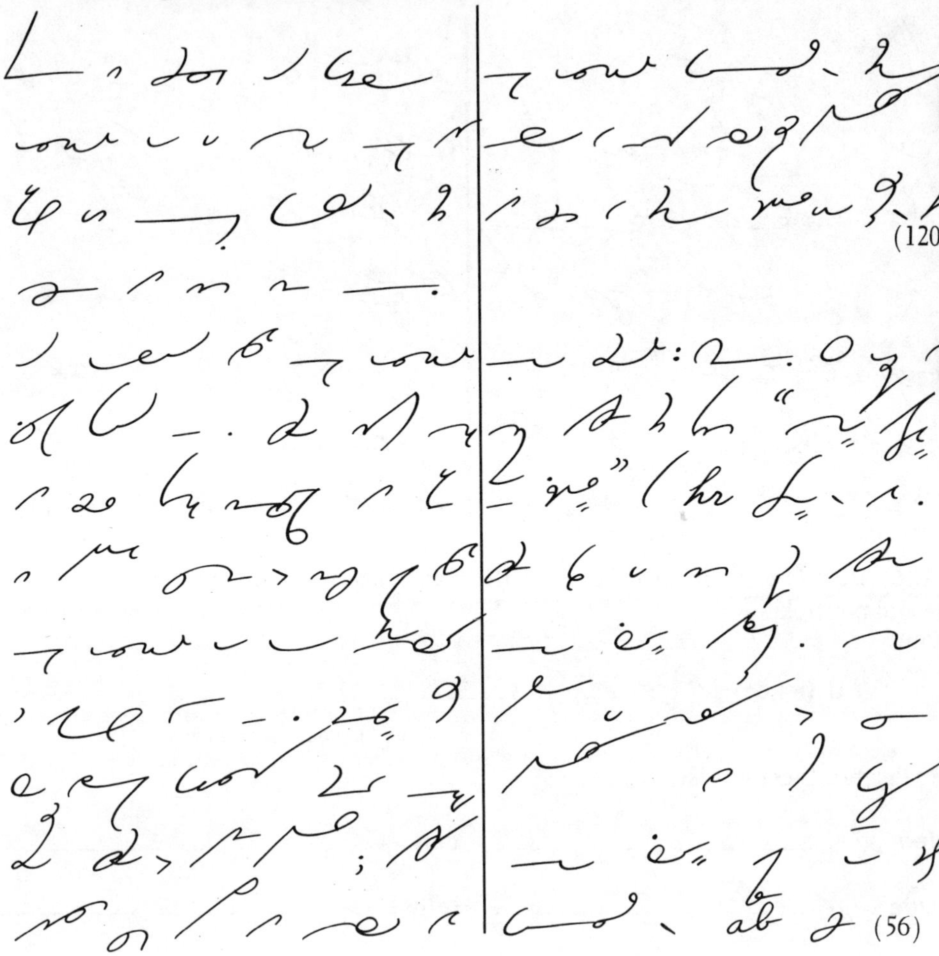

(120)

Record 3 Side 2 Band 2

Record 3 Side 2 Band 3

(56)

118. Brief Forms. Practice these brief forms until you know them thoroughly.

Brief Forms

present	______	must	______
company	______	opportunity	______
part	______	after	______
advertise	______	immediate	immediately
wish	______		______

usual

QUICK CHECK *(Read)*

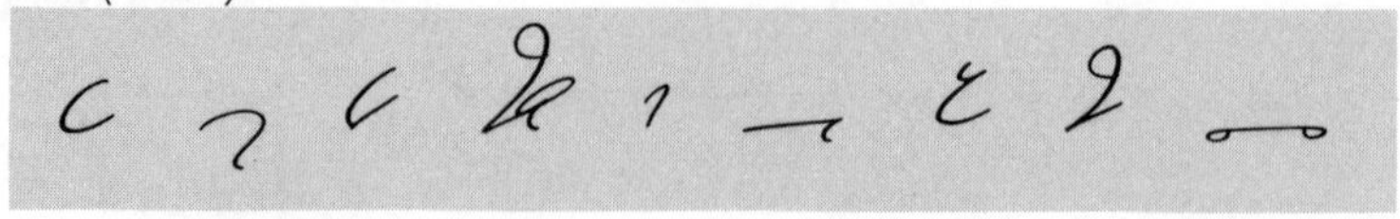

119. Reading and Self-Dictation Practice

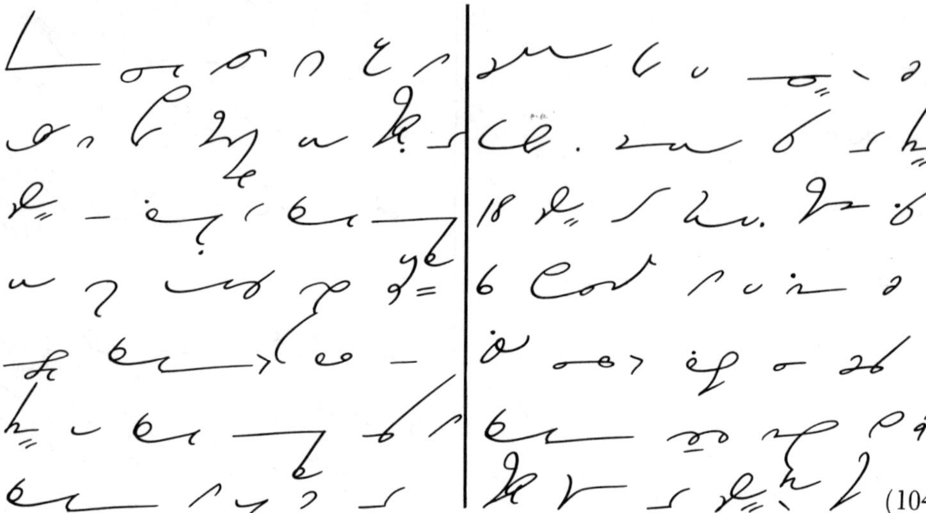

(104)

U

120. U. The sound of *u* heard in the word *view* is represented by joining the e and oo strokes.

U (e+oo) 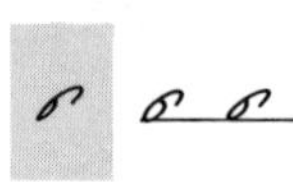

(Write several times, saying **u** aloud each time.)

Practice these words:

few	**unit**
cute	**refuse**
unite	**unique**
reviewed	**usual**

QUICK CHECK *(Read)*

-ment

121. Word Ending -ment. The word ending *-ment* is represented by the shorthand stroke for *m*.

Practice the following words:

arrangements 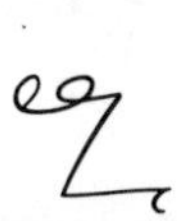 ____________ advertisement  ____________

garments  ____________ shipments 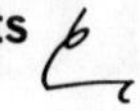 ____________

assignment  ____________ payment  ____________

Note: In the word *assignment*, the *m* for *-ment* is joined to the *n* with a jog.

122. Reading and Self-Dictation Practice

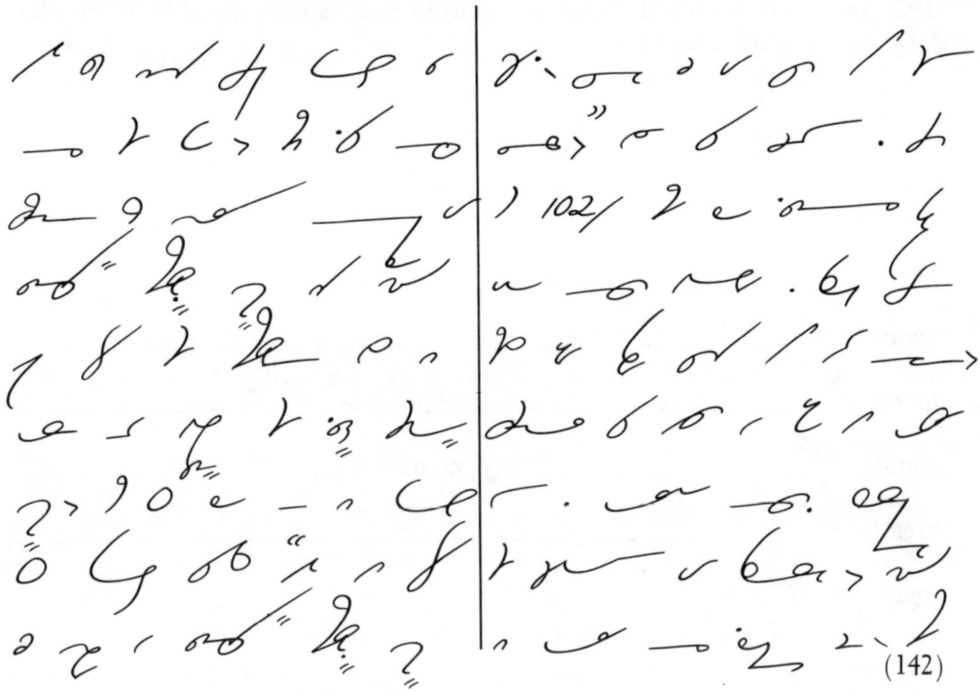

(142)

SELF-CHECK 15

It is time again to test yourself to determine your progress. Complete Self-Check 15; then check you work against the key in your Transcript.

RECORDED DICTATION

You are ready to take from dictation the letters in Paragraph 117, which are dictated at 50 words a minute on Record 3, Side 2, Bands 2 and 3.

Play the record from the beginning, using Band 1 as a warm-up.

SECTION 16

ow

In this section you will study the character for another vowel sound, one word ending, two word beginnings, another block of brief forms, and another blend.

123. Ow. The sound of *ow*, as in the word *now*, is represented by joining the large *a* circle and the *oo* hook.

Ow (Write several times, saying **ow** aloud each time.)

Practice these words:

now **allow**

ounce

found **account**

doubt **amount**

proud

QUICK CHECK *(Read)*

-ther

124. Word Ending -ther. The word ending *-ther* is represented by the *th* stroke.

Practice these words:

other **leather**

whether

mother **either**

neither ______________ bothered ______________

rather ______________ ______________

QUICK CHECK (Read)

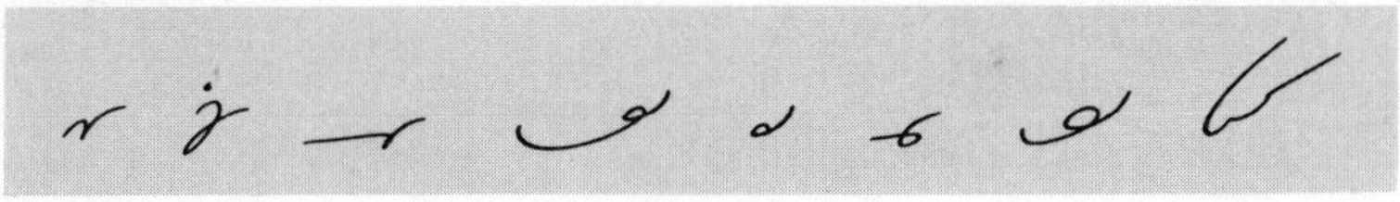

125. Reading and Self-Dictation Practice

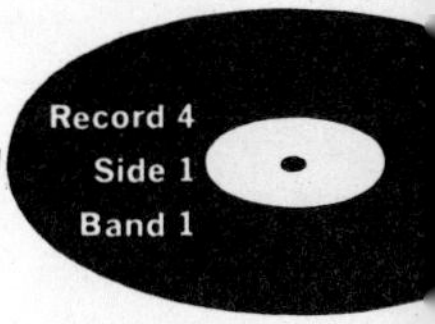

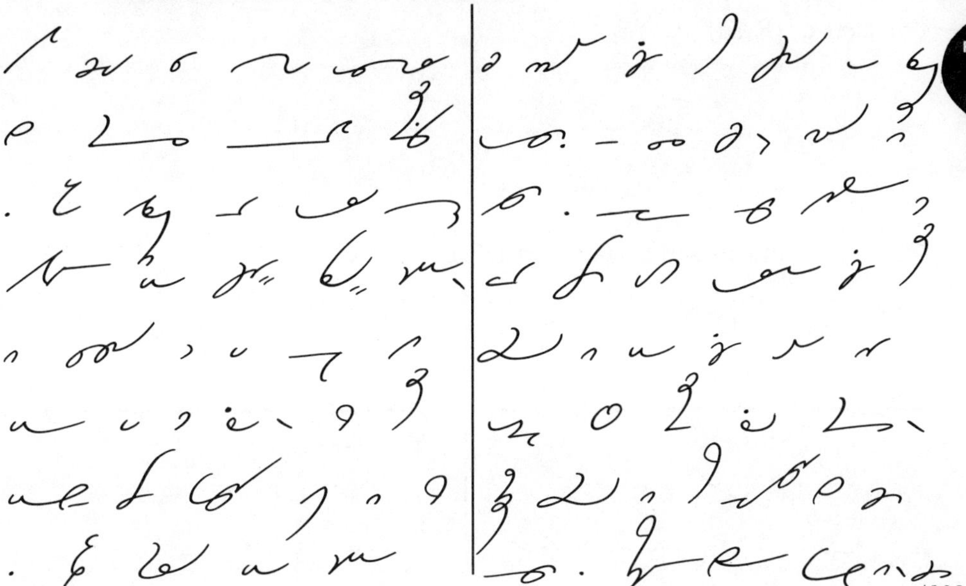

(108)

126. Word Beginning Con-. The word beginning *con-* is represented by the shorthand stroke for *k*.

Con-

Practice these words:

concern ______________ consisted ______________

consider ______________ ______________

contract ______________ controlled ______________

confer ______________ ______________

QUICK CHECK (Read)

127. Word Beginning Com-. The word beginning *com-* is also represented by the shorthand stroke for *k*.

Practice these words:

combine **complain** **compare** **complete** **comply** **compete**

QUICK CHECK *(Read)*

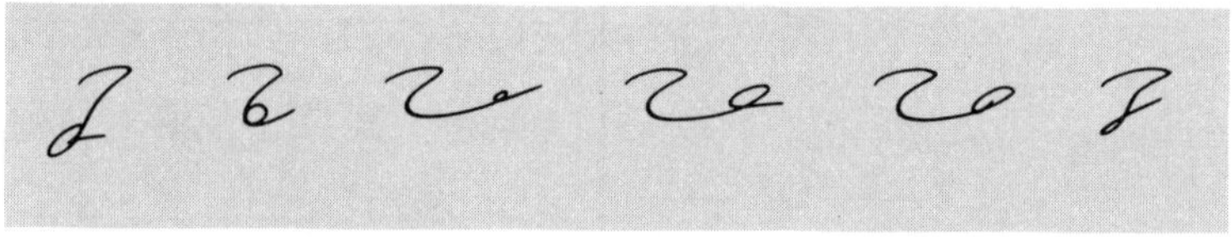

128. Reading and Self-Dictation Practice

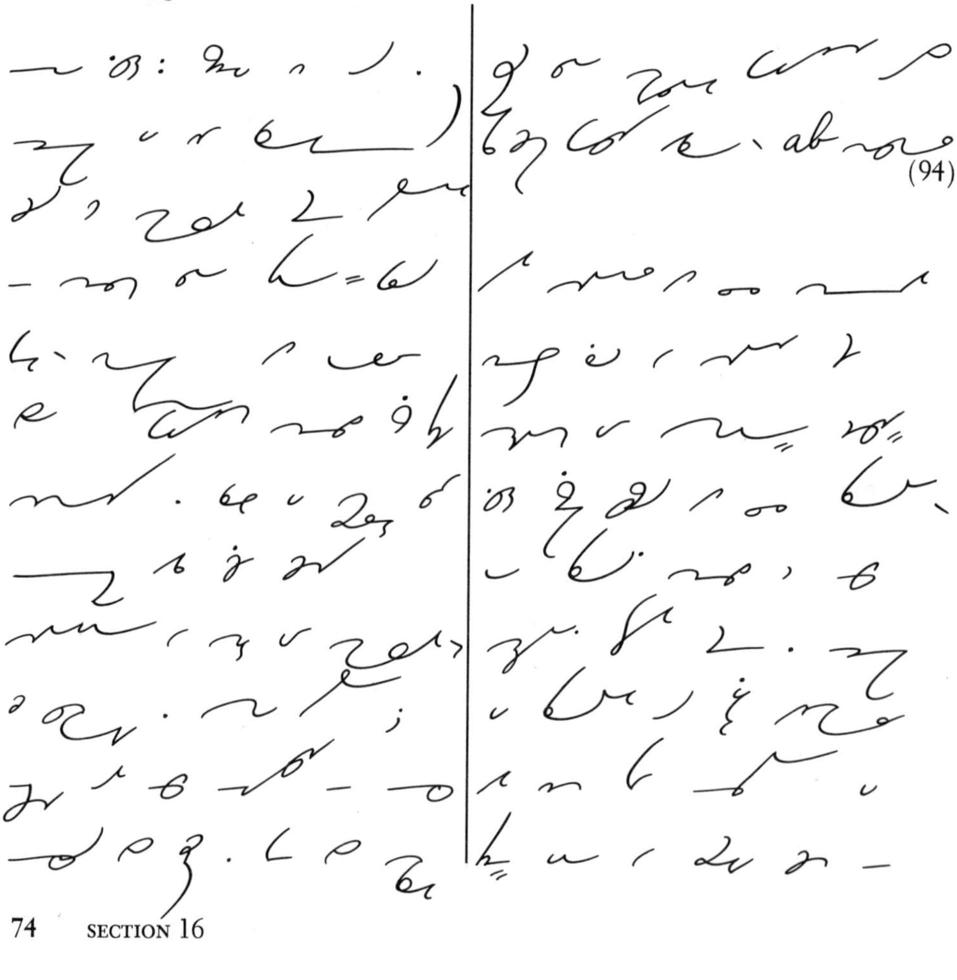

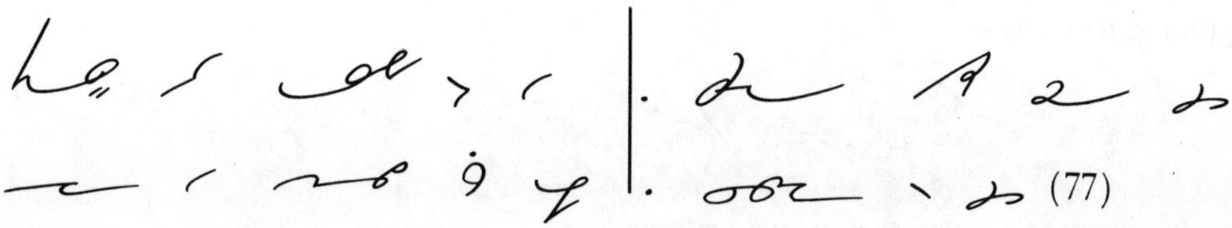

(77)

129. Brief Forms. Practice the following brief forms, saying the words aloud as you write.

advantage ____________ suggest ____________

correspond, correspondence ____________ ____________

____________ use ____________

such ____________ how, out ____________

big ____________ several ____________

ever, every ____________ ____________

QUICK CHECK *(Read)*

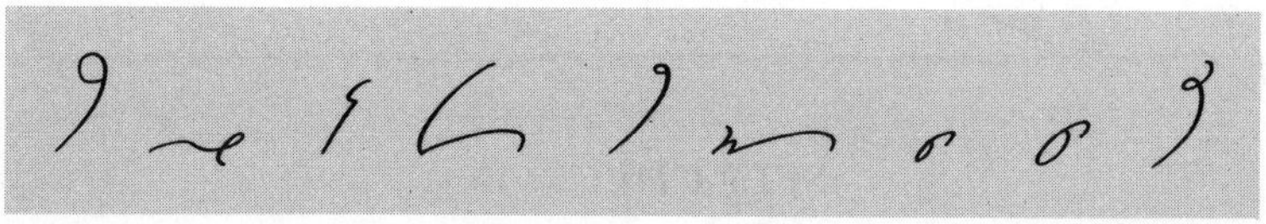

130. Den. When *d* and *n* come together, the angle is rounded off to form the *den* blend.

Den ____________

(Write several times, saying **den** aloud each time.)

Practice the following words:

sudden ____________ confidently ____________

dentist ____________ ____________

____________ wooden ____________

president ____________ danger ____________

evidently ____________ ____________

____________ dinner ____________

QUICK CHECK *(Read)*

131. Reading and Self-Dictation Practice

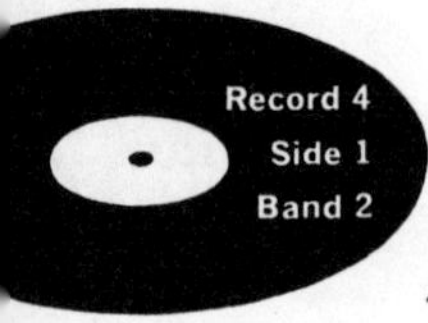

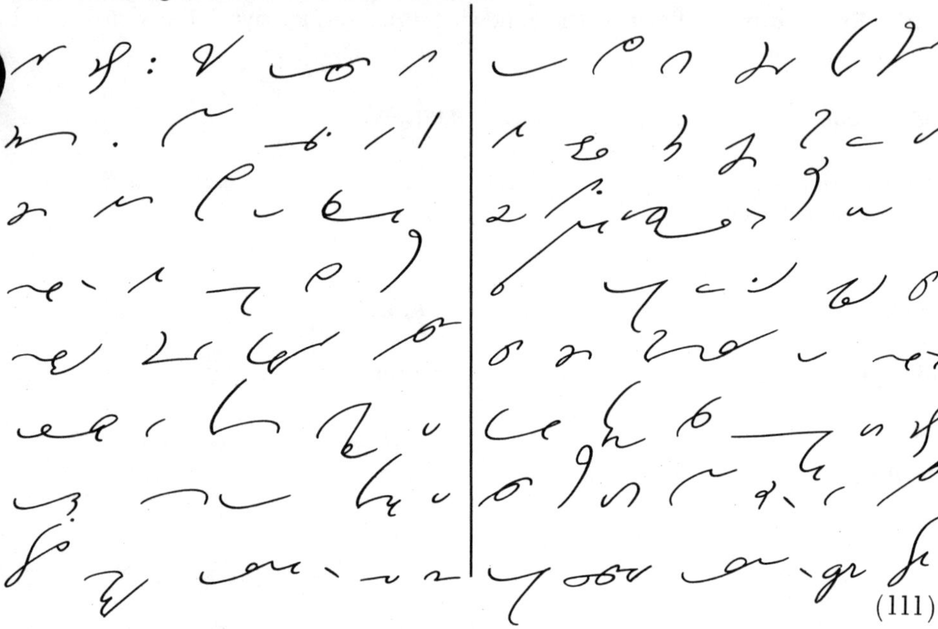

(111)

SELF-CHECK 16

You are now ready to complete Self-Check 16 and test your mastery of the shorthand principles in this section. Be sure to check your work against the key in your Transcript.

RECORDED DICTATION

You are now ready to take from dictation at 60 words a minute Record 4, Side 1, Bands 1 and 2.

Band 1 contains the material from Paragraph 125.

Band 2 contains the material from Paragraph 131.

SECTION 17

In this section you will continue your study of facile blends and useful business phrases.

Ten

132. Ten. The blend that represents *den* also represents *ten.*
Practice these words:

attend   **bulletin**

attention

written   **remittance**

sentence

tend   **stand**

gotten   **tonight**

QUICK CHECK *(Read)*

Tain

133. Tain. The blend that represents *den, ten* also represents *tain.*
Practice these words:

attain   **retain**

obtain   **maintain**

detain

certain   **container**

contain

QUICK CHECK *(Read)*

134. Reading and Self-Dictation Practice

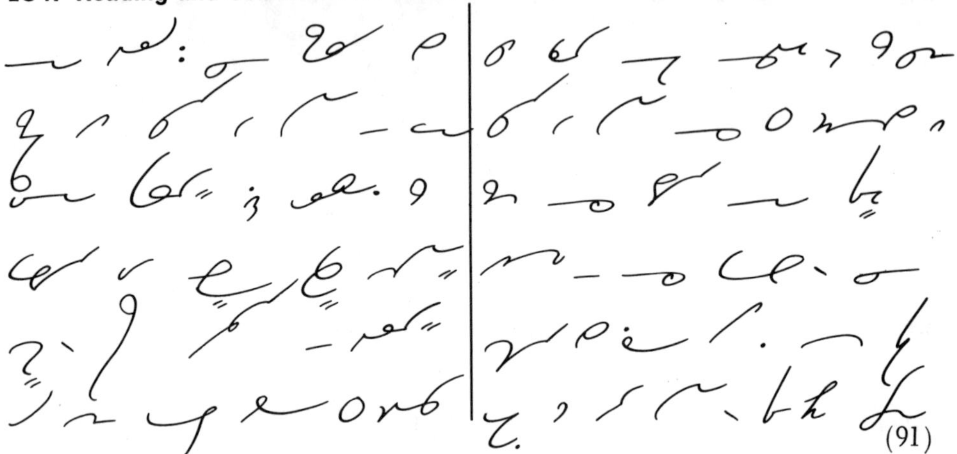

(91)

Dem

135. Dem. When *d* and *m* come together, the angle is rounded off to form the *dem* blend.

Dem 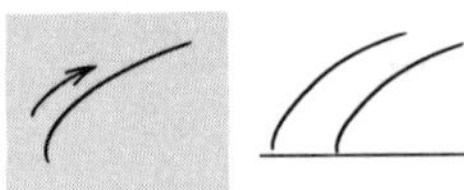

(Write several times, saying **dem** aloud each time.)

Practice the following words:

demonstrate 

freedom 

demand 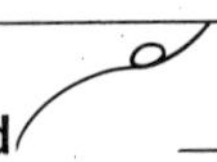

seldom 

condemn 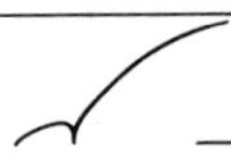

domestic 

damage 

medium 

QUICK CHECK *(Read)*

Tem

136. Tem. The stroke that represents *dem* also represents *tem*. Practice the following words:

temper	**temporary**
attempt	
system	**customer**
item	
estimate	**tomorrow**

QUICK CHECK *(Read)*

137. Reading and Self-Dictation Practice

Record 4
Side 1
Band 3

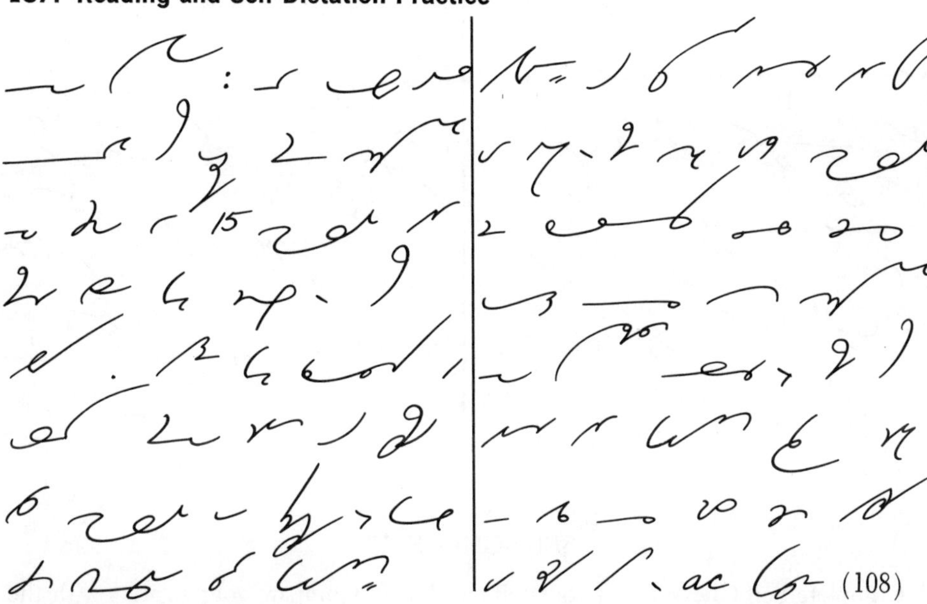

(108)

Business Phrases

138. Business Abbreviations. Here are a few very common business letter salutations and closings. Practice them.

Dear Mr.	**Dear Miss**
Dear Mrs.	**Cordially yours**

Yours sincerely ______________ Very cordially yours ______________

QUICK CHECK (*Read*)

Useful Phrases

139. Useful Phrases. Here are three useful phrases formed with the *ten* and *tem* blends. Practice them.

to know ______________ to make ______________

to me ______________ ______________

QUICK CHECK (*Read*)

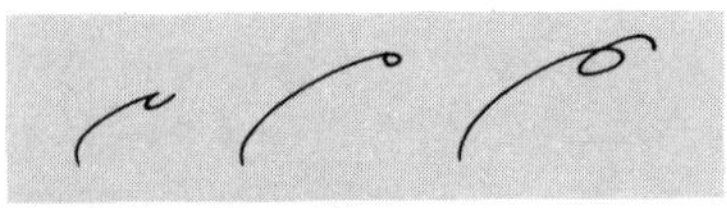

140. Reading and Self-Dictation Practice

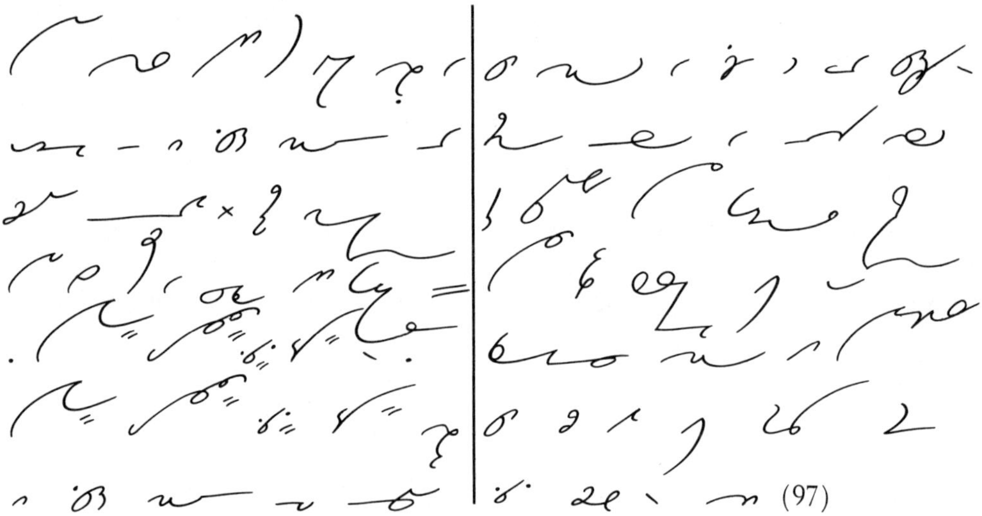

(97)

SELF-CHECK 17

Complete Self-Check 17 on your self-check pad. Compare your answers with the key in your Transcript.

RECORDED DICTATION

You can now take from dictation Record 4, Side 1, Band 3, which contains the material from Paragraph 137 dictated at 60 words a minute.

Play the record from the beginning, using Bands 1 and 2 as a warm-up.

SECTION 18

This section again presents considerable variety: shorthand forms for the days of the week and the months of the year, another block of brief forms, another fluent blend, and a principle of vowel omission.

Days

141. Days of the Week. Practice these outlines, which are very easy to remember.

Sunday ________________ **Wednesday** ________________

Monday ________________ **Thursday** ________________

________________ **Friday** ________________

Tuesday ________________ **Saturday** ________________

QUICK CHECK *(Read)*

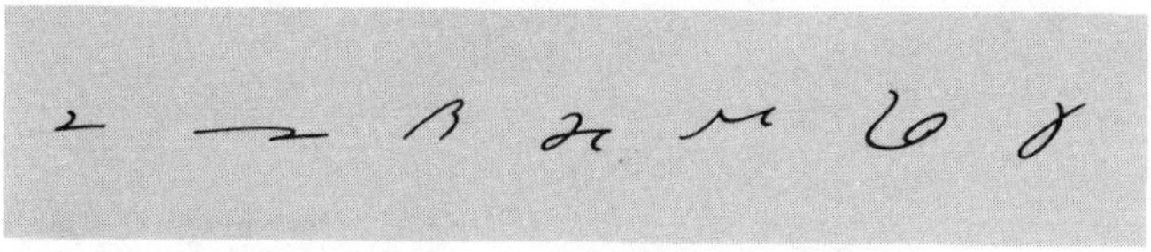

Months

142. Months of the Year. Some of these are abbreviated; some are written out. Practice them.

January ________________ **July** ________________

February ________________ **August** ________________

March ________________ **September** ________________

April ________________ **October** ________________

May ________________ **November** ________________

June ________________ **December** ________________

QUICK CHECK *(Read)*

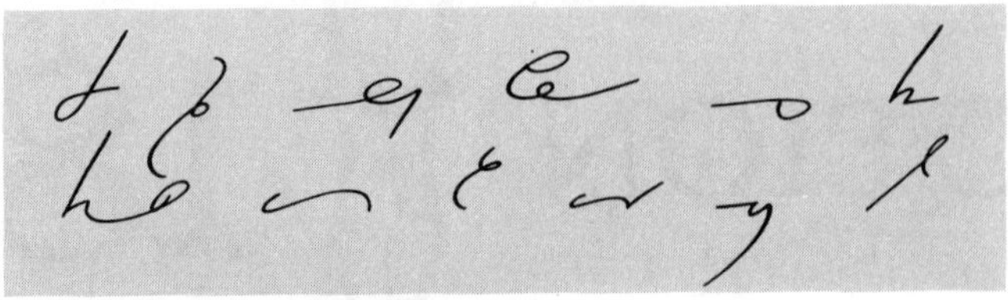

143. Reading and Self-Dictation Practice

Record 4
Side 2
Band 1

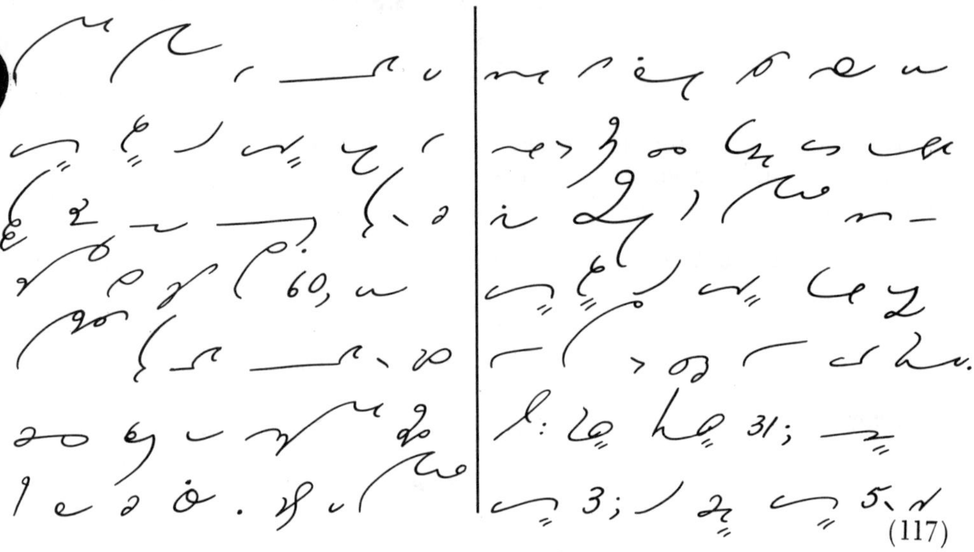

(117)

Brief Forms

144. Brief Forms. Practice these useful brief forms.

time ______ **gone** ______

question ______ ______

during ______ **yet** ______

general ______ **worth** ______

acknowledge ______ ***over** ______

*The brief form over is written above the following character. It is also used as a prefix form, as in overcame.

Practice these words:

overcame ______ **overtake** ______

oversight ______ **overcoat** ______

QUICK CHECK *(Read)*

145. Reading and Self-Dictation Practice

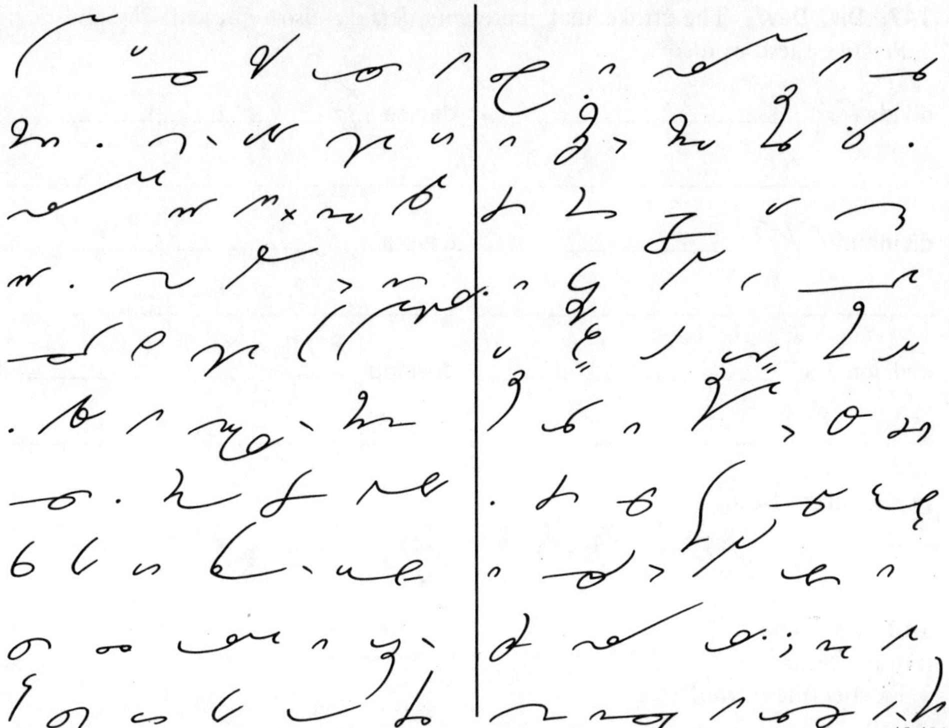

(141)

146. Def, Dif. By rounding off the angle between *d* and *f*, we obtain the fluent *def, dif* blend.

Def

Dif

Def, Dif  (Write several times, saying **def, dif** aloud each time.)

Practice these words:

definite  **defined** 

defeat  **different** 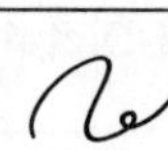

defied  **difference** 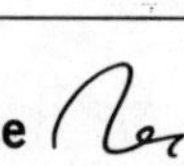

QUICK CHECK *(Read)*

Div Dev

147. Div, Dev. The stroke that represents *def, dif* also represents *div* and *dev.* Practice these words:

divide	**devise**
dividend	**devote**
division	**develop**

QUICK CHECK *(Read)*

Vowel Omission

148. Omission of E in U. The *oo* hook is often used to represent the sound of *u* in *new, suit.*

Practice these words:

new	**avenues**
continued	**issue**
	induce
due	**suits**

QUICK CHECK *(Read)*

149. Reading and Self-Dictation Practice

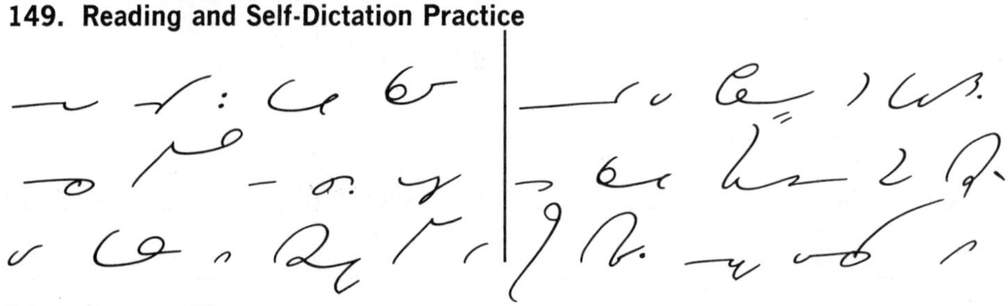

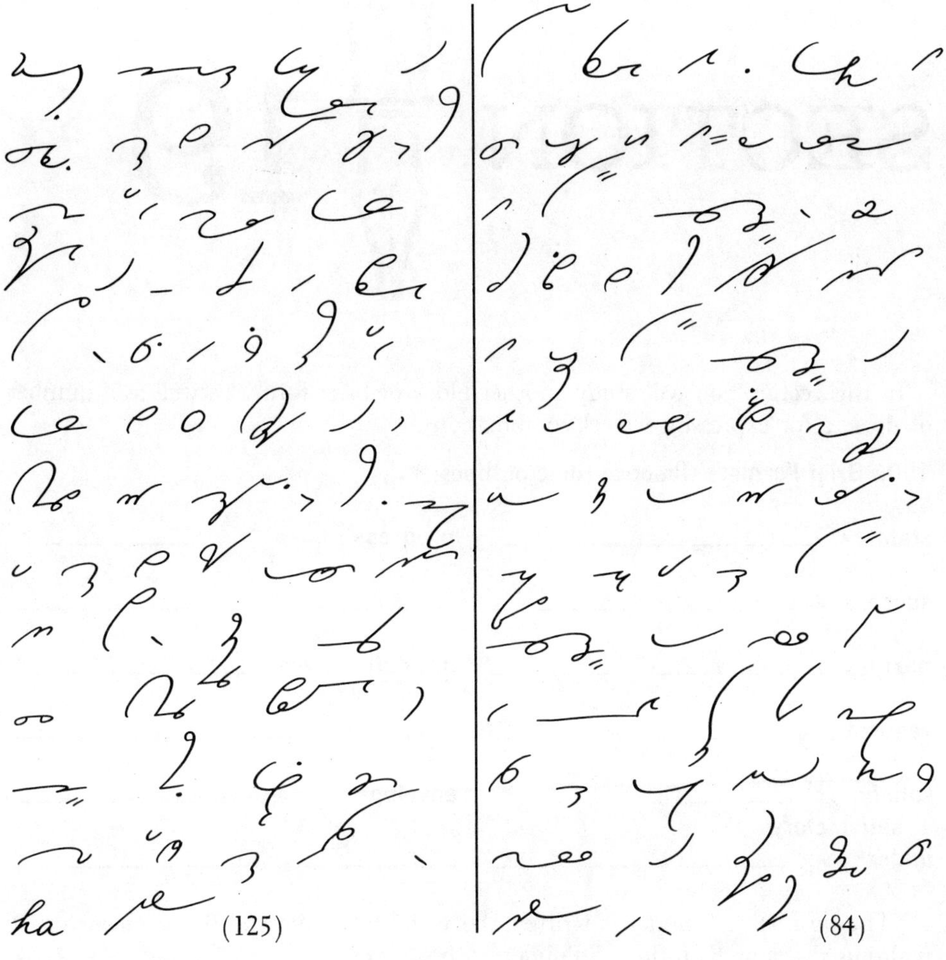

(125) (84)

SELF-CHECK 18

Complete Self-Check 18 on your pad of self-checks. Check your work with the key in your Transcript.

RECORDED DICTATION

You are now ready to take the dictation on Record 4, Side 2, Band 1, which contains the material in Paragraph 143 dictated at 60 words a minute.

Be sure to read Paragraph 143 and make a shorthand copy of it, if time permits, before you turn on the record player.

PRACTICE HINT: When you have completed your work on this section, turn to the brief-form chart on page 175 and review all the brief forms you have studied thus far.

SECTION 19

In this section you will study another block of brief forms, as well as a number of devices for expressing vowel combinations.

Brief Forms

150. Brief Forms. Practice these outlines:

state	**progress**
success	
next	**difficult**
request	
satisfy, satisfactory	**envelope**
under*	

*The *oo* hook for *under* is written above the following shorthand character. It is also used as a prefix form, as in *underneath*.

Practice these words:

underneath	**underpay**
undertake	**undergo**

QUICK CHECK *(Read)*

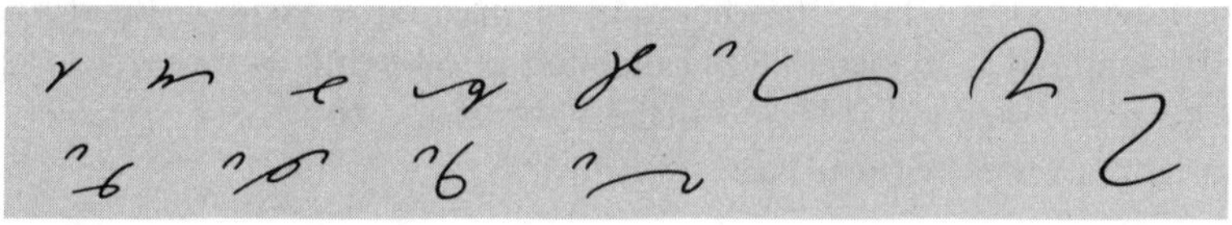

151. Brief-Form Derivatives. Here are some useful derivatives of the brief forms in paragraph 150. Practice them.

satisfied	**progressed**
difficulty	

states ______________________ understand ______________________

requests ______________________ ______________________

QUICK CHECK (*Read*)

152. Reading and Self-Dictation Practice

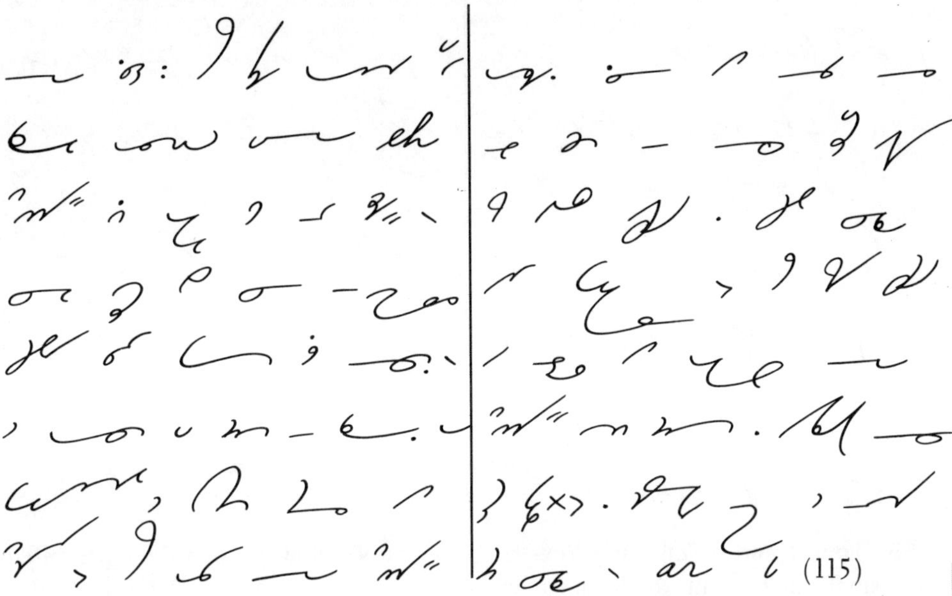

(115)

Phrases

153. Useful Business Phrases. The following phrases are used so frequently in business that special forms have been provided for them. Practice these phrases until you know them thoroughly.

of course ______________________ we hope ______________________

as soon as ______________________ let us ______________________

as soon as possible ______________________ ______________________

to do ______________________ to us ______________________

I hope ______________________ your order ______________________

QUICK CHECK (*Read*)

154. Reading and Self-Dictation Practice

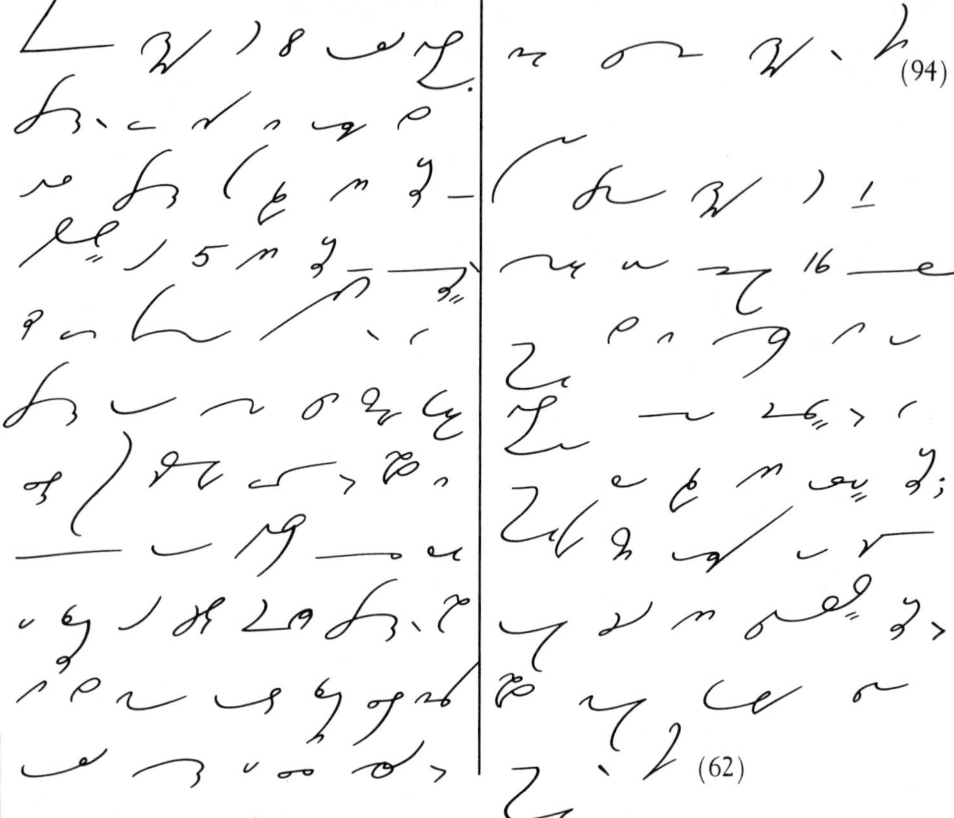

155. Long I and a Following Vowel.

Any vowel following long *i* is represented by a small circle within the large circle.

COMPARE: line  lion 

Practice these words:

trial  ______________

prior  ______________

____

science  ______________

appliance  ______________

diet  ______________

____

reliance  ______________

quiet  ______________

____

QUICK CHECK *(Read)*

IA

156. Ia, Ea. The sounds of *ia,* as in *piano,* and *ea,* as in *create,* are represented by a large circle with a dot placed within it.

Ia

Ea

Practice these words:

area  ____________________ initiate  ____________________

create  ____________________ variation  ____________________

piano  ____________________ brilliant  ____________________

appreciate  ____________________ ____________________

QUICK CHECK *(Read)*

157. Reading and Self-Dictation Practice

Record 4
Side 2
Band 2

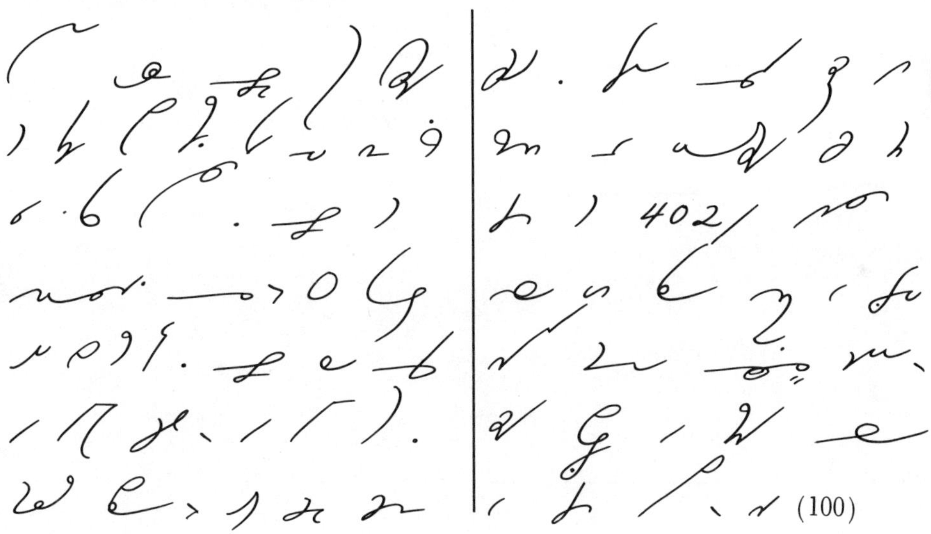

(100)

SELF-CHECK 19

You are now ready to complete Self-Check 19. After completing the self-check, compare your work with the key in your Transcript.

RECORDED DICTATION

You can now play Record 4, Side 2, Band 2, which contains the material in Paragraph 157 dictated at 60 words a minute.

Use Band 1 as a warm-up.

For extra dictation, replay Records 1-3. They will give you a good review as well as provide an opportunity for you to improve your shorthand penmanship.

SECTION 20

In this section you will study three new prefixes, another block of brief forms, two new strokes, and a principle of vowel omission.

In-
Un-
En-

158. Word Beginnings In-, Un-, En-. Each of these word beginnings is represented by the *n* stroke *if a consonant immediately follows.*

Practice these words:

In-

insist ______ **invest** ______

indeed ______ **increased** ______

instant ______ **injured** ______

QUICK CHECK *(Read)*

Un-

unfair ______ **uncertain** ______

until ______ ______

______ **unpaid** ______

unfilled ______ **unless** ______

______ ______

QUICK CHECK *(Read)*

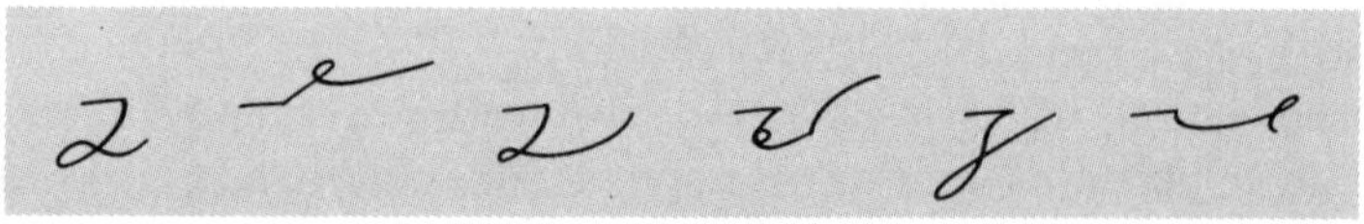

En-

enjoy ________	**endeavor** ________
enrolled ________	**engaged** ________
encouragement ________	**enlarge** ________

QUICK CHECK *(Read)*

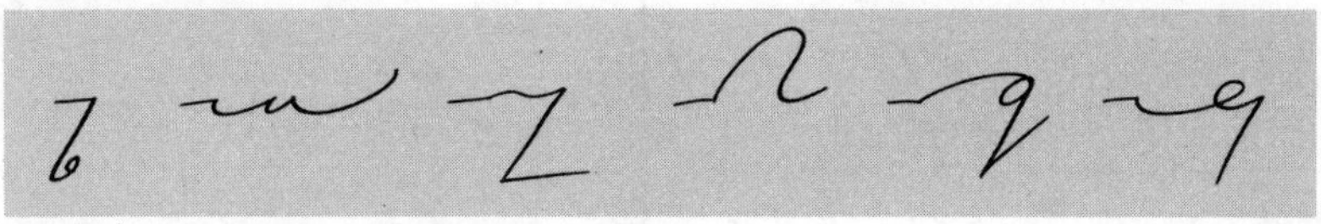

159. Reading and Self-Dictation Practice

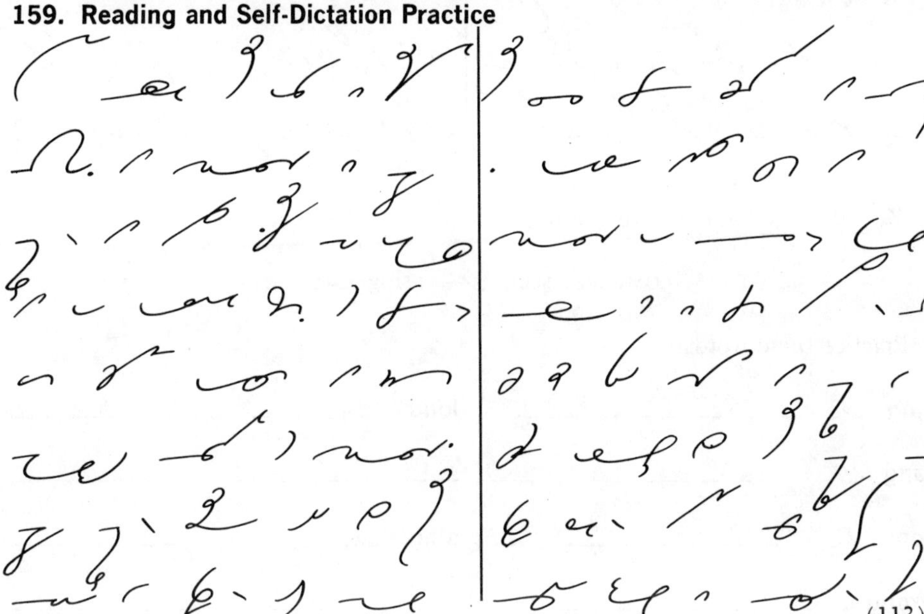

(113)

160. Brief Forms. Practice these brief forms:

particular ________	**newspaper** ________
idea ________	**upon** ________
speak ________	**probable** ________
street ________	**regular** ________
subject ________	

Brief Forms

QUICK CHECK *(Read)*

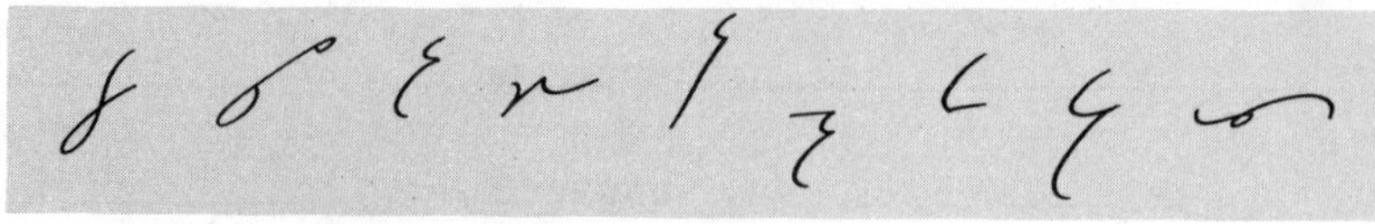

161. Reading and Self-Dictation Practice

Record 4
Side 2
Band 3

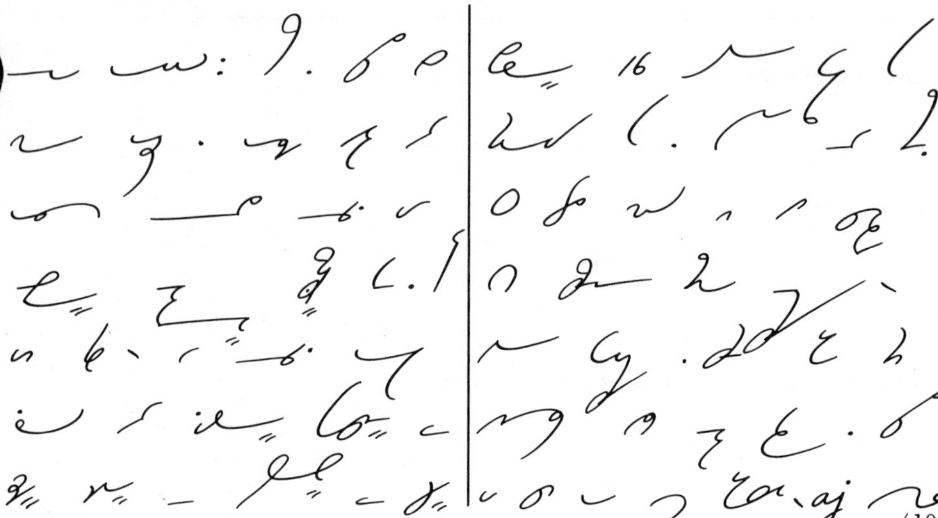

(105)

NG

162. Ng. The sound of *ng*, as in *sing*, is represented by

COMPARE: seen sing

Practice these words:

sing	________	**long**	________
rang	________		________
song	________	**single**	________
wrong	________		________
bring	________	**strong**	________

QUICK CHECK *(Read)*

Ngk

163. Ngk. The sound of *ngk* (spelled *nk*) is written

COMPARE: seem sink

Practice these words:

rank ______ blank ______

drink ______ ______

bank ______ frank ______

ink ______ ______

tank ______ shrink ______

QUICK CHECK *(Read)*

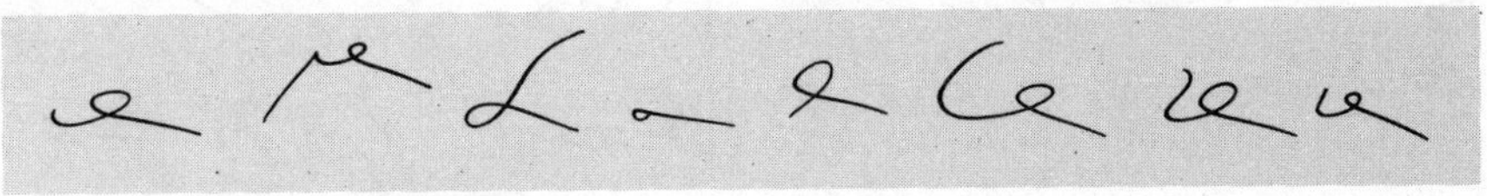

Vowel Omission

164. Omission of Vowel Preceding -tion, -sion. When *t, d, n,* or *m* is followed by *-ition, -ation,* the circle is omitted.

Practice these words:

admission ______ commission ______

______ ______

quotations ______ conditions ______

______ ______

reputation ______ addition ______

______ ______

QUICK CHECK *(Read)*

165. Reading and Self-Dictation Practice

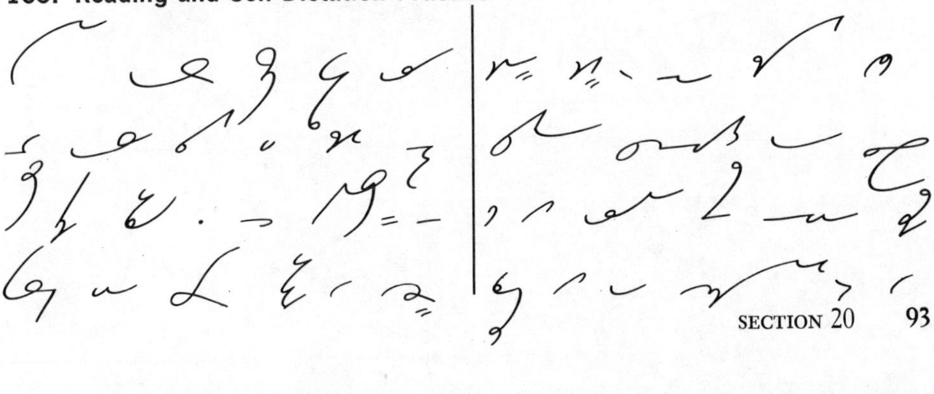

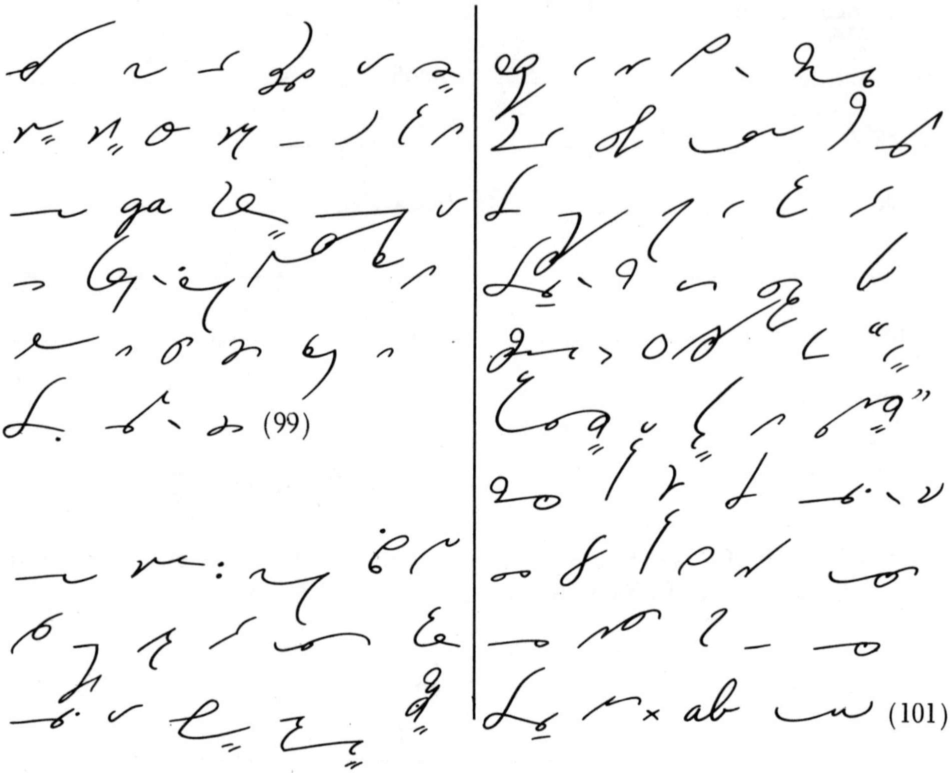

SELF-CHECK 20

Complete Self-Check 20 on your self-check pad and compare your work with the key in your Transcript.

RECORDED DICTATION

You can now take from dictation Record 4, Side 2, Band 3, which contains the material in Paragraph 161 dictated at 60 words a minute.

Play the record from the beginning, using Bands 1 and 2 for warm-up.

SECTION 21

This section presents a number of additional ways to express vowel combinations, another new stroke, and a new principle of vowel omission.

Ah

Aw

166. Ah, Aw. A dot is used for *a* in words that begin with *ah* and *aw*, such as *ahead, await.*

Practice the following words:

ahead  ______________

await  ______________

awoke  ______________

away  ______________

awake  ______________

aware  ______________

QUICK CHECK *(Read)*

Y

167. Y. Before *o* and *oo*, *y* is expressed by the small circle. *Ye* is expressed by a *small* loop; *ya*, by a *large* loop.

Practice the following words:

yawn  ______________

yield  ______________

youth  ______________

yell  ______________

yarn  ______________

yard  ______________

QUICK CHECK *(Read)*

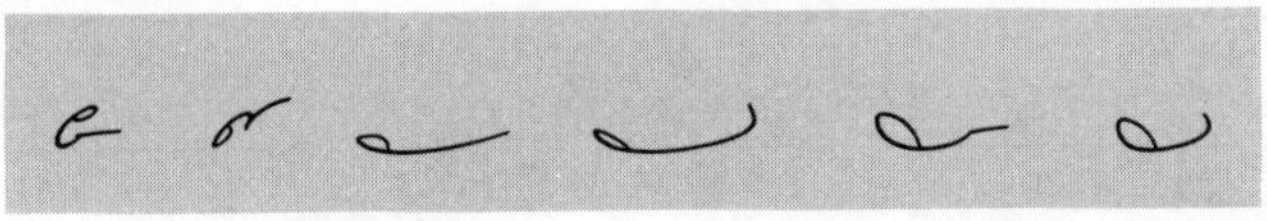

168. Reading and Self-Dictation Practice

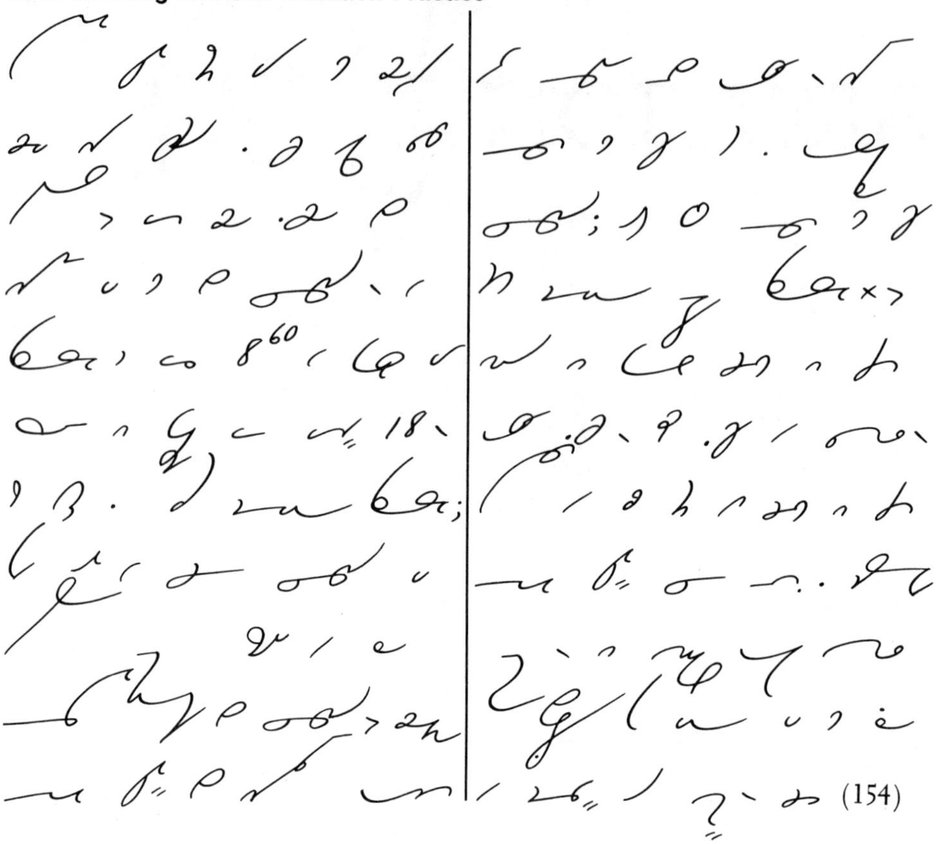

X

169. X.

The letter x is usually represented by an s stroke written with a slightly backward slant.

COMPARE: miss mix

fees fix

Practice these words:

box **relaxes**

tax

relax **boxes**

taxes

QUICK CHECK *(Read)*

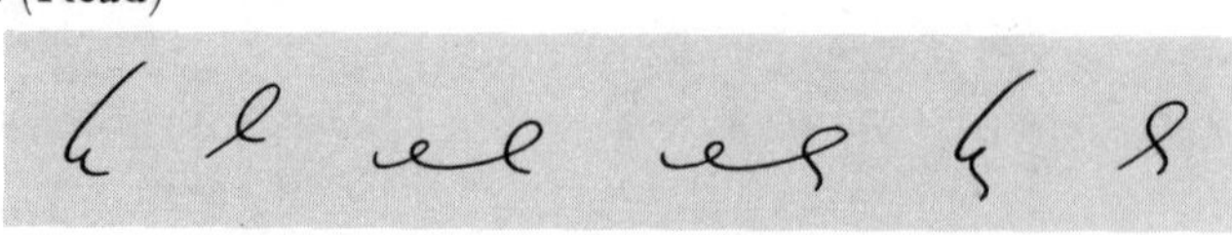

170. Reading and Self-Dictation Practice

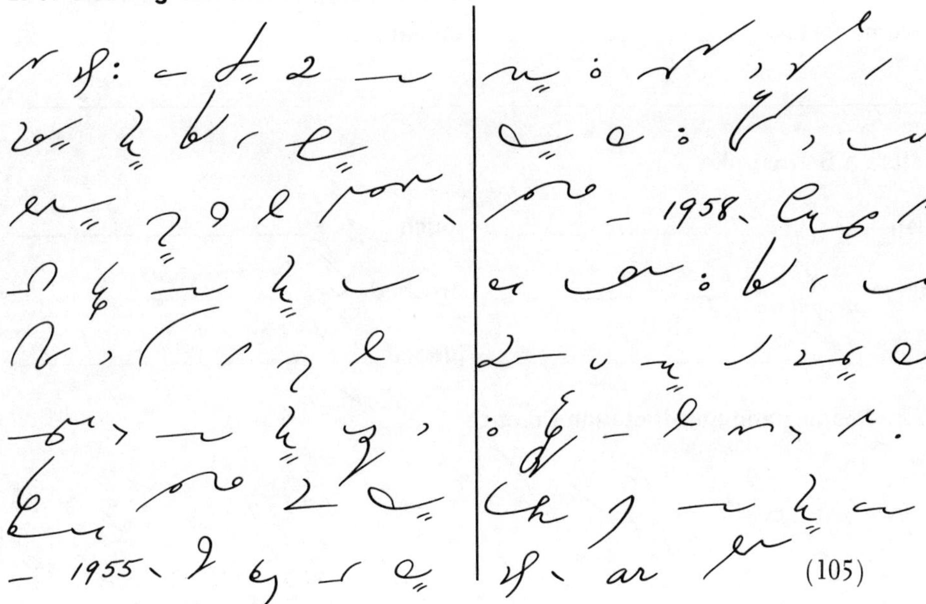

171. Omission of Short U.

In the body of a word, short *u* is omitted before *n, m,* or a straight *downstroke.*

Practice these outlines:

Vowel Omission

Before N

son ____________ **ton** ____________

gun ____________ **fun** ____________

____________ **begun** ____________

done ____________ ____________

QUICK CHECK *(Read)*

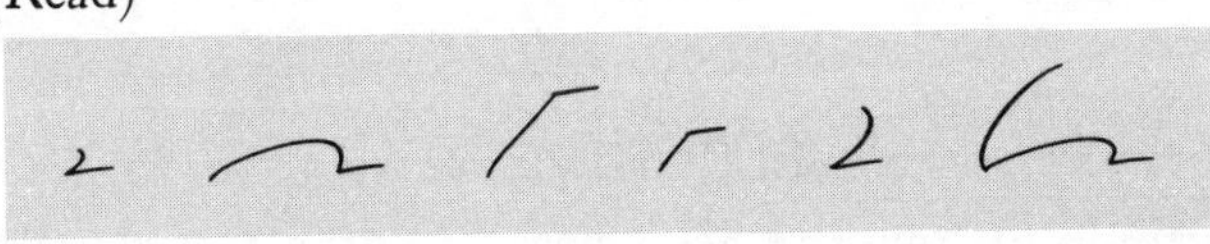

Before M

some ____________ **come** ____________

____________ ____________

lumber ____________ **summer** ____________

____________ ____________

become ______________ column ______________

______________ ______________

Before a Downstroke

rush ______________ touch ______________

budget ______________ brushed ______________

much ______________ judged ______________

172. Reading and Self-Dictation Practice

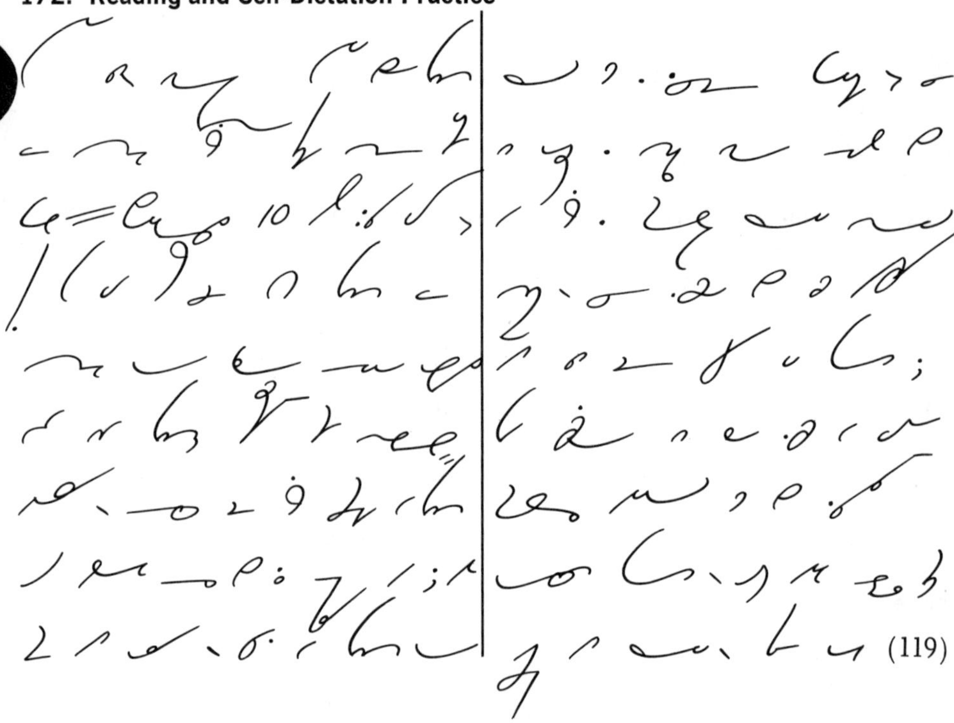

(119)

SELF-CHECK 21

You are now ready to complete Self-Check 21. After you complete your work on this self-check, compare it with the key in your Transcript.

RECORDED DICTATION

You can now take from dictation Record 5, Side 1, Band 1. This band contains the material from Paragraph 172, which you should practice before you turn on your record player. The material is dictated at 70 words a minute.

If time is available, replay Records 1 through 4; this repetition practice will have a wholesome effect on your shorthand writing speed.

SECTION 22

In this section you will encounter another block of brief forms, a new word beginning, a new blend, and three common word endings.

Brief Forms

173. Brief Forms. Practice these brief forms:

purpose 

public 

responsible 

opinion 

ordinary 

circular 

regard 

publish, publication 

organize 

QUICK CHECK *(Read)*

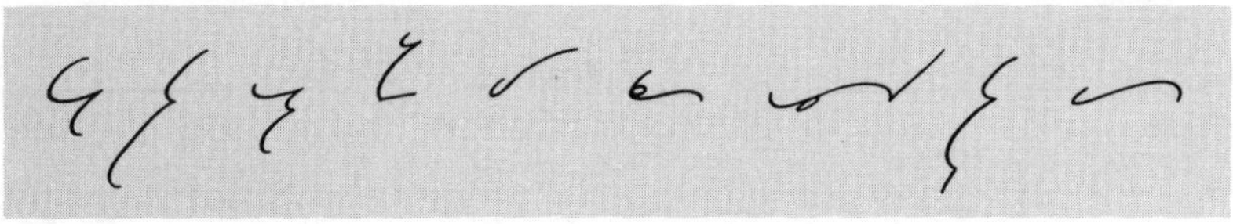

Ex-

174. Word Beginning Ex-. The word beginning ex- is represented by es. Practice these words:

expense 

expert 

express 

explain 

extra 

extend 

excel 

examine 

QUICK CHECK *(Read)*

175. Reading and Self-Dictation Practice

Record 5
Side 1
Band 2

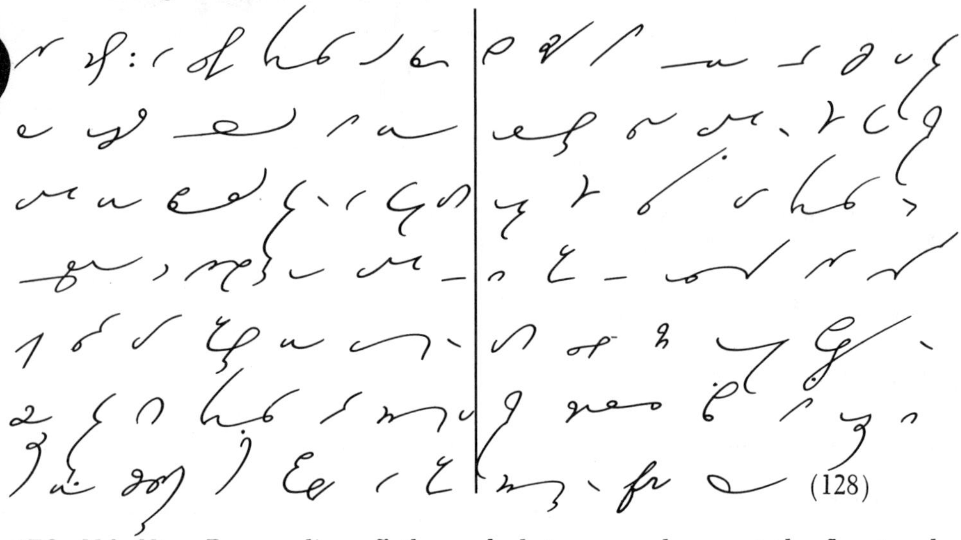

(128)

Md
Mt

176. Md, Mt. By rounding off the angle between *m-d*, we get the fluent *md* blend. The same stroke is used to represent *mt*.

Md, Mt 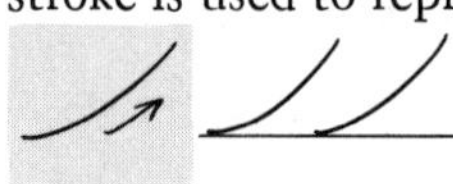 (Write several times.)

COMPARE: seem  seemed 

Practice the following words:

named 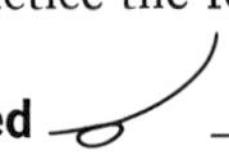 **framed** 

claimed  **prompt** 

trimmed 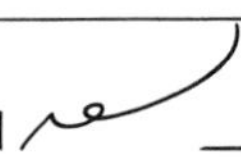 **empty** 

QUICK CHECK *(Read)*

-ful

177. Word Ending -ful. The word ending *-ful* is represented by the shorthand stroke for *f*.

Practice the following words:

careful ________ **helpful** ________

useful ________ ________

hopeful ________ **gratefully** ________

awful ________ ________

beautiful ________ **doubtful** ________

QUICK CHECK *(Read)*

178. Reading and Self-Dictation Practice

Record 5
Side 1
Band 3

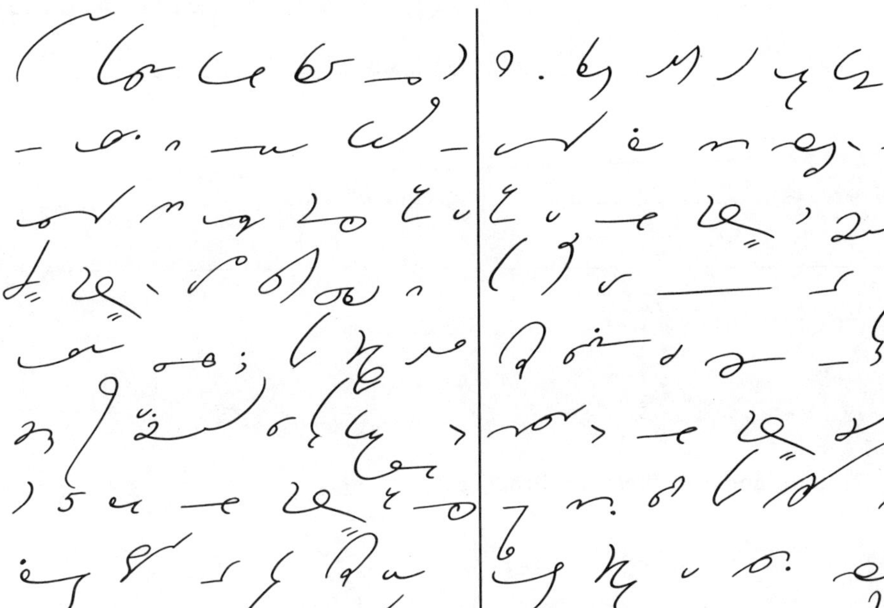

(135)

-ure

179. Word Ending -ure. The word ending *-ure* is represented by the *r* stroke.

Practice these words:

failure ________ **nature** ________

________ **natural** ________

figure

procedure

secure

picture

procure

QUICK CHECK *(Read)*

-ual

180. Word Ending -ual. The word ending *-ual* is represented by the *l* stroke. Practice these words:

annual

eventual

actual

annually

equal

gradually

QUICK CHECK *(Read)*

181. Reading and Self-Dictation Practice

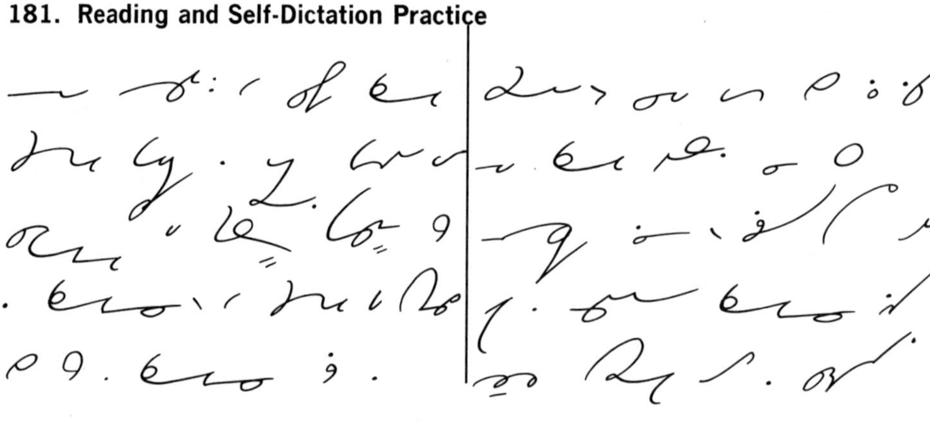

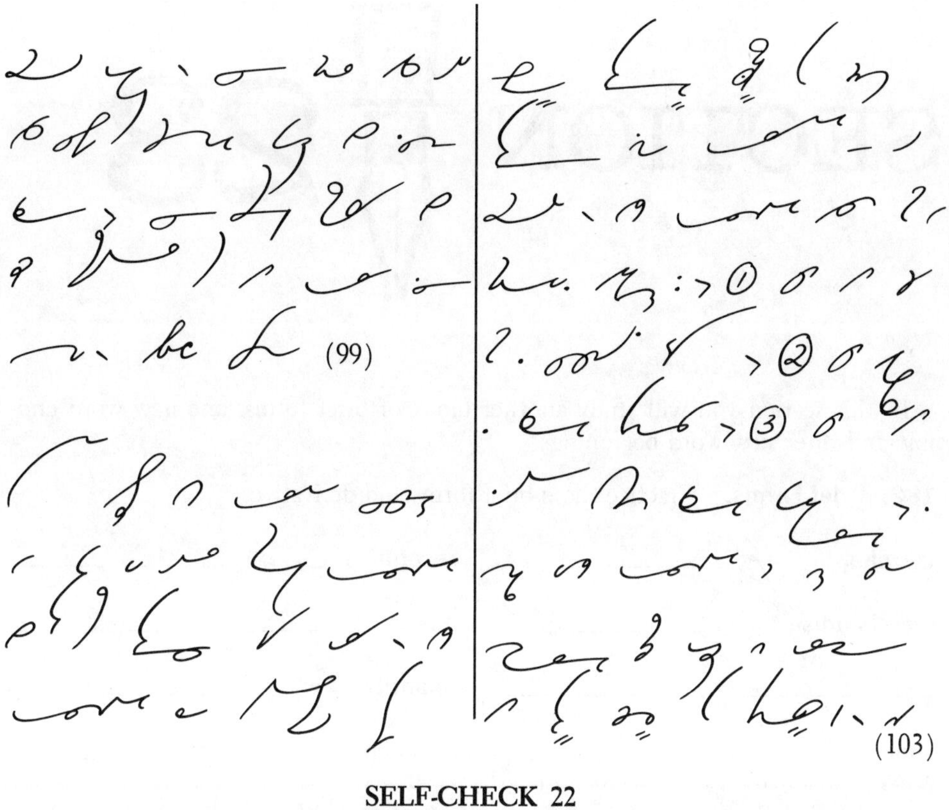

SELF-CHECK 22

Turn to Self-Check 22 in your self-check pad. After you have completed the self-check, compare your work with the key in your Transcript.

RECORDED DICTATION

You can now take from dictation Record 5, Side 1, Band 2, which contains the material from Paragraph 175; and Band 3, which contains the material from Paragraph 178. The material is dictated at 70 words a minute.

Be sure to practice reading and copying these paragraphs before you take the dictation from these bands.

SECTION 23

In this section you will study another block of brief forms, one new word ending, and three new word beginnings.

Brief Forms

182. Brief Forms. Practice these brief forms and derivatives:

merchant	**recognize**
merchandise	**never**
	quantity
short	**between**
experience	**situation**

Derivatives

merchants	**shortly**
quantities	**recognized**
situations	

QUICK CHECK *(Read)*

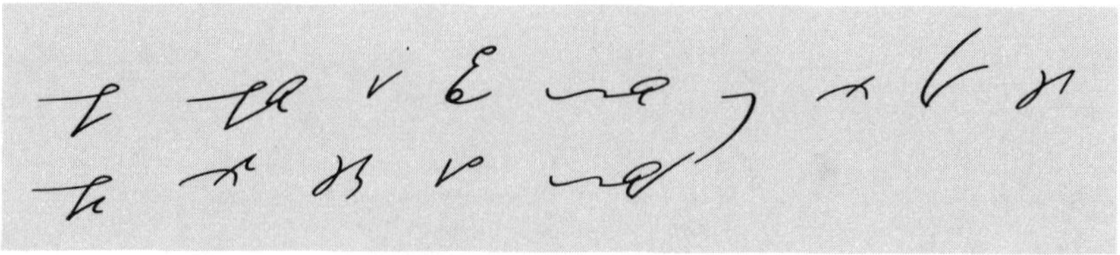

183. Reading and Self-Dictation Practice

Record 5
Side 2
Band 1

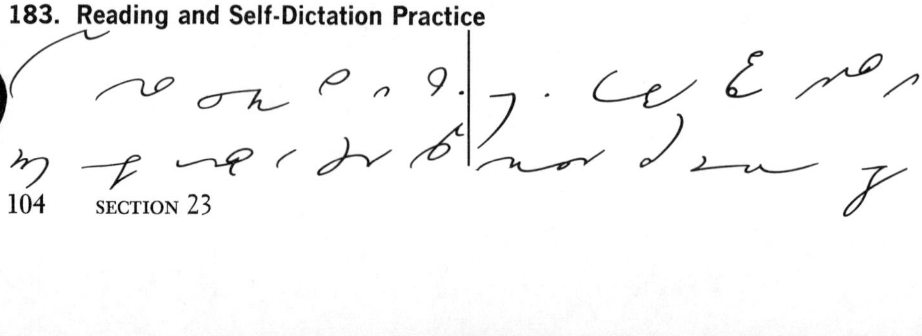

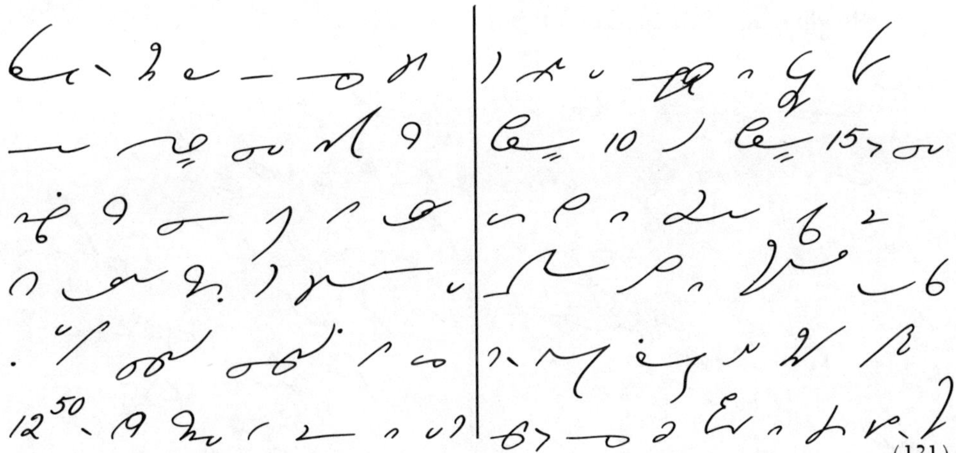

(131)

184. Word Ending -ily. The word ending *-ily* is expressed by a narrow *loop*. Practice the following words:

-ily

easily ______ temporarily ______

heavily ______ ______

hastily ______ heartily ______

families ______ speedily ______

______ ______

QUICK CHECK *(Read)*

185. Word Beginning Al-. The word beginning *al-* is represented by the o hook. Practice the following words:

Al-

also ______ altogether ______

although ______ ______

already ______ almost ______

______ alter ______

QUICK CHECK *(Read)*

186. Reading and Self-Dictation Practice

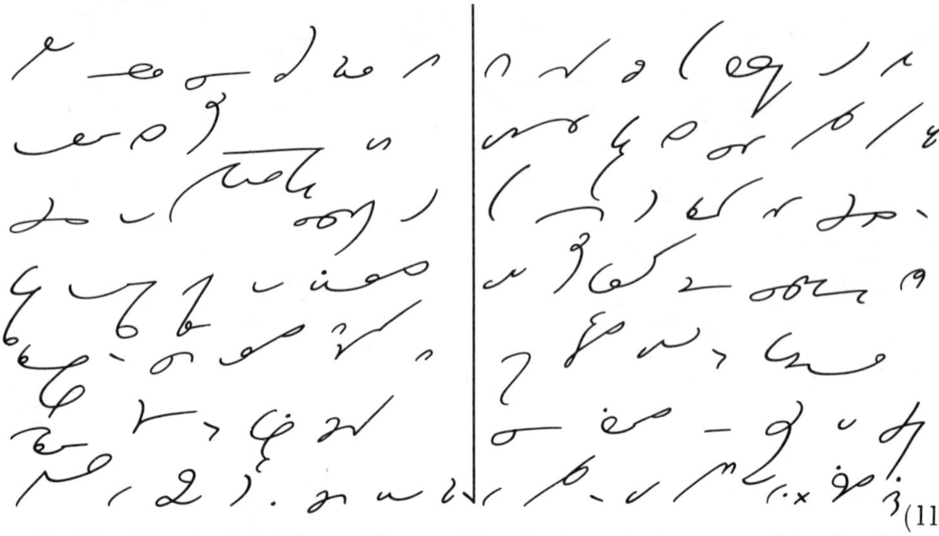

(112)

Mis-

187. Word Beginning Mis-. The word beginning *mis-* is expressed in shorthand by *m-s*.

Practice the following words:

mistake  ______ misprint  ______

misplaced  ______ mistaken  ______

mislead  ______ misery  ______

QUICK CHECK (Read)

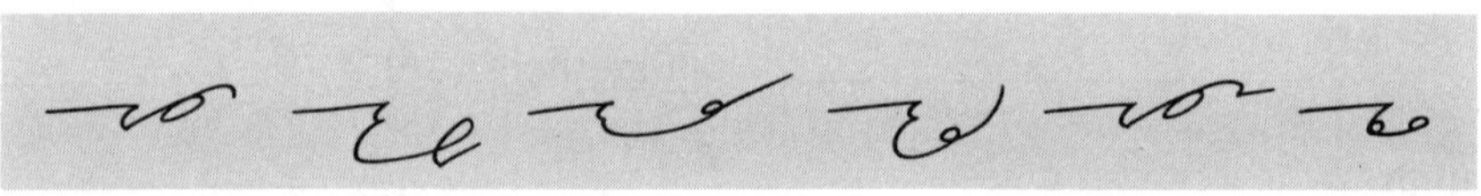

Dis-

Des-

188. Word Beginnings Dis-, Des-. The word beginnings *dis-* and *des-* are expressed by *d-s*.

Practice the following words:

dispose  ______ describe  ______

distance  ______

dispute  ______ description  ______

discover 

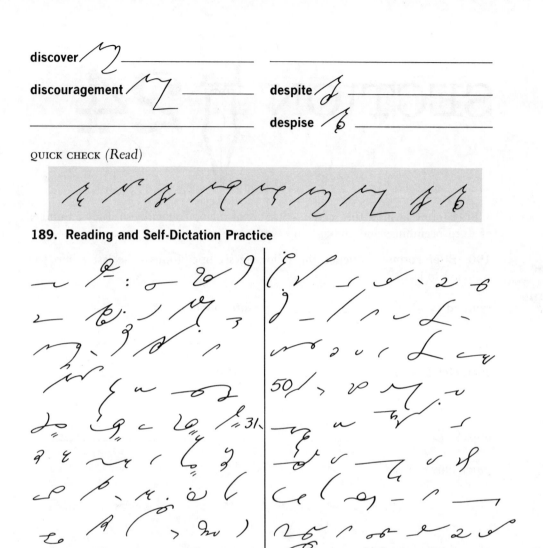

discouragement 

despite 

despise 

QUICK CHECK *(Read)*

189. Reading and Self-Dictation Practice

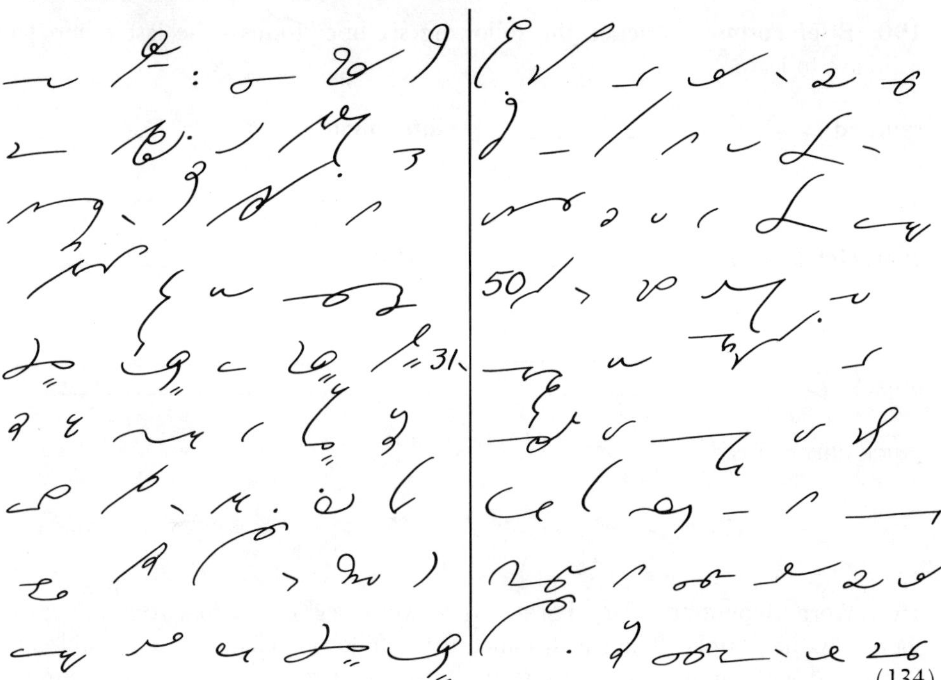

(134)

SELF-CHECK 23

Check your mastery of Section 23 by completing Self-Check 23. Compare your work with the key in your Transcript.

RECORDED DICTATION

You can now take from dictation Record 5, Side 2, Band 1, which contains the material from Paragraph 183 dictated at 70 words a minute.

Be sure to practice Paragraph 183 before you take Band 1 from dictation.

SECTION 24

Brief forms again in this section — just six of them. You will also study a number of word beginnings and endings and two very useful phrasing principles.

Brief Forms

190. Brief Forms. Practice the following six brief forms — the last group you will have to learn.

railroad ______

throughout ______

character ______

world ______

govern ______

object ______

QUICK CHECK *(Read)*

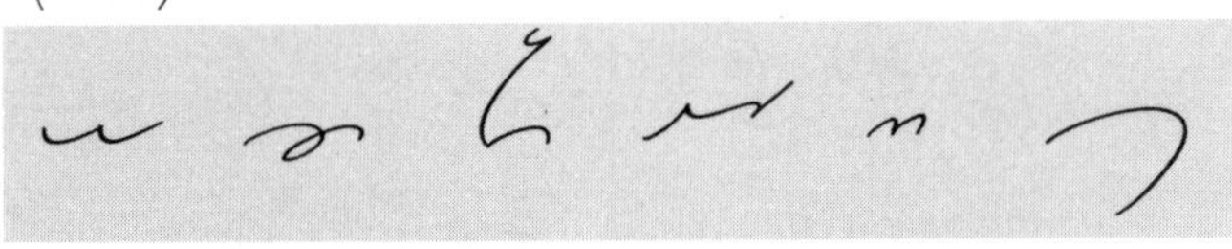

For- **Fore-**

191. Word Beginnings For-, Fore-. The word beginnings *for-, fore-* are represented by the *f* stroke. The *f* is disjoined if the following character is a vowel. The *f* is joined with an angle to *r* or *l* to indicate that it represents a word beginning.

Practice these words:

forget ______

forth ______

informed ______

forgive ______

forever ______

foreclose ______

forerunner ______

form ______ forlorn ______

force ______ ______

QUICK CHECK *(Read)*

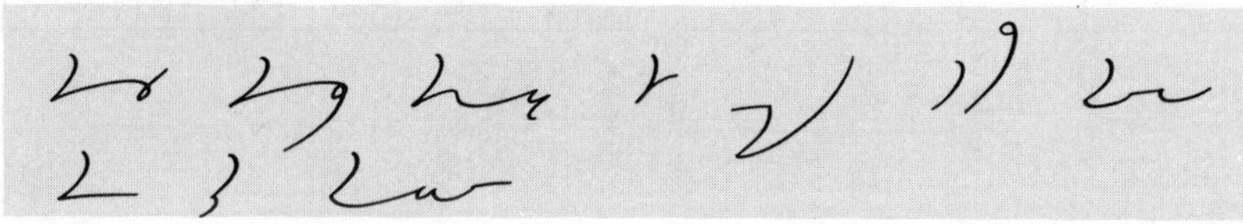

Fur-

192. Word Beginning Fur-. The word beginning *fur-* is expressed by *f.* Practice the following words:

furnace ______ furnishing ______

furniture ______ further ______

furnished ______ furlough ______

QUICK CHECK *(Read)*

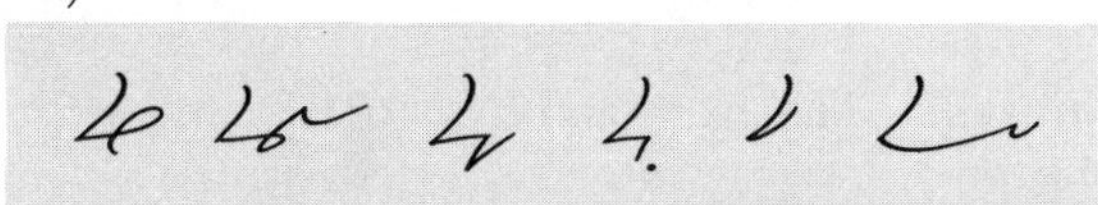

193. Reading and Self-Dictation Practice

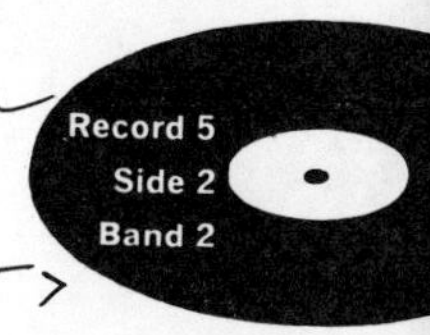

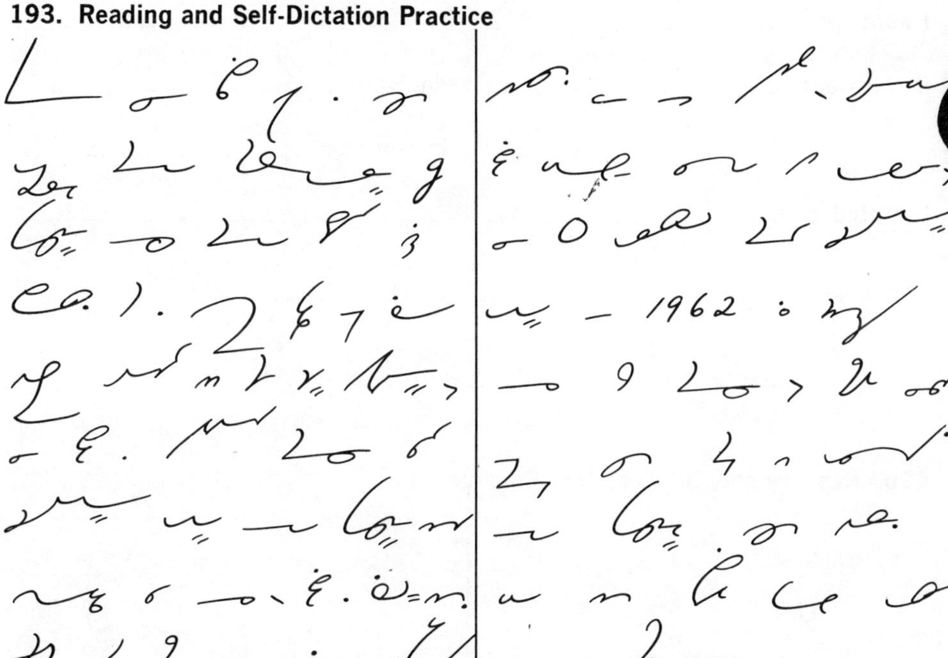

(131)

AGO in Phrases

194. Ago in Phrases. In many phrases, the word *ago* may be represented by the g (gay) stroke.

Practice the following phrases:

days ago ______ **weeks ago** ______

long ago ______ **years ago** ______

minutes ago ______ **months ago** ______

QUICK CHECK *(Read)*

WANT in Phrases

195. Want in Phrases. The word *want* is conveniently represented in many phrases by the *nt* blend.

I want ______ **he wants** ______

if you want ______ **you want** ______

do you want ______

I wanted ______

QUICK CHECK *(Read)*

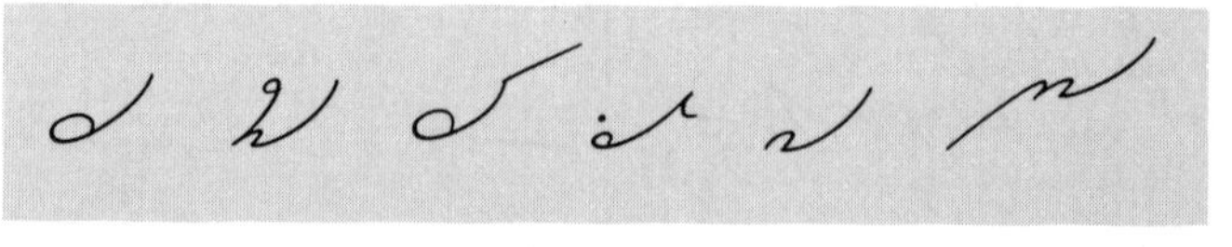

196. Reading and Self-Dictation Practice

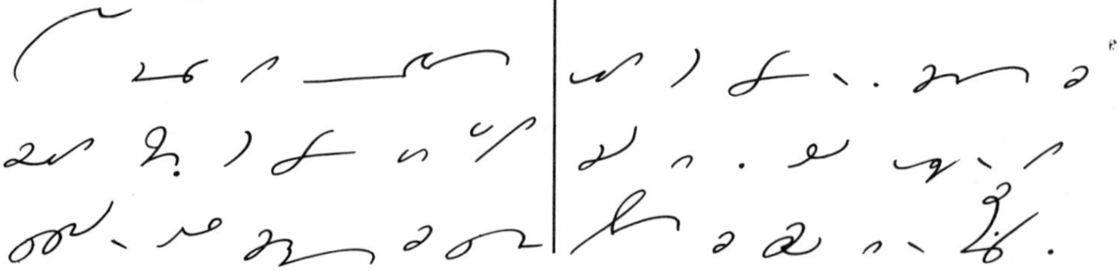

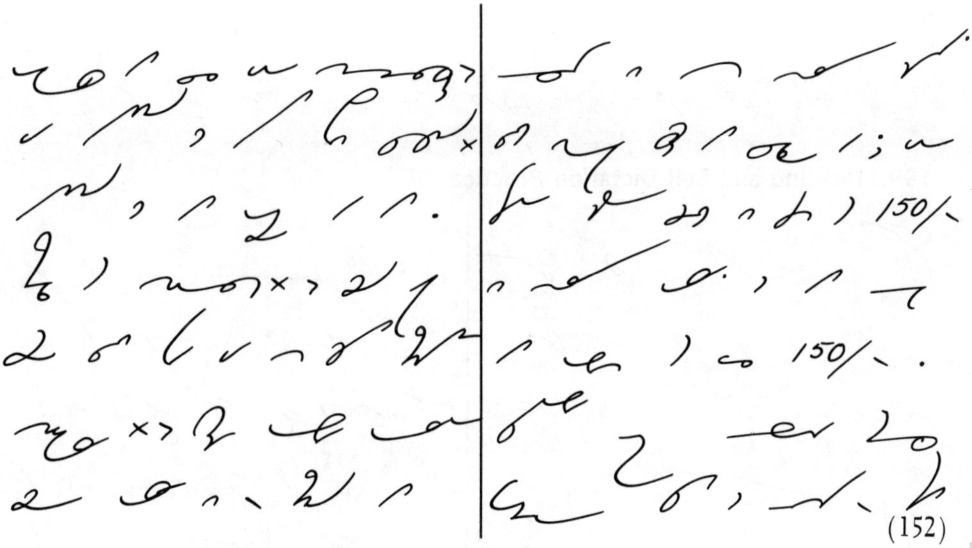

(152)

-Ort

197. Ort. In the combination *ort*, the *r* is omitted.

Practice the following words:

report ____________	**quart** ____________
support ____________	**quarter** ____________
export ____________	**resort** ____________
assort ____________	**portable** ____________

QUICK CHECK *(Read)*

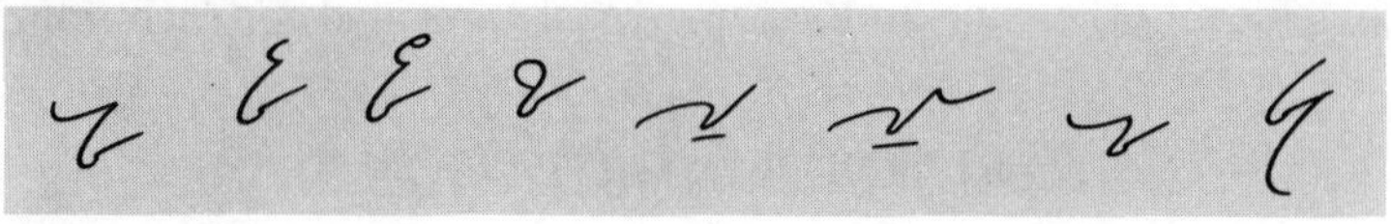

R Omitted

198. Omission of R. The *r* is omitted in the combinations *tern, term, dern, thern.*

Practice the following words:

turn ____________	**term** ____________
return ____________	**determine** ____________
eastern ____________	____________
western ____________	**modern** ____________
southern ____________	____________

QUICK CHECK *(Read)*

199. Reading and Self-Dictation Practice

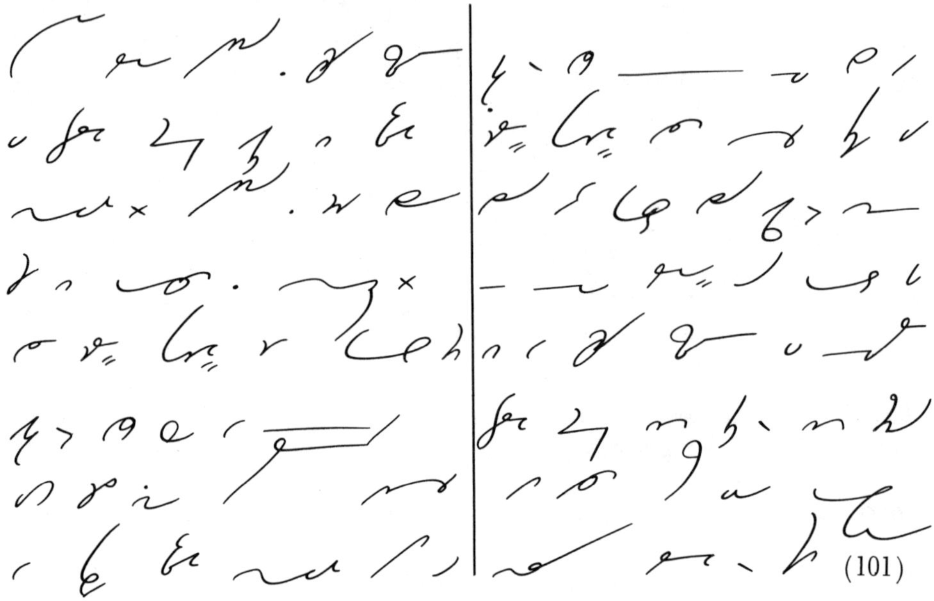

(101)

SELF-CHECK 24

Time for another test to check up on your progress. Turn to Self-Check 24 and complete both parts. Don't forget to check your work against the key in your Transcript.

Are you achieving the time and accuracy goals provided for each self-check?

RECORDED DICTATION

You can now take from dictation Record 5, Side 2, Band 2, which contains the material in Paragraph 193 dictated at 70 words a minute.

Use Band 1 as a warm-up.

SECTION 25

This section presents several additional, useful word beginnings and word endings, as well as another timesaving phrasing principle.

-cal

-cle

200. Word Endings -cal, -cle. The word endings *-cal, -cle* are represented by a disjoined *k* stroke, written below the end of the preceding character.

Practice the following words:

chemical  ____________ **critical**  ____________

articles  ____________ **practical**  ____________

political  ____________ **physically**  ____________

QUICK CHECK *(Read)*

201. Reading and Self-Dictation Practice

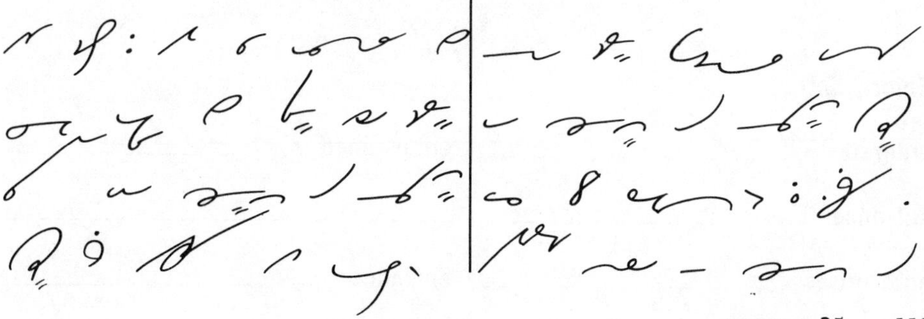

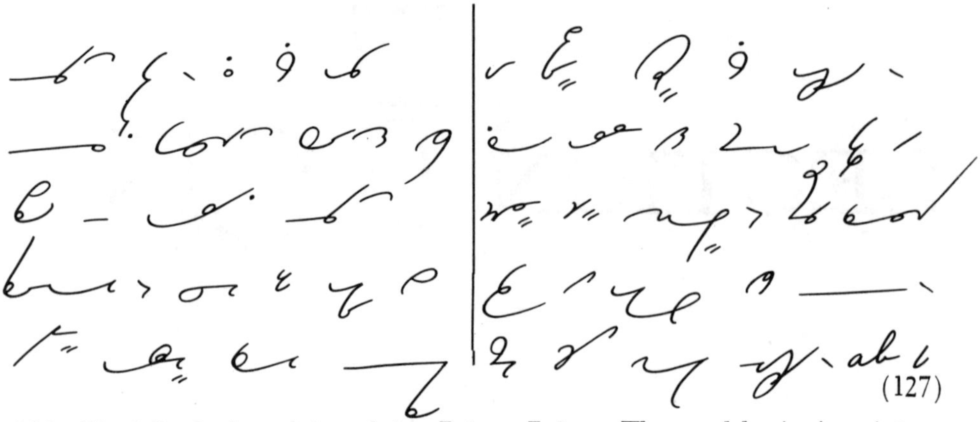

(127)

Inter- etc.

202. Word Beginnings Inter-, Intr-, Enter-, Entr-. The word beginnings *inter-*, *intr-*, *enter-*, *entr-* are represented by the *n* stroke written just above the character that follows it.

Practice the following words:

Inter-

interest | **interrupt**

interpret | **intervene**

interval | **interview**

QUICK CHECK (*Read*)

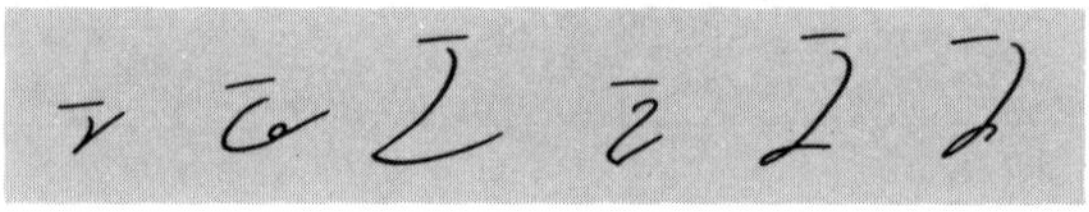

Intr-

introduce | **intricate**

introduces | **intrigue**

QUICK CHECK (*Read*)

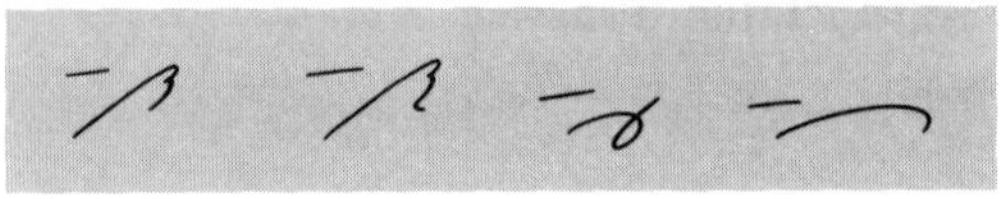

Enter-, Entr-

entered | **entertained**

entrance

enterprises | **entrances**

QUICK CHECK *(Read)*

203. Reading and Self-Dictation Practice

Record 5
Side 2
Band 3

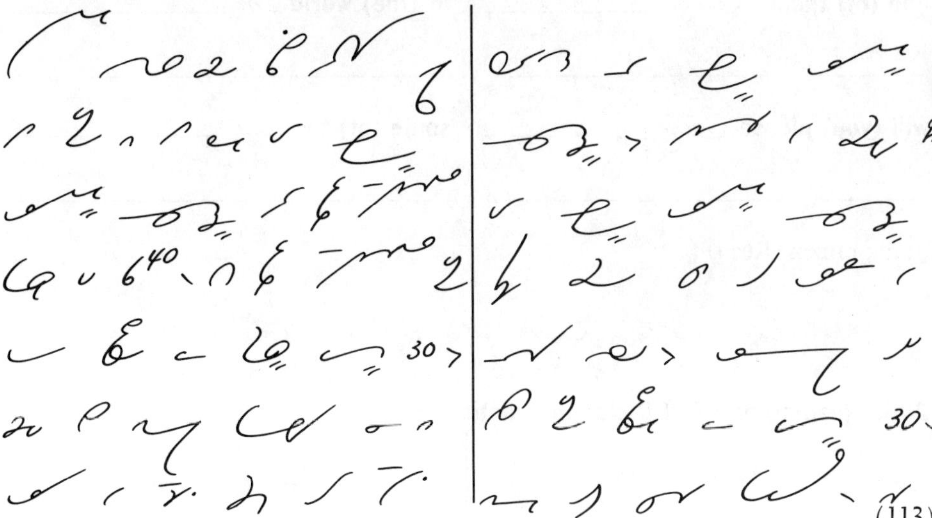

(113)

-ings

204. Word Ending -ings. The word ending *-ings* is represented by a disjoined left *s*.

Practice these words:

openings  ____________ **proceedings**  ____________

meetings  ____________ **holdings**  ____________

clippings  ____________ **evenings**  ____________

QUICK CHECK *(Read)*

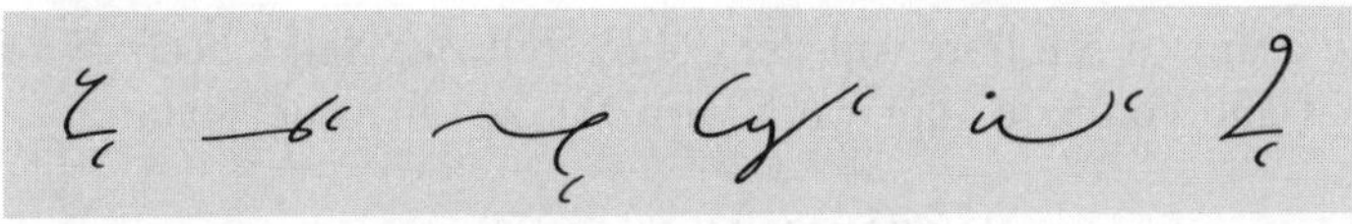

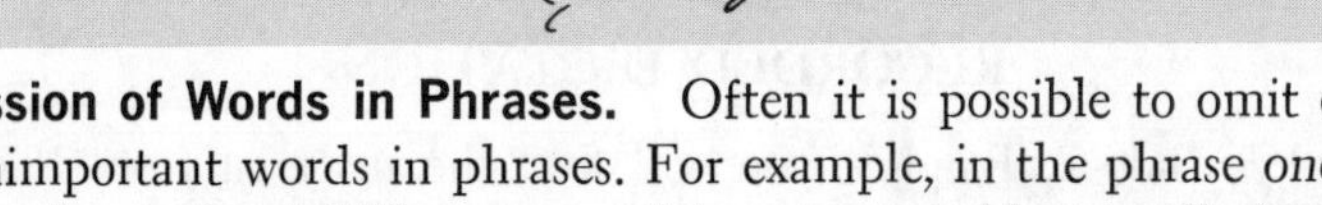

Phrases

205. Omission of Words in Phrases. Often it is possible to omit one or more small or unimportant words in phrases. For example, in the phrase *one of the*, the word *of* may be omitted. When transcribing, you would naturally insert the word *of*, as the phrase without that word would make no sense.

Practice the following phrases:

one (of) the ____________ **up (to) date** ____________

one (of) them ____________ **in (the) world** ____________

will (you) please ____________ **some (of) the** ____________

QUICK CHECK *(Read)*

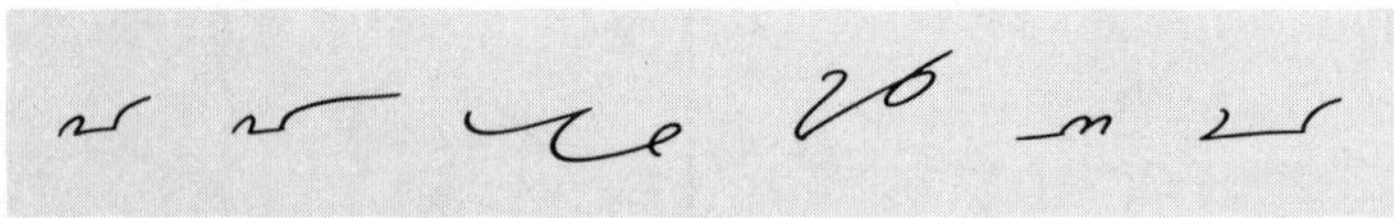

206. Reading and Self-Dictation Practice

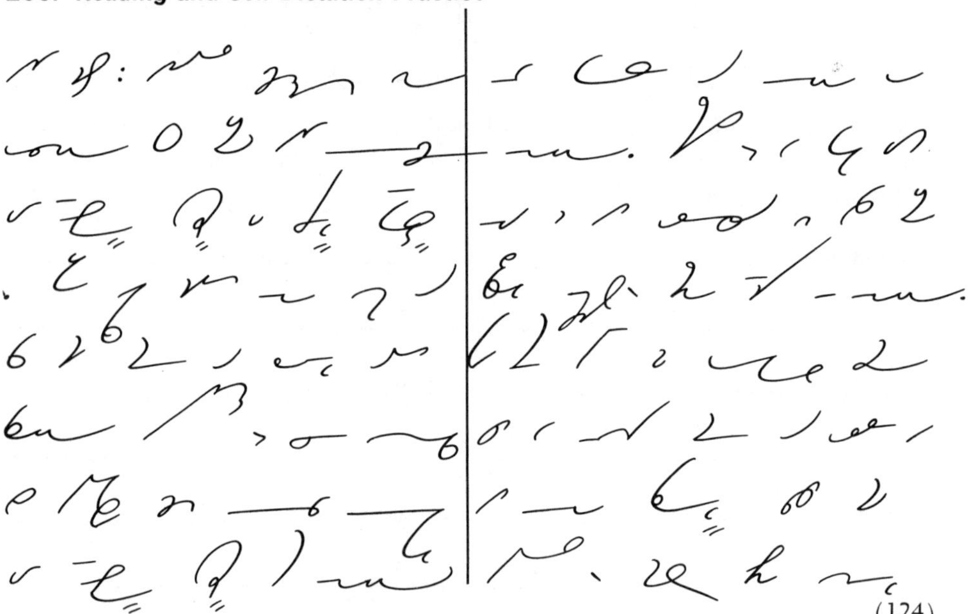

(124)

SELF-CHECK 25

It is time again to see how you are doing! Fill out Self-Check 25 on your pad of self-checks and compare your work with the key in your Transcript.

RECORDED DICTATION

On Record 5, Side 2, Band 3, you will find the material from Paragraph 203 dictated at 70 words a minute. Take Bands 1 and 2 from dictation as a warm-up; then take Band No. 3.

SECTION 26

In this section you will learn a number of additional word beginnings and endings, as well as another principle for the omission of minor vowels.

-ingly

207. Word Ending -ingly. The word ending *-ingly* is represented by a disjoined e circle.

Practice these words:

accordingly 

increasingly 

surprisingly 

exceedingly 

willingly 

knowingly 

QUICK CHECK *(Read)*

Vowel Omission

208. Omission of Minor Vowels. When two vowel sounds come together, the minor vowel may often be omitted.

Practice the following words:

courteous 

genuine 

period 

serious 

ideal 

theory 

QUICK CHECK *(Read)*

209. Reading and Self-Dictation Practice

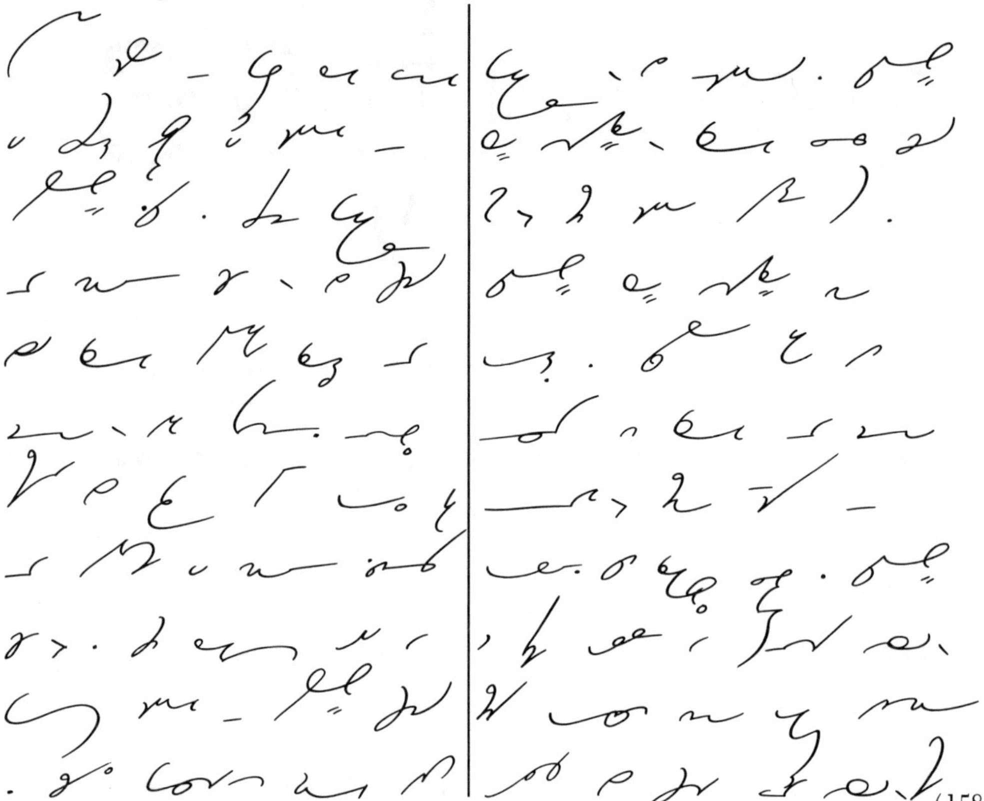

(158)

Im-

Em-

210. Word Beginnings Im- Em-.

The word beginnings *im-*, *em-* are represented by the *m* stroke.

Practice the following words:

Im-

import 

impose 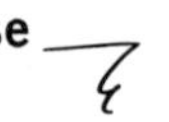

improve 

impressed 

impossible 

improperly 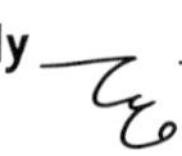

QUICK CHECK *(Read)*

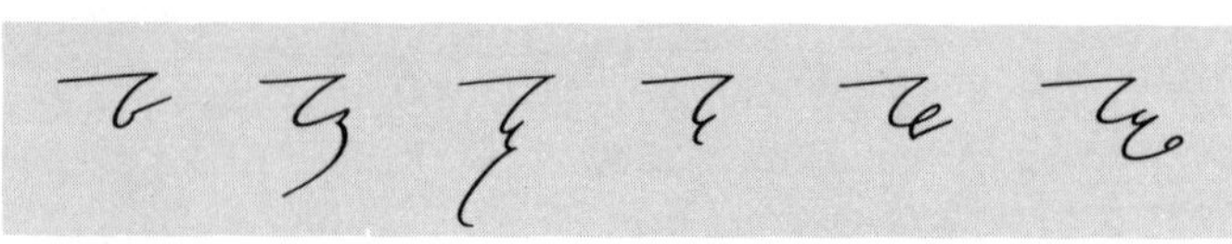

Em-

employment ________	**embrace** ________
emphatically ________	**emphasis** ________
empire ________	**embarrass** ________

QUICK CHECK *(Read)*

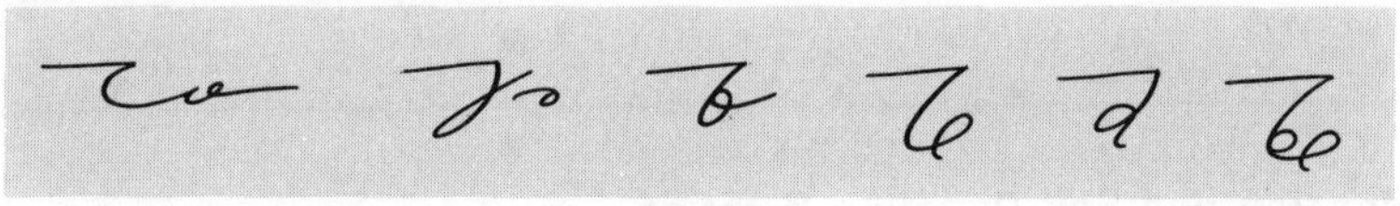

211. Reading and Self-Dictation Practice

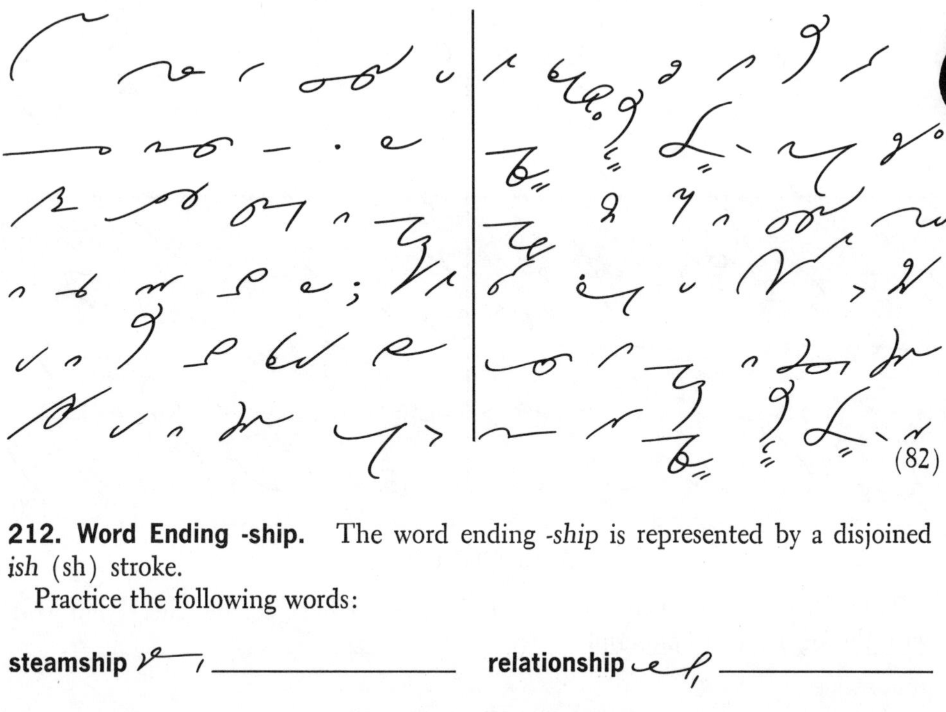

(82)

212. Word Ending -ship. The word ending *-ship* is represented by a disjoined *ish* (sh) stroke.

Practice the following words:

steamship ________	**relationship** ________
friendship ________	**ownership** ________
membership ________	**hardship** ________

-ship

Sub-

213. Word Beginning Sub-. The word beginning *sub-* is represented by an s stroke.

Practice the following words:

submit  ________________	**substantial**  ________________
________________	________________
subdivided  ________________	**sublet**  ________________
________________	________________
subscribe  ________________	**suburbs**  ________________
________________	________________

214. Reading and Self-Dictation Practice

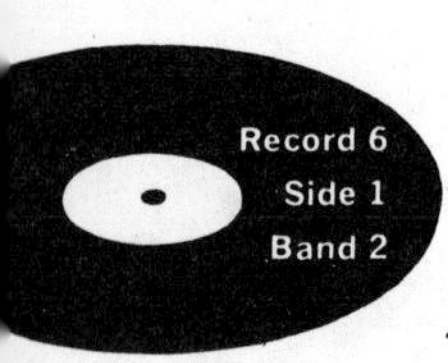

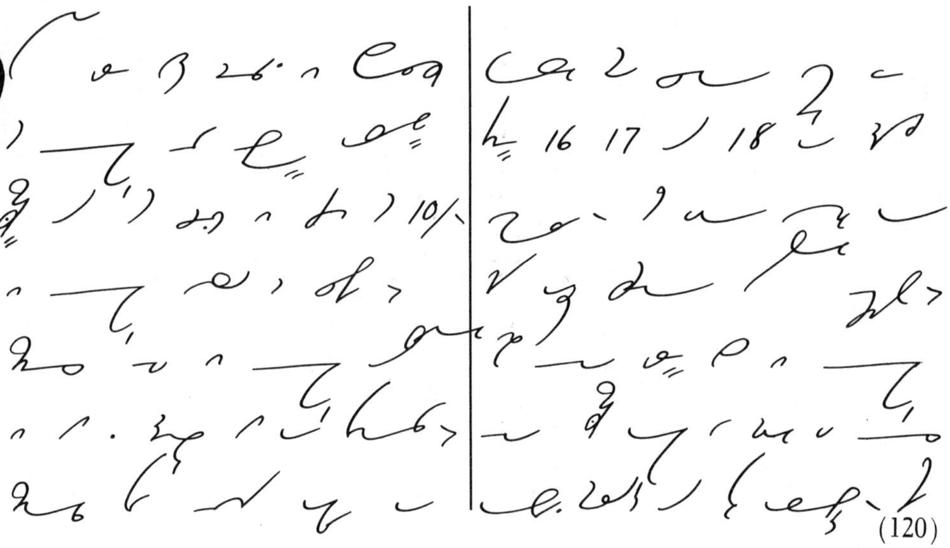

(120)

SELF-CHECK 26

Time for you to test yourself again! Fill out Self-Check 26, and check your work with the key in your Transcript.

RECORDED DICTATION

You can now take from dictation Record 6, Side 1, Band 1, which contains the material from Paragraph 211; and Band 2, which contains the material from Paragraph 214 dictated at 80 words a minute.

Read and copy these paragraphs before you take them from dictation.

SECTION 27

In this section you will learn a number of additional word endings. In addition, you will learn a useful, timesaving principle of abbreviation.

-rity

215. Word Ending -rity. The word ending *-rity* is represented by a disjoined *r* stroke.

Practice the following words:

security  ______

minority  ______

authority  ______

sincerity  ______

prosperity  ______

majority  ______

maturity  ______

QUICK CHECK *(Read)*

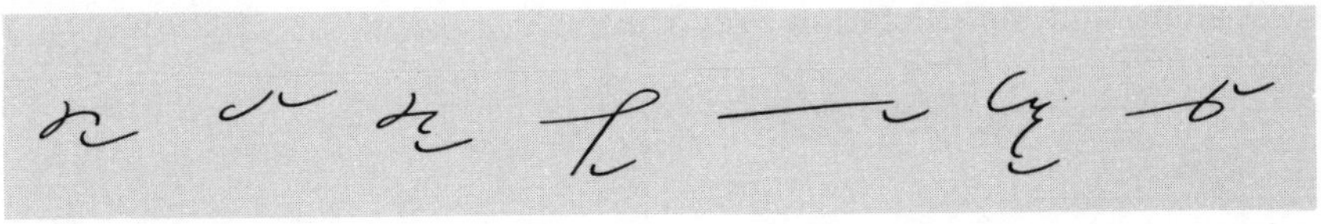

-lity
-lty

216. Word Endings -lity, -lty. The word endings *-lity, -lty* are represented by a disjoined *l* stroke.

Practice these words:

-lity

ability  ______

possibility  ______

locality  ______

facilities  ______

reliability

qualities

utility

personality

vitality

QUICK CHECK *(Read)*

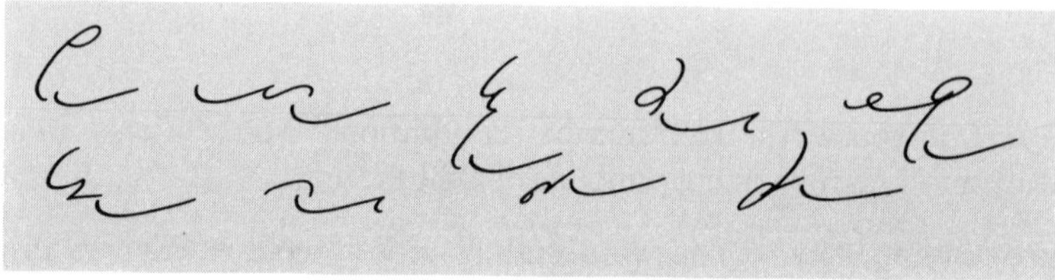

-lty

penalty

loyalty

royalty

faculty

QUICK CHECK *(Read)*

217. Reading and Self-Dictation Practice

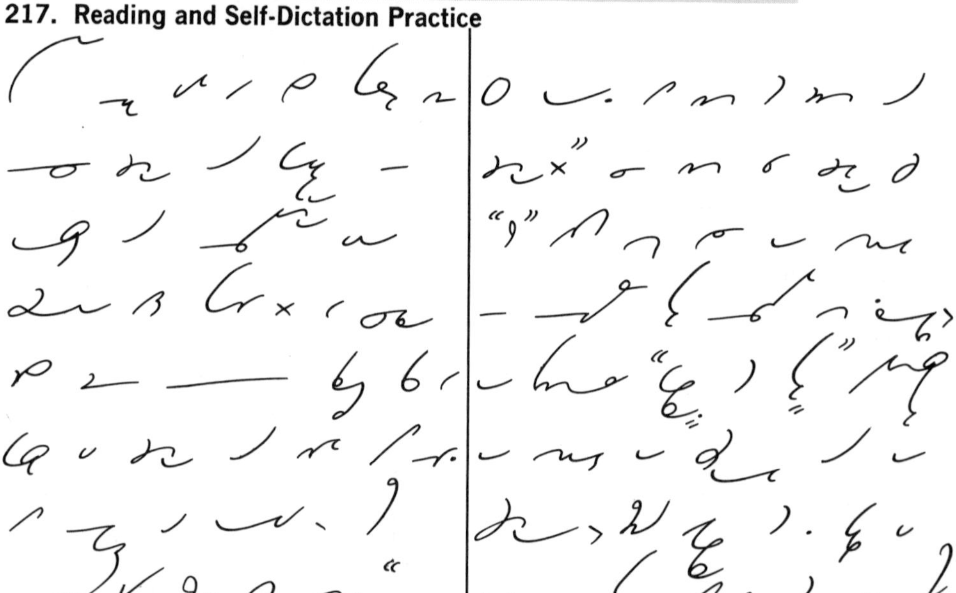

(120)

-self

-selves

218. Word Endings -self, -selves. The word ending *-self* is represented by an *s* stroke; *-selves,* by the *ses* stroke.

Practice these words:

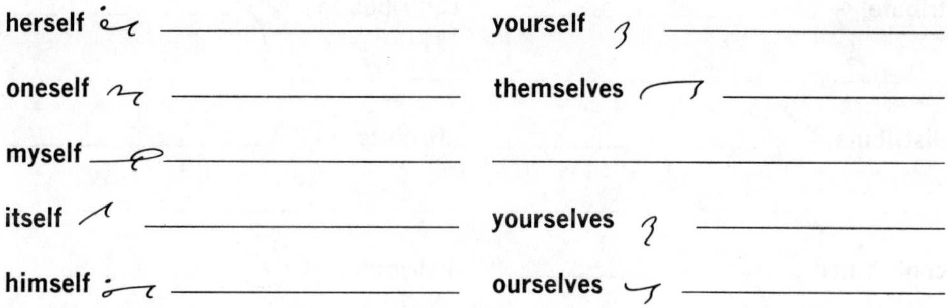

QUICK CHECK *(Read)*

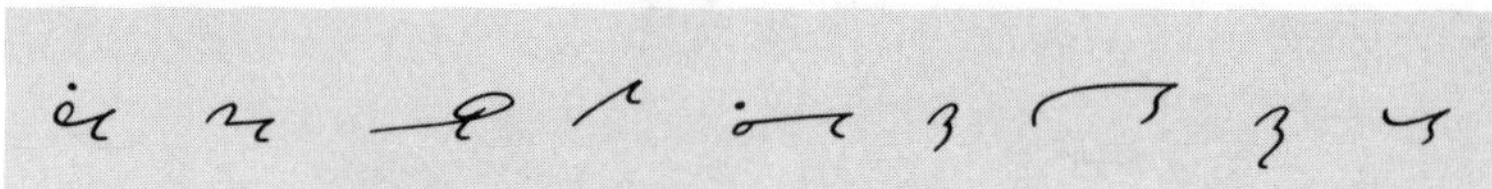

219. Reading and Self-Dictation Practice

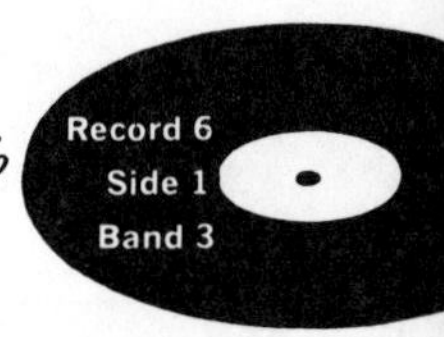

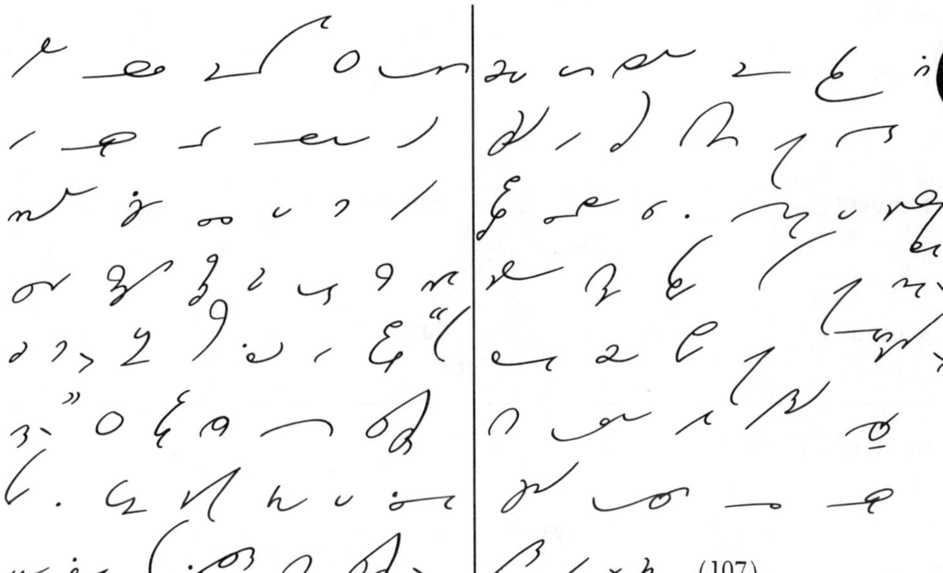

(107)

220. Abbreviated Words. Shorthand itself is an abbreviated form of writing. We can save still more time, however, by shortening the outlines for many long words by dropping their endings – just as we do in longhand (*Jan.* for *January,* etc.). Of course, one person may find it possible to abbreviate much more than another – it depends upon one's familiarity with the words and the nature of the subject matter. You will notice that many words fall into families of similar endings that can easily be abbreviated.

Abbreviation

Practice these groups:

-tribute

tribute  ______ **contribution**  ______

distribute  ______ **attribute**  ______

contributed  ______ **distributor**  ______

QUICK CHECK *(Read)*

-quent

consequent  ______ **subsequently**  ______

frequent  ______ **consequently**  ______

subsequent  ______ **eloquent**  ______

QUICK CHECK *(Read)*

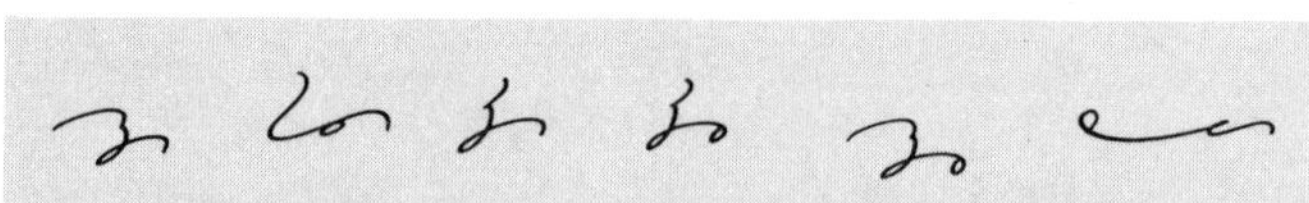

-quire

require  ______ **inquiries**  ______

inquire  ______ **requirement**  ______

acquire  ______

QUICK CHECK *(Read)*

221. Reading and Self-Dictation Practice

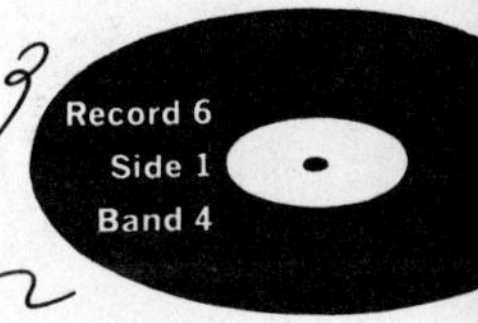

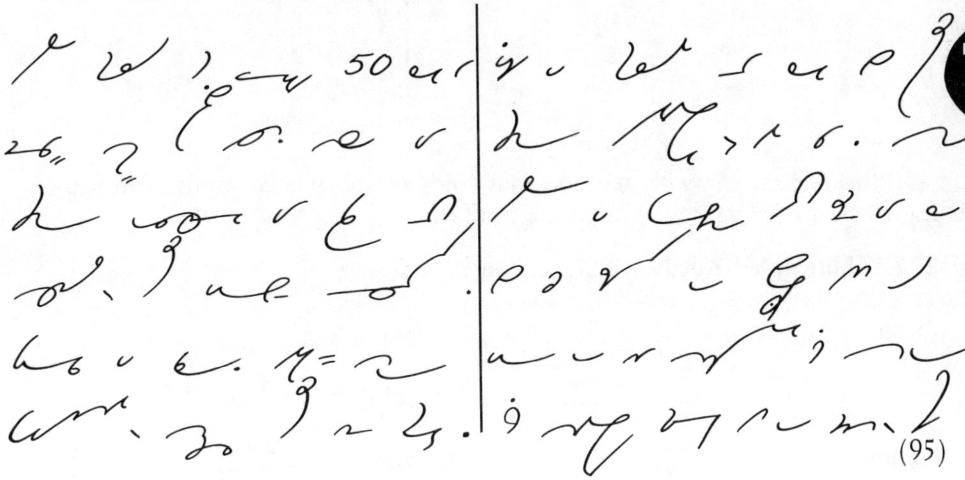

(95)

SELF-CHECK 27

Fill out Self-Check 27 and compare your work with the key in your Transcript.

RECORDED DICTATION

You can now take from dictation Record 6, Side 1, Band 3, which contains the material from Paragraph 219; and Band 4, which contains the material from Paragraph 221 dictated at 80 words a minute.

Use Bands 1 and 2 for warm-up purposes and penmanship improvement.

SECTION 28

In this section you will continue your study of abbreviated words. You will also learn a number of new word beginnings and endings.

Abbreviation

222. Abbreviated Words. Practice these words:

-titute

substitute ______ **substitution** ______

institute ______ **institution** ______

constitute ______ **constitution** ______

-titude

aptitude ______ **gratitude** ______

latitude ______ ______

______ **attitude** ______

QUICK CHECK *(Read)*

223. Reading and Self-Dictation Practice

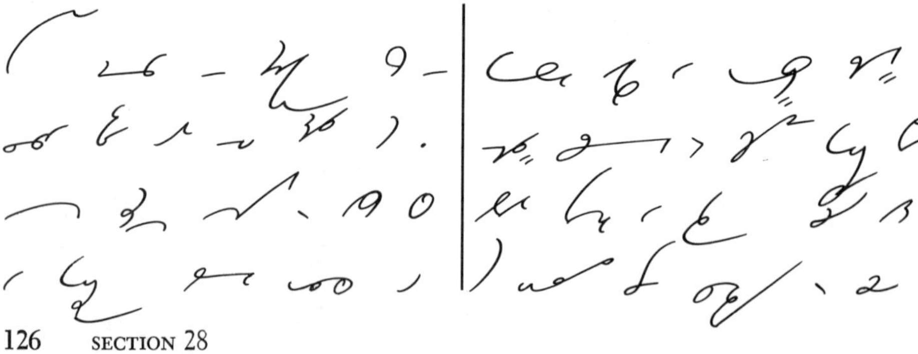

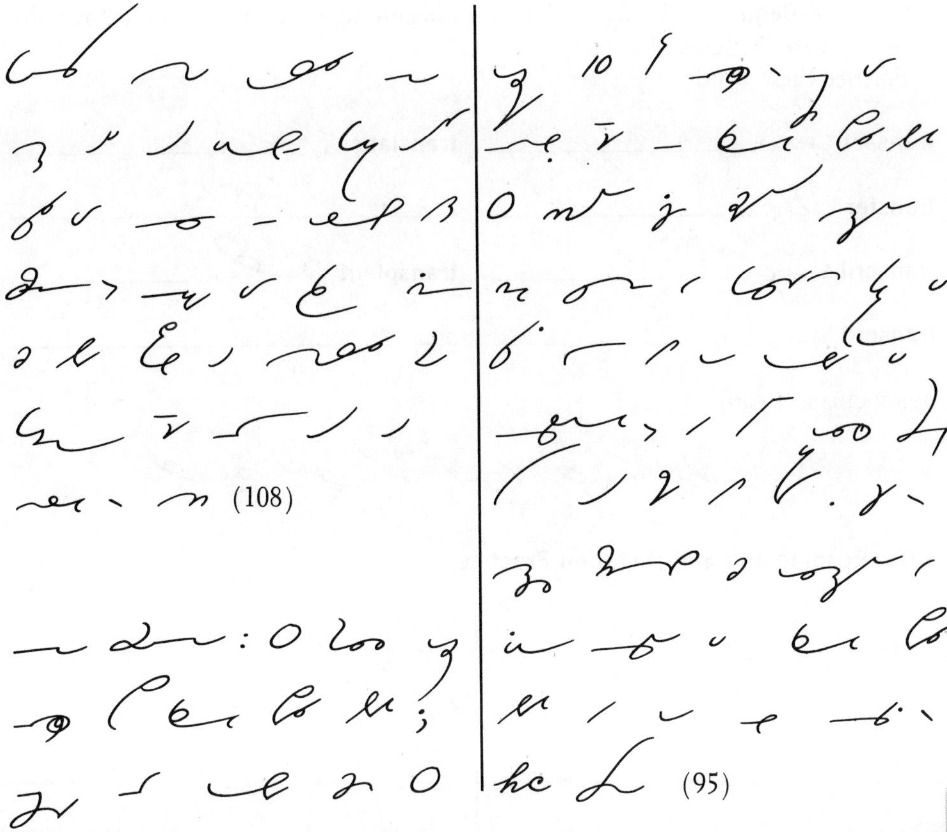

224. Miscellaneous Abbreviated Words. Many words which do not fall in groups such as those you have studied may be abbreviated by omitting their endings. **Abbreviation**

Practice these words:

convenient, convenience  ______

equivalent  ______

privilege  ______

memorandum ______

reluctance  ______

privileges  ______

QUICK CHECK *(Read)*

Trans-

225. Word Beginning Trans-. The word beginning *trans-* is represented by a disjoined *t* stroke. Note its placement.

Practice these words:

transact ____________ translate ____________

transfer ____________ ____________

transcribe ____________ transplant ____________

transmit ____________ ____________

QUICK CHECK *(Read)*

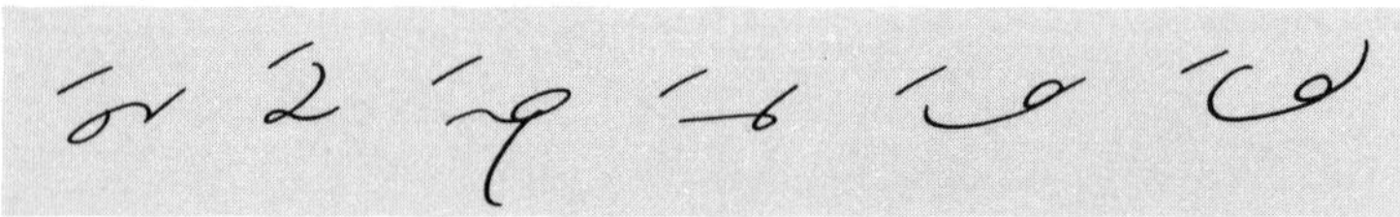

226. Reading and Self-Dictation Practice

Record 6 Side 2 Band 1

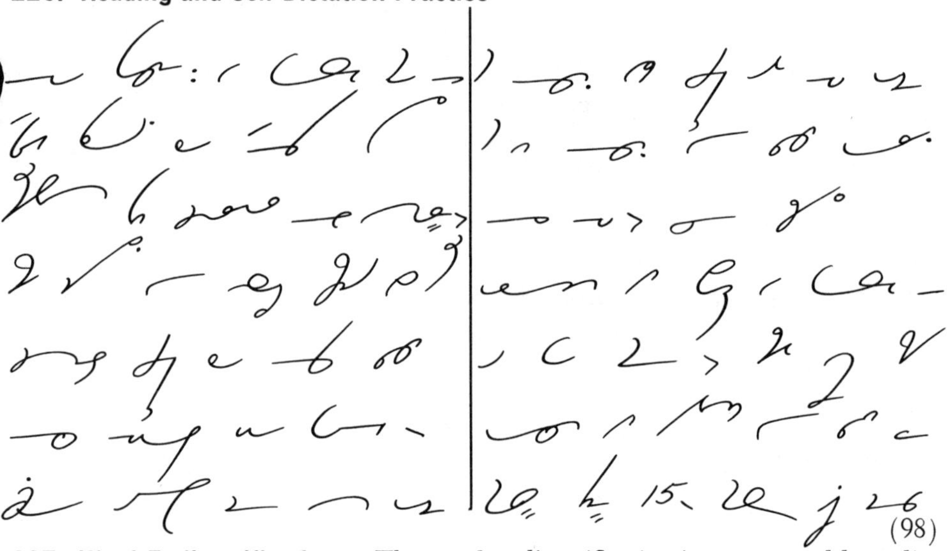

(98)

-ification

227. Word Ending -ification. The word ending *-ification* is represented by a disjoined *f* stroke. Note its placement.

Practice the following words:

classification ____________ notification ____________

____________ ____________

specification ____________ qualifications ____________

modification ____________ ____________

____________ justification ____________

QUICK CHECK (*Read*)

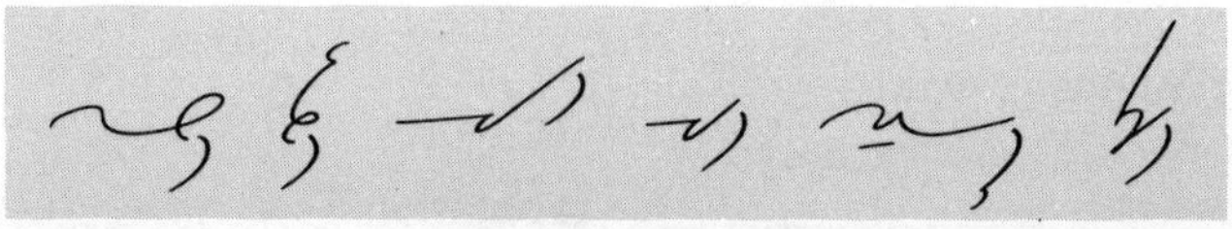

228. Reading and Self-Dictation Practice

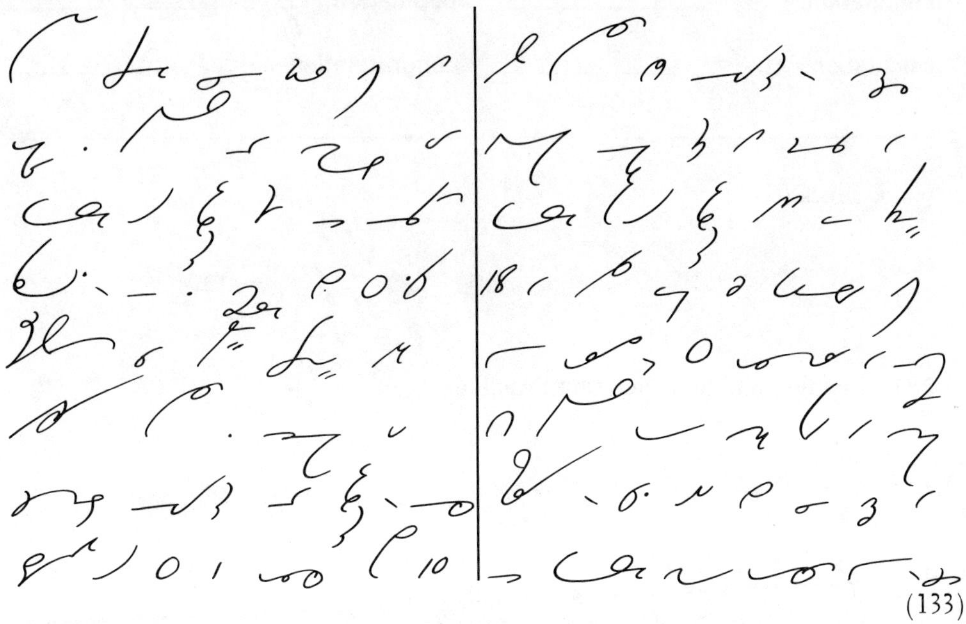

(133)

229. Word Ending -ulate.

-ulate

The word ending *-ulate* is represented by a disjoined oo hook.

Practice the following words:

accumulate ____________

tabulate  ____________

regulate  ____________

circulate 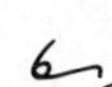 ____________

congratulate  ____________

stipulated  ____________

QUICK CHECK (*Read*)

-ulation

230. Word Ending -ulation. The word ending *-ulation* is represented by disjoined *oo-tion.*

Practice the following words:

circulation  ______	**tabulation**  ______
stimulation  ______	**population**  ______
calculation  ______	**congratulation**  ______
______	______

QUICK CHECK *(Read)*

231. Reading and Self-Dictation Practice

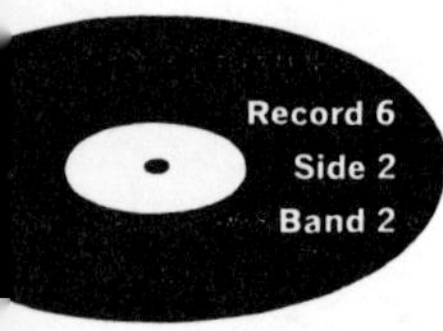

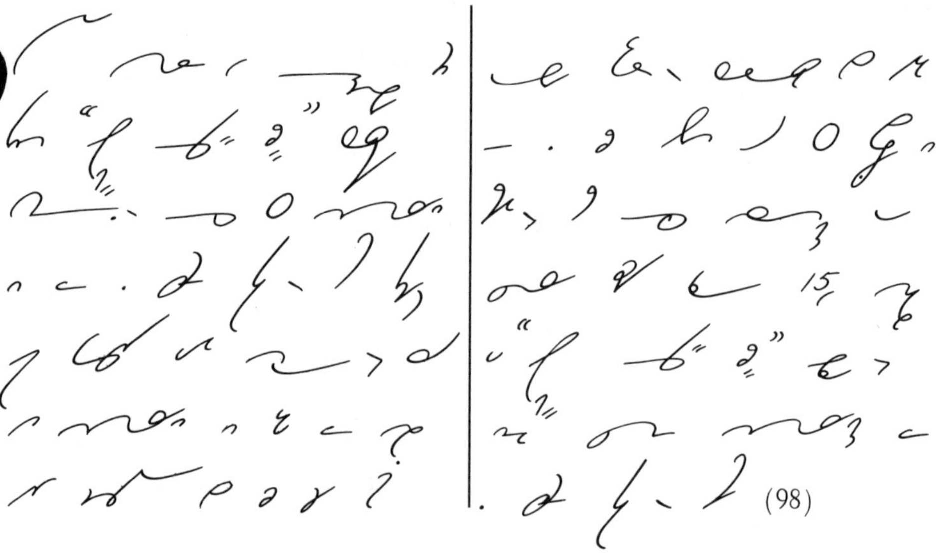

(98)

SELF-CHECK 28

Complete Self-Check 28 on your pad of self-checks. Then compare your answers with the key to Self-Check 28 in your Transcript.

RECORDED DICTATION

You can now take from dictation Record 6, Side 2, Band 1, which contains the material in Paragraph 226; and Band 2, which contains the material in Paragraph 231 dictated at 80 words a minute.

SECTION 29

In this section you will study a number of additional word beginnings and endings.

Post-

232. Word Beginning Post-. The word beginning *post-* is represented by a disjoined *p* stroke. It is placed slightly above the following character.

Practice these words:

postage ________ post office ________

postpone ________ postman ________

postmark ________ ________

________ postponed ________

QUICK CHECK *(Read)*

Super-

233. Word Beginning Super-. The word beginning *super-* is represented by a disjoined comma *s*. Notice its placement.

Practice these words:

supervise ________ superimpose ________

supervision ________ ________

supervisor ________ superintend ________

superhuman ________ ________

________ superior ________

QUICK CHECK *(Read)*

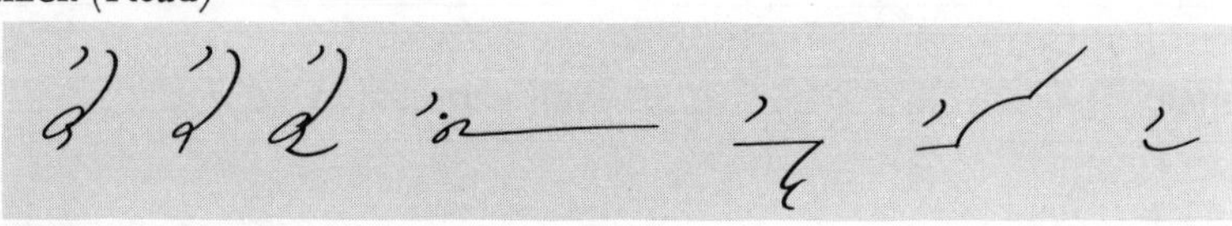

Record 6
Side 2
Band 3

234. Reading and Self-Dictation Practice

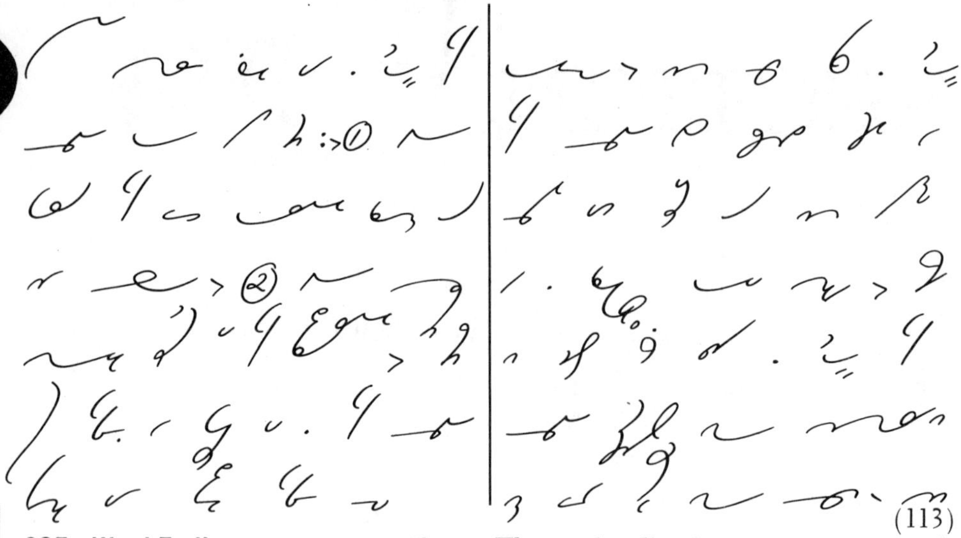

(113)

-sume

-sumption

235. Word Endings -sume, -sumption.

The word ending for *-sume* is represented by the shorthand strokes *s-m*; *-sumption*, by *s-m-tion*.

Practice the following words:

resume ______	**consumption** ______
consume ______	______
presume ______	**resumption** ______
assume ______	______

QUICK CHECK *(Read)*

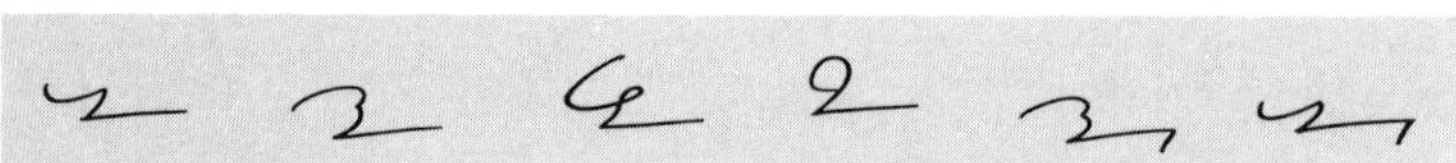

Self-

236. Word Beginning Self-.

The word beginning *self-* is represented by a disjoined left *s*.

Practice the following words:

self-confident ______	**self-reliant** ______
______	______
self-made ______	**self-assurance** ______
______	______
self-defense ______	**self-expression** ______
______	______

QUICK CHECK *(Read)*

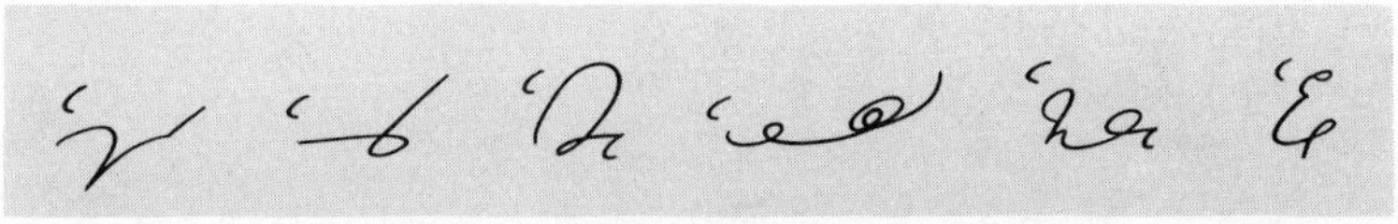

237. Word Beginning Circum-.

Circum-

The word beginning *circum-* is also represented by a disjoined left *s*.

Practice the following words:

circumstance  ______________ **circumstances**  ______________

circumstantial  ______________ **circumvent**  ______________

QUICK CHECK *(Read)*

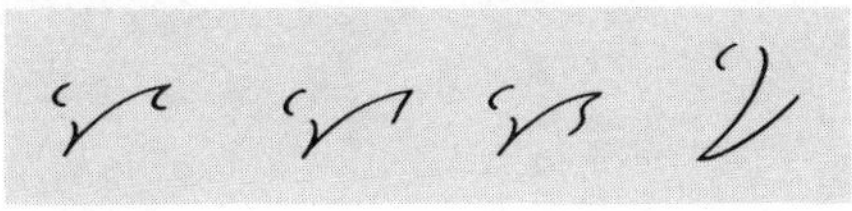

238. Reading and Self-Dictation Practice

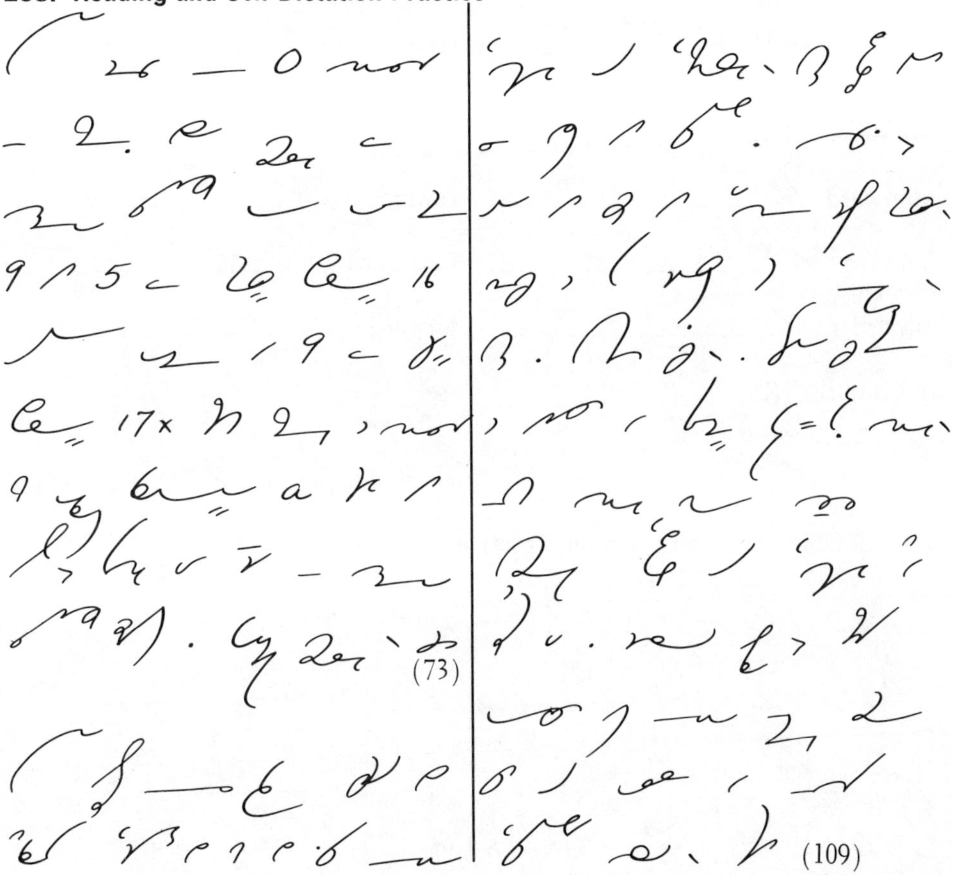

(73) (109)

-hood

-ward

239. Word Endings -hood, -ward. The word endings *-hood* and *-ward* are represented by a disjoined *d* stroke.

Practice these words:

-hood

neighborhood  **manhood** 

childhood  **brotherhood** 

motherhood  **likelihood** 

QUICK CHECK *(Read)*

-ward

afterward  **reward** 

outward  **backward** 

onward  **forward** 

QUICK CHECK *(Read)*

240. Reading and Self-Dictation Practice

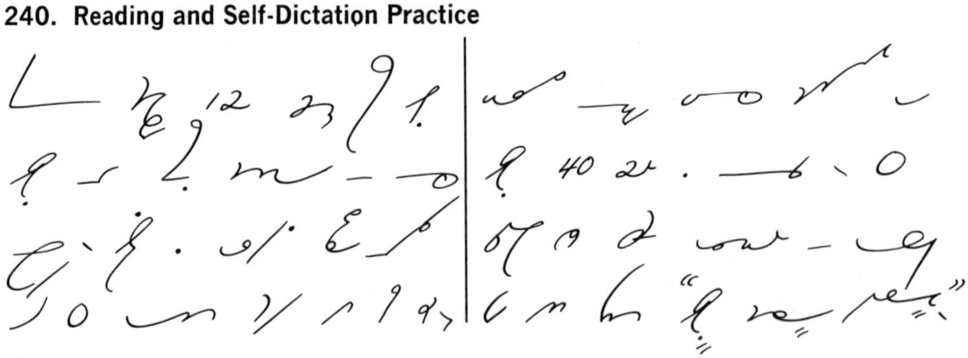

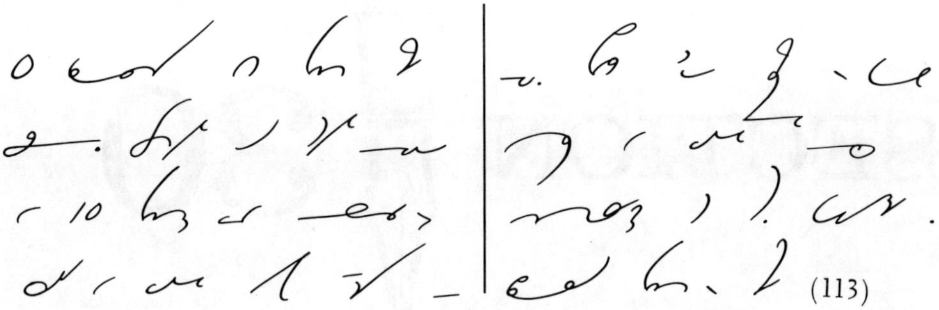

(113)

SELF-CHECK 29

Take inventory of your mastery of Section 29 by completing Self-Check 29 on your pad of self-checks. Compare your work with the key to Self-Check 29 in your Transcript.

RECORDED DICTATION

You can now take from dictation Record 6, Side 2, Band 3, which contains the material in Paragraph 234 dictated at 80 words a minute.

Use Bands 1 and 2 for warm-up and penmanship practice.

SECTION 30

This is the last section in which new shorthand principles are presented. After you have learned the abbreviating devices in this unit, you should be able to construct a readable outline for any word in the English language.

UL

241. Ul. The combination *ul* is represented by the *oo* hook when it precedes a forward or upward stroke.

Practice these words:

consult ______ **culminate** ______

result ______

insult ______ **multiply** ______

adult ______

QUICK CHECK *(Read)*

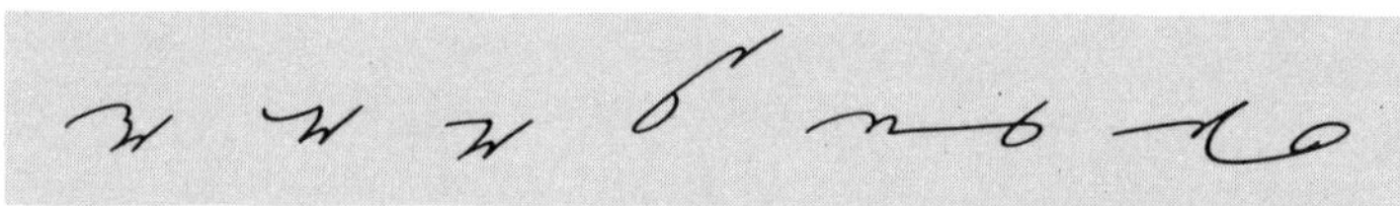

Amounts

242. Quantities and Amounts. Here are additional abbreviations for quantities and amounts.

Practice:

$500 ______ **a million** ______

5 million ______ **a dollar** ______

several dollars ______

5 billion ______ **4 pounds** ______

8 feet ______

Note: The *m* for *million* is written beside the figure as a positive distinction from *hundred,* in which the *n* is written underneath the figure.

QUICK CHECK *(Read)*

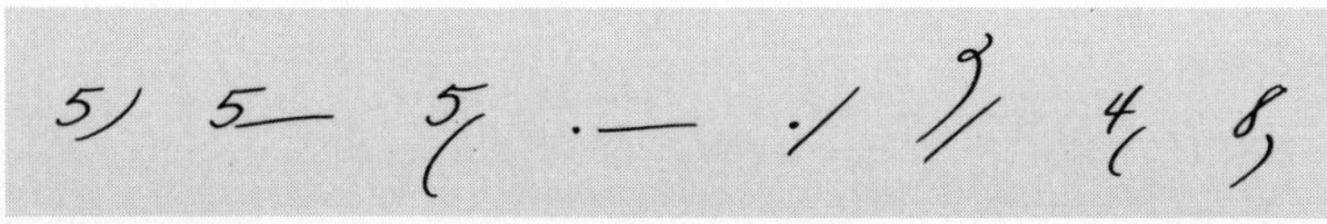

243. Reading and Self-Dictation Practice

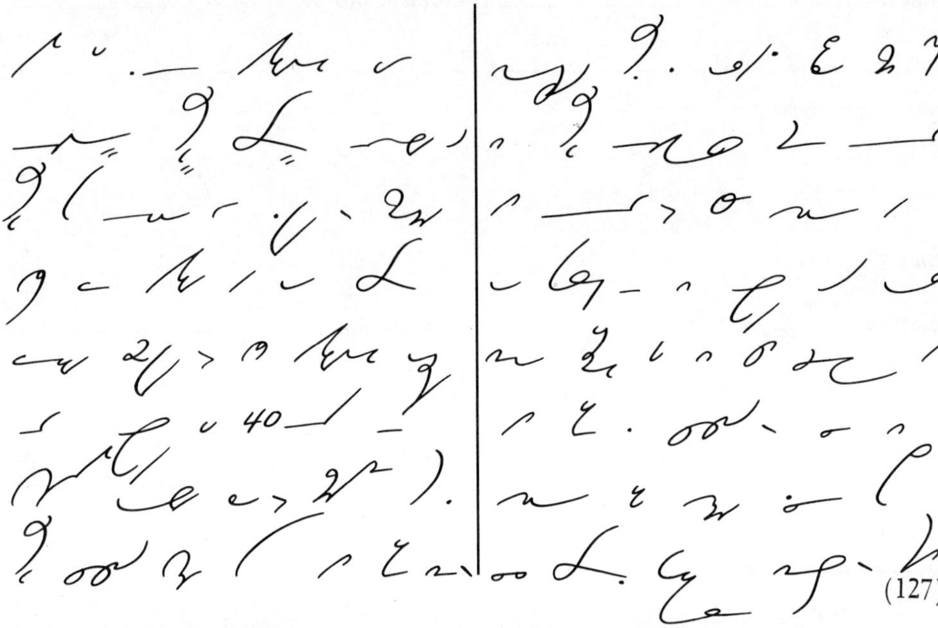

(127)

-gram

244. Word Ending -gram. The word ending *-gram* is represented by a disjoined g (gay) stroke. Note its placement.

Practice the following words:

telegram  ____________ **diagram**  ____________

programs  ____________ **cablegram**  ____________

QUICK CHECK *(Read)*

Electr-

Electric

245. Word Beginnings Electr-, Electric-. The word beginnings *electr-* and *electric-* are represented by a disjoined *el* stroke.

Practice the following words:

Electric-

electric ______________ electric wire ______________

electrical ______________ electric motor ______________

QUICK CHECK *(Read)*

Electr-

electronic ______________ electrician ______________

electricity ______________ electrotype ______________

QUICK CHECK *(Read)*

Compounds

246. Compounds. Most compound words are formed simply by joining the outlines for the words that make up the compounds. In some words, however, it is helpful to modify the outline for one of the words in order to obtain a facile joining.

Practice the following compounds:

anyhow ______________ notwithstanding ______________

anywhere ______________

anybody ______________ however ______________

within ______________ worthwhile ______________

withstand ______________ someone ______________

QUICK CHECK *(Read)*

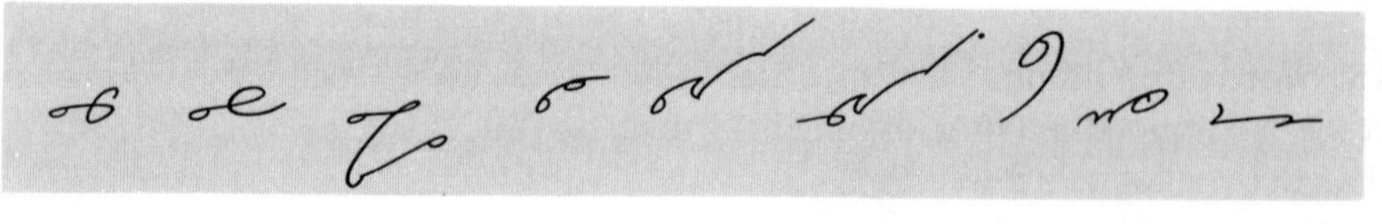

247. Reading and Self-Dictation Practice

Record 6 Side 2 Band 4

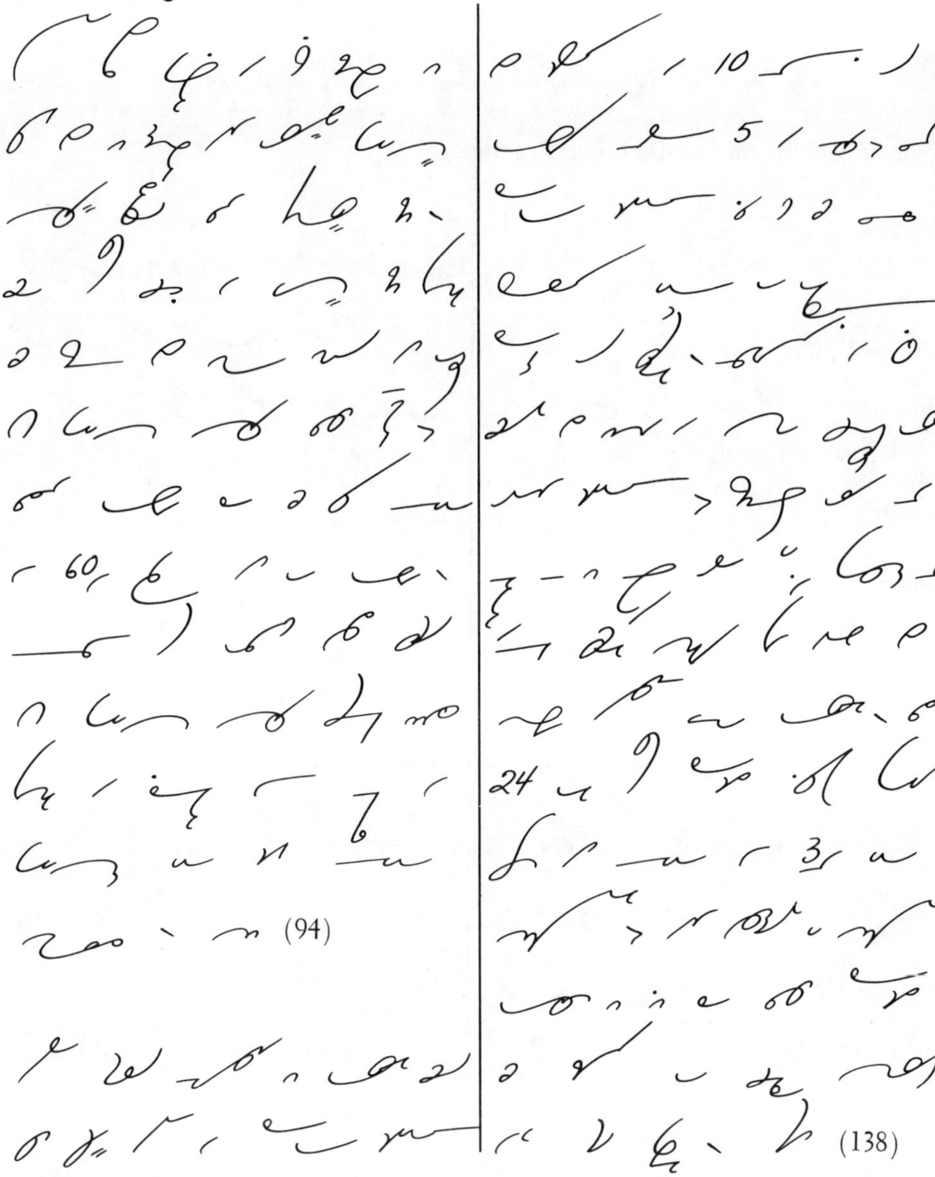

248. Intersection. Intersection—the writing of one character through another—is sometimes useful for special phrases. Intersection should be used only for phrases that occur quite frequently in the writing you do. These phrases are suggestive only.

Intersection

Practice the following:

a.m. ______________________ **vice versa** ______________________

p.m. ______________________ **Chamber of Commerce** ______________________

Associated Press ______________________ **school board** ______________________

QUICK CHECK *(Read)*

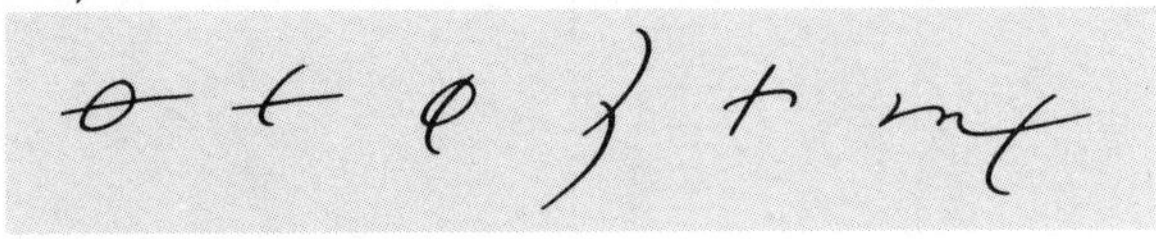

249. Reading and Self-Dictation Practice

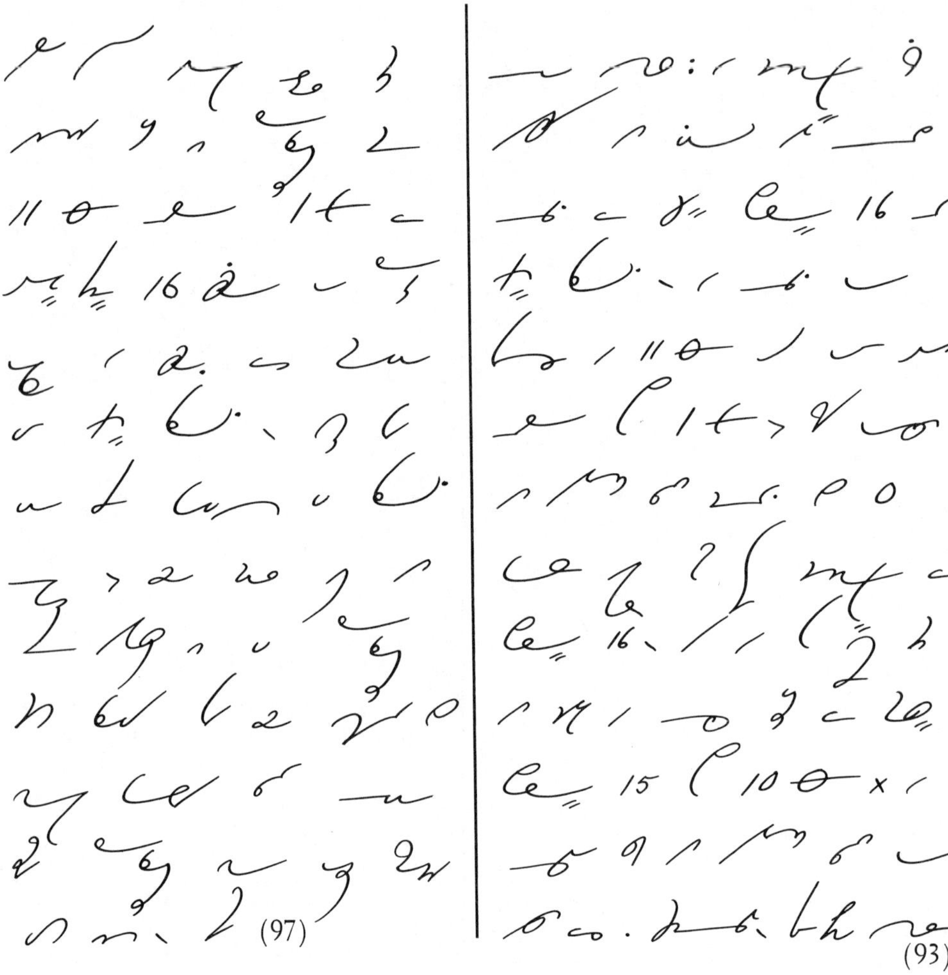

(97) (93)

SELF-CHECK 30

Check your mastery of the principles of Section 30. Complete Self-Check 30, and check it against the key in your Transcript.

RECORDED DICTATION

You are now ready to take from dictation Record 6, Side 2, Band 4, which contains the material in Paragraph 247 dictated at 80 words a minute.

Play the record from the beginning, using Bands 1, 2, and 3 for warm-up and penmanship practice.

Part Two

Review and Reinforcement

Review Sections

In Sections 1-30 you studied all the shorthand strokes and word-building principles that you need in order to be able to construct a legible shorthand outline for any word in the language. You are now familiar with the shorthand alphabet and the abbreviating devices such as brief forms, word beginnings and endings, and phrases that will be helpful in developing shorthand speed.

The review sections in Part Two of your textbook are designed to reinforce and strengthen your knowledge of the system and to develop your skill in the application of the principles to a constantly expanding vocabulary.

Each section of Part Two concentrates on a major division of Gregg Shorthand as follows:

REVIEW SECTION 1: *Brief Forms*
REVIEW SECTION 2: *Phrases*
REVIEW SECTION 3: *Joined Word Beginnings*
REVIEW SECTION 4: *Joined Word Endings*
REVIEW SECTION 5: *Disjoined Word Beginnings*
REVIEW SECTION 6: *Disjoined Word Endings*
REVIEW SECTION 7: *Blends*
REVIEW SECTION 8: *Omission of Vowels*
REVIEW SECTION 9: *Brief Forms*
REVIEW SECTION 10: *Phrases*

Each section consists of two parts. Part One is an Evolution Drill that develops your writing power by teaching you to construct shorthand outlines for new words from shorthand outlines that you already know. Part Two is a Reading and Self-Dictation Practice that is "packed" with illustrations of the major shorthand divisions listed above.

Recorded Dictation

Throughout your work with Sections 1-30, you had for home practice the six dictation records included in your kit. You can continue to use those records to advantage as you work with the review sections in Part Two. The dictation on these records will provide you with a fine review as well as give you an opportunity to improve your shorthand penmanship. From this point on, however, your shorthand speed development will depend to a considerable degree on the amount of dictation practice you do on new, ungraded business-letter material.

If you are attending class, you will undoubtedly receive a great deal of dictation from your instructor. If you can supplement this with outside-of-class dictation practice, your progress will quite naturally be so much more rapid.

The Gregg Division of the McGraw-Hill Book Company has made available a large selection of dictation records at all speeds. The material on these dictation records has been carefully selected, timed, and expertly dictated. If you would like complete information about the Gregg dictation records that are available, write to the Recordings and Supplies Department, McGraw-Hill Book Company, 330 West 42 Street, New York, New York 10036.

Your Practice Program for Part Two

Evolution Drills. In each Evolution Drill, you will be given the shorthand for the first item on a line. Using that outline as a guide, you are to fill in the shorthand outlines for the rest of the items on the line.

Examples

WORDS. In the Evolution Drill you will find:

hope  -s -ing -d

The completed drill will look like this:

hope  -s  -ing  -d 

WORD BEGINNINGS. In the Evolution Drill you will find:

*overcoat  -stay -bid -come

*All the items on the line are to be based on the underscored syllable, word, or phrase.

The completed drill will look like this:

overcoat  -stay  -bid  -come 

WORD ENDINGS. In the Evolution Drill you will find:

neatly  great- nice- fair-

The completed drill will look like this:

neatly  great-  nice-  fair- 

PHRASES. In the Evolution Drill you will find:

in the  -that -this -those

or

in the  on- at- with-

The completed drill will look like this:

in the  -that  -this  -those 

or

in *the*  on-  at-  with- 

Practice the Evolution Drills in this way:

1. Say aloud the shorthand word or phrase that introduces each drill.
2. Write the shorthand outlines for the remaining items on the line, saying each word or phrase aloud as you write.
3. Whenever you meet a form for which you cannot immediately construct an outline, make a stab at it and proceed at once to the next outline. Don't spend more than a few seconds on any outline.
4. After you have completed the drill, check your outlines with those in the Transcript.

Reading and Self-Dictation Practice. Continue to practice the Reading and Self-Dictation Practice exercises in Part Two as you practiced those in Part One; that is,

1. Read the shorthand, referring to the Transcript whenever you cannot read an outline.
2. Make a shorthand copy of the material.

Review Self-Checks

After you have completed your work on each review section, complete the corresponding self-check on your pad of self-checks. Check your answers with the key in the Transcript.

REVIEW SECTION 1

EVOLUTION DRILLS — Brief Forms

In the spaces provided, write the correct shorthand forms.

1. send	-s	-ing	-r
2. work	-s	-ed	-r
3. order	-s	-ing	-ly
4. great	-r	-ly	-ness
5. business	-s	-men	-man
6. manufacture	-ing	-r	-rs
7. present	-ly	-ing	-s
8. part	-ly	-s	-ed
9. advertise	-s	-ing	-ment
10. wish	-s	-ing	-ed
11. use	-s	-ing	-ful
12. suggest	-s	-ed	-tion
13. correspond	-s	-ing	-ed
14. out	-come	-side	-let
15. time	-s	-ing	-r
16. acknowledge	-s	-ment	-ments

The key to these drills appears on page 38 of the Transcript.

Reading and Self-Dictation Practice

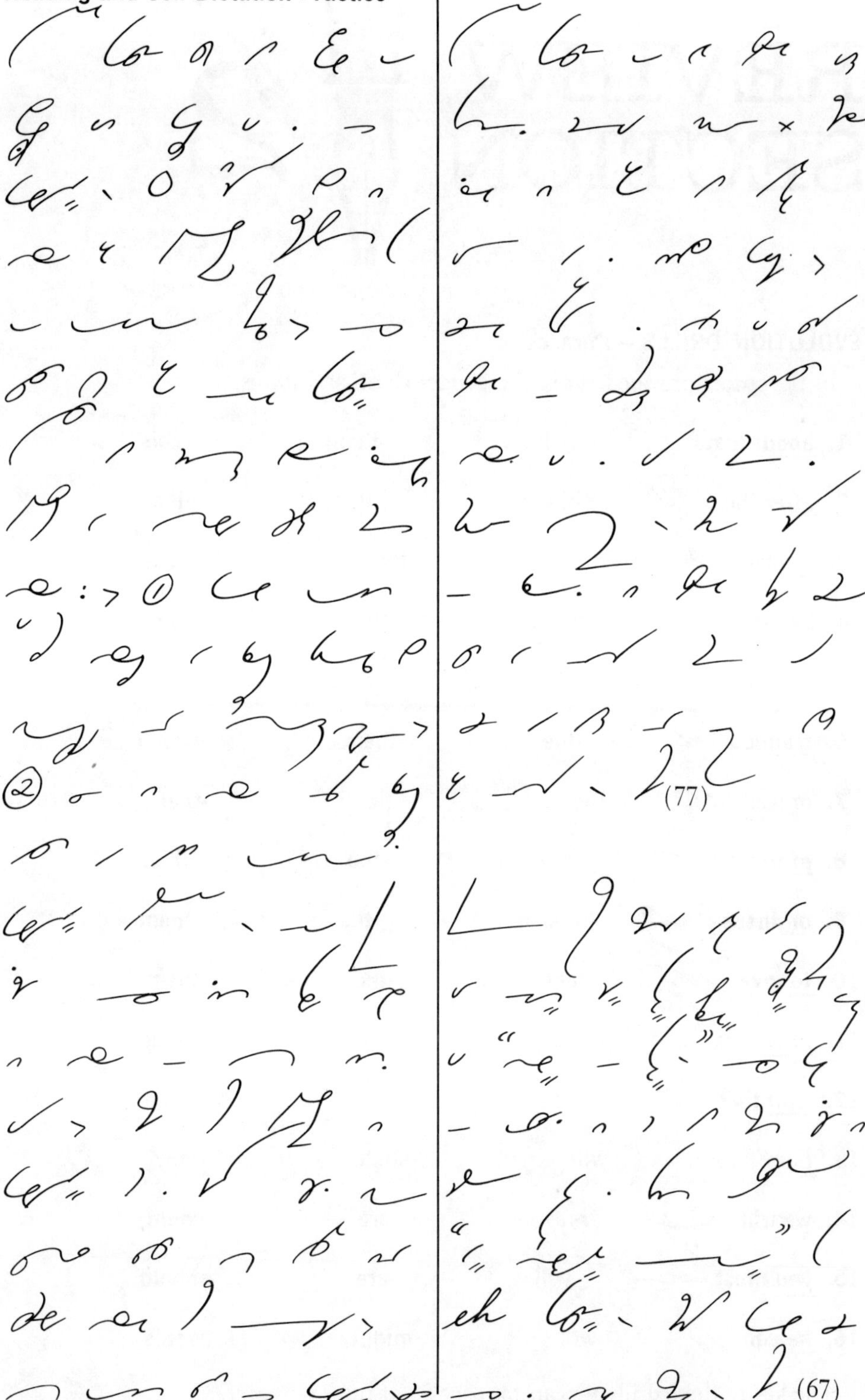

(77)

(142)

(67)

REVIEW SECTION 2

EVOLUTION DRILLS — Phrases

In the spaces provided, write the correct shorthand forms.

1. about that		-the	-them	-this
2. after the		-them	-this	-that
3. at this		-that	-these	-those
4. by that		-this	-them	-us
5. for them		-these	-those	-my
6. from our		-the	-them	-which
7. in it		-the	-this	-that
8. of them		-our	-the	-this
9. on these		-those	-the	-them
10. to give		-take	-the	-them
11. upon this		-that	-them	-our
12. with that		-them	-our	-the
13. I am		-will	-shall	-may
14. we will		-may	-are	-could
15. you must		-will	-are	-should
16. he can		-will	-might	-would

The key to these drills appears on page 38 of the Transcript.

Reading and Self-Dictation Practice

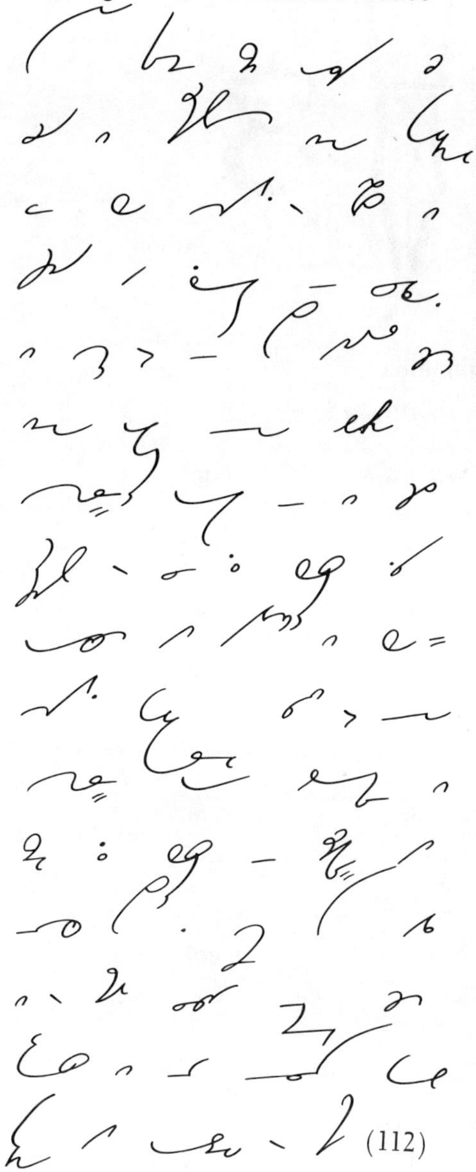

(112)

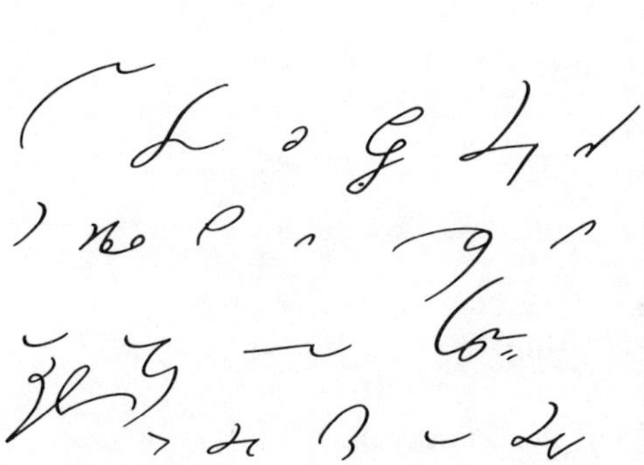

(103)

(84)

REVIEW SECTION 3

EVOLUTION DRILLS — Joined Word Beginnings

In the spaces provided, write the correct shorthand forms.

1.	alter		-s	-ed	-ation
2.	become		-ing	-s	-ingly
3.	concern		-s	-ed	-ing
4.	complete		-s	-ing	-d
5.	deliver		-s	-ed	-ery
6.	describe		-s	-ing	-d
7.	employ		-s	-ing	-ment
8.	engage		-s	-d	-ment
9.	intend		-s	-ing	-ed
10.	examine		-s	-r	-ation
11.	furnish		-s	-ed	-ings
12.	repel		-s	-ing	-ed
13.	unfold		-s	-ing	-ed
14.	subscribe		-s	-d	-r
15.	impress	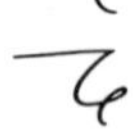	-ed	-ing	-s

The key to these drills appears on page 38 of the Transcript.

Reading and Self-Dictation Practice

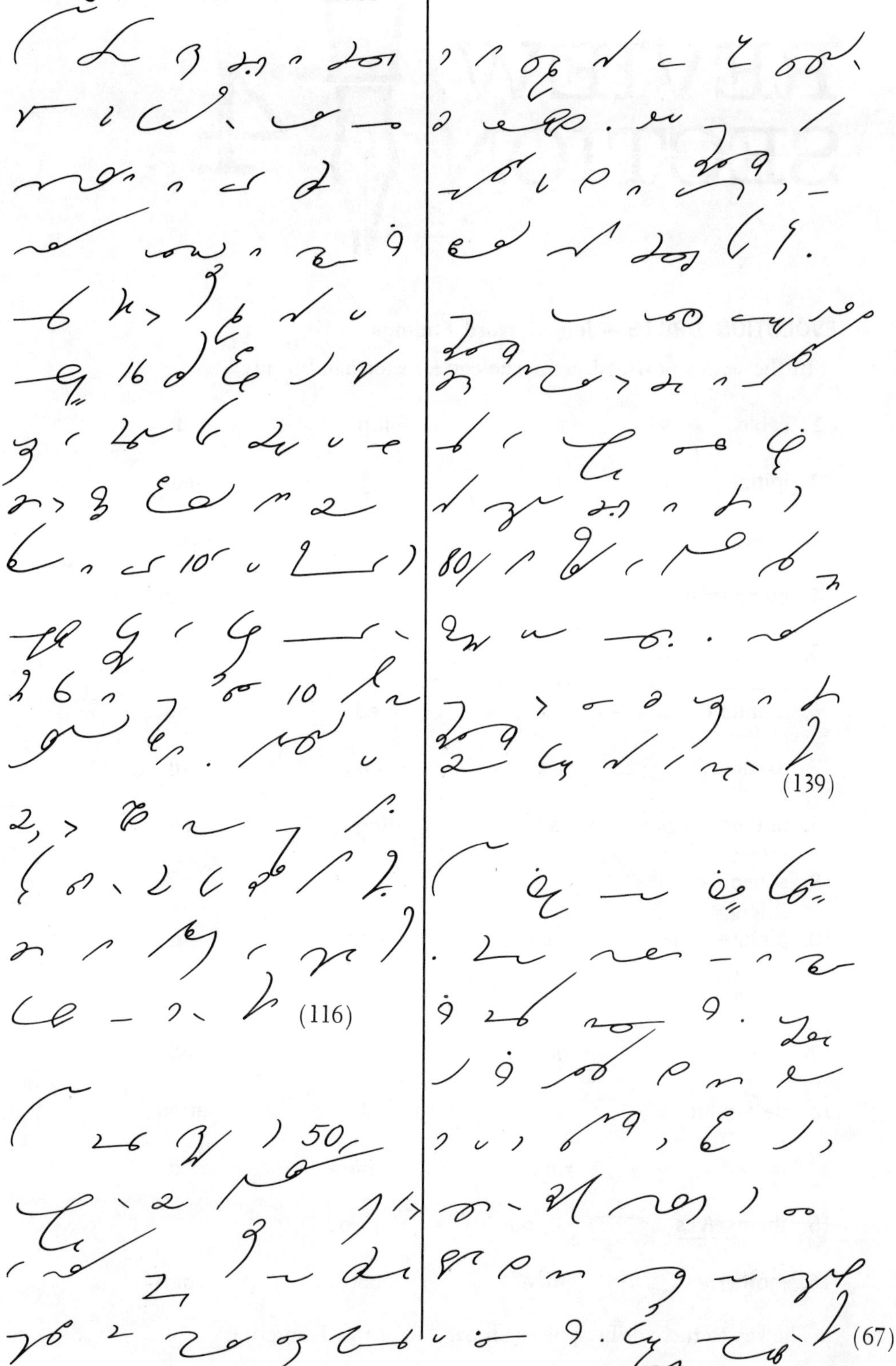

(116)

(139)

(67)

REVIEW SECTION 4

EVOLUTION DRILLS — Joined Word Endings

In the spaces provided, write the correct shorthand forms.

1. cable		-s	-ing	-d
2. initial		-s	-ing	-ed
3. care		-s	-d	-ful
4. compliment		-s	-ing	-ary
5. report		-s	-ed	-r
6. mention		-s	-ed	-ing
7. assume		-s	-ing	-d
8. bother		-s	-ing	-ed
9. schedule		-s	-ing	-d
10. picture		-s	-ing	-d
11. contain		-s	-d	-r
12. return		-s	-ing	-ed
13. determine	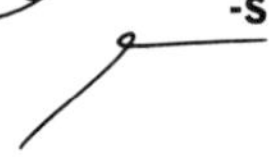	-s	-d	-ation
14. my*self*		your-	him-	it-
15. them*selves*		our-	your-	
16. mother*ly*		nice-	bare-	part-

The key to these drills appears on page 38 of the Transcript.

Reading and Self-Dictation Practice

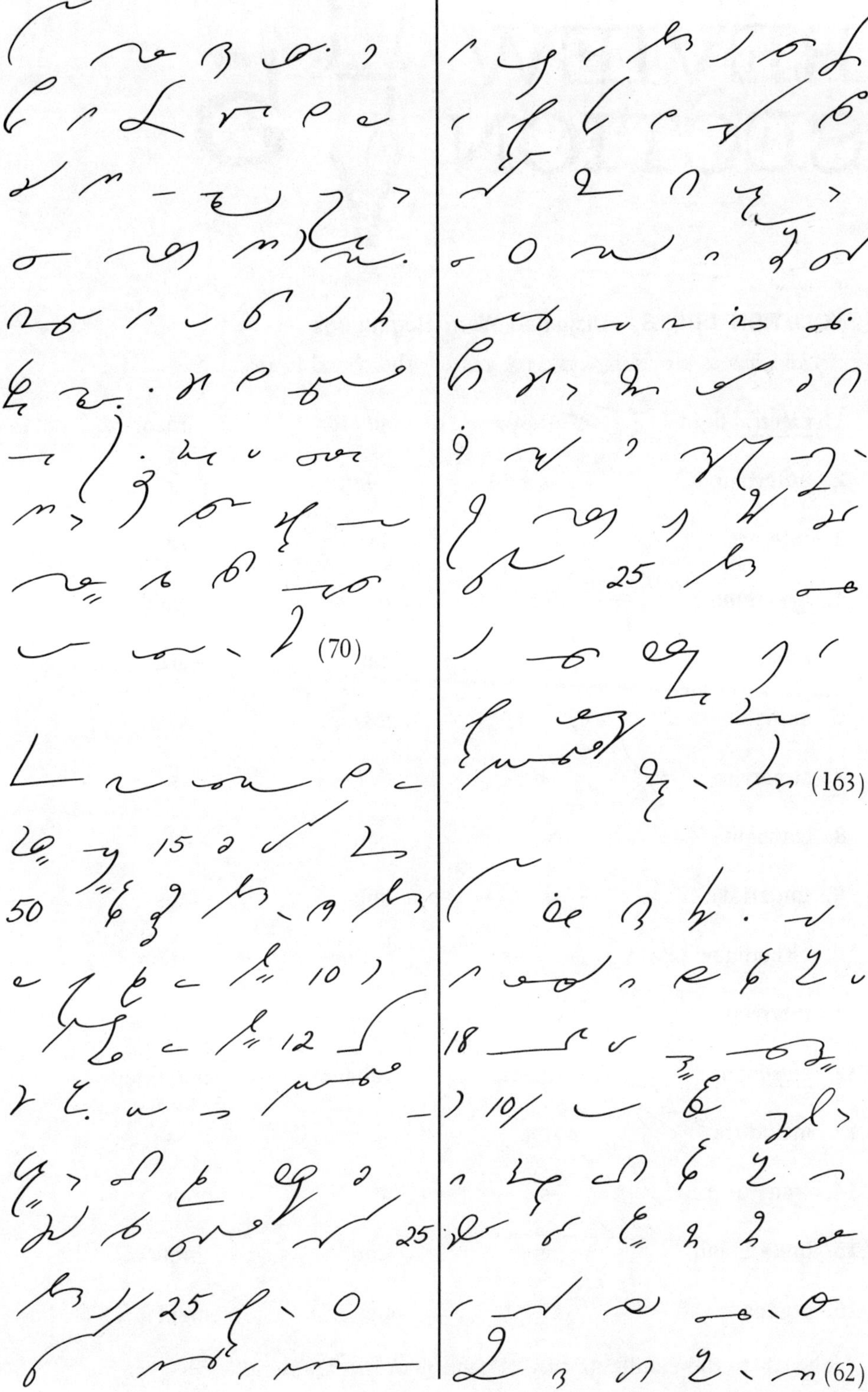

REVIEW SECTION 5

EVOLUTION DRILLS — Disjoined Word Beginnings

In the spaces provided, write the correct shorthand forms.

1. *electric* light	 -fan	-motor	-razor
2. entertain		-s	-ing	-r
3. interest		-s	-ing	-ed
4. *over*come		-step	-throw	-paid
5. *post*al		-age	-man	-card
6. selfish		-ly	-ness	
7. supervise		-d	-r	-rs
8. transmit		-s	-ed	-al
9. undertake		-s	-ing	-ings
10. circumnavigate		-s	-ing	-ation
11. interrupt		-s	-ing	-ed
12. *self*-made		-confident	-reliant	-contented
13. introduce		-ing	-d	-s
14. transform		-s	-r	-ation
15. understand		-s	-ing	-ingly
16. postpone		-s	-ing	-ment

The key to these drills appears on page 39 of the Transcript.

Reading and Self-Dictation Practice

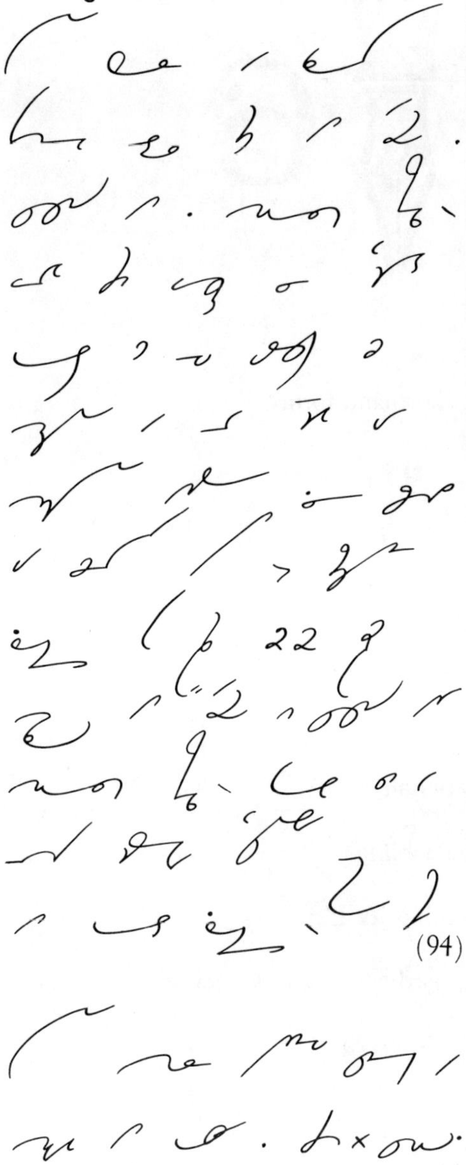

(94)

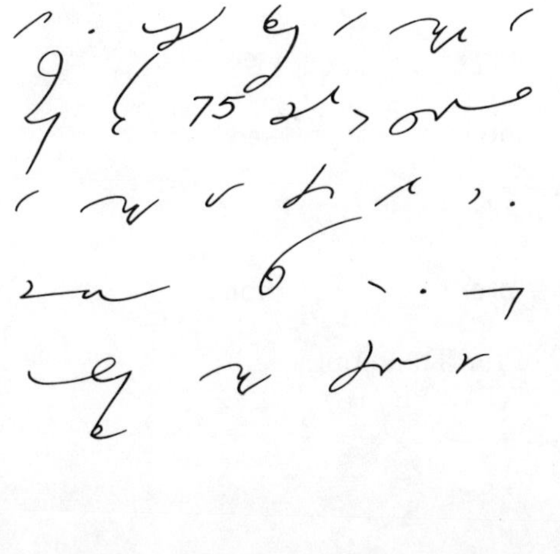

(159)

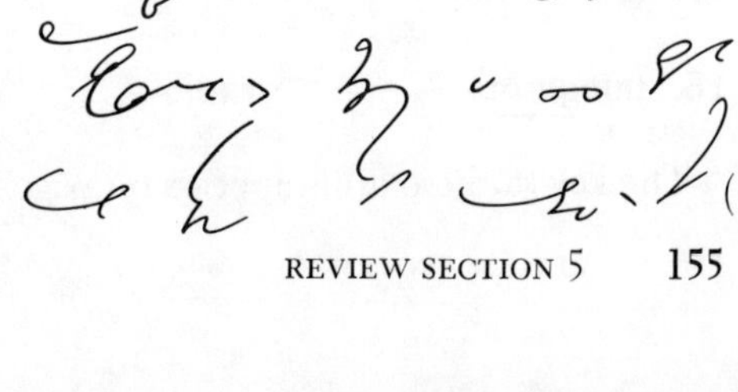

(41)

REVIEW SECTION 6

EVOLUTION DRILLS — Disjoined Word Endings

In the spaces provided, write the correct shorthand forms.

1. chemical	-s	-ly	
2. neighbor*hood*	parent-	child-	boy-
3. note	-s	-ation	-ification
4. surpris*ingly*	know-	will-	seem-
5. bear*ings*	find-	paint-	mail-
6. faculty	-s	penalty	-s
7. facility	-s	possibility	-s
8. majority	-s	minority	-s
9. steam*ship*	hard-	author-	fellow-
10. stipulate	-s	-ing	-d
11. tabulate	-s	-ing	-d
12. class	-s	-ical	-ification
13. forward	-s	-ing	-ed
14. reward	-s	-ing	-ed
15. logic	-ical	-ically	
16. tele*gram*	radio-	pro-	mono-

The key to these drills appears on page 39 of the Transcript.

Reading and Self-Dictation Practice

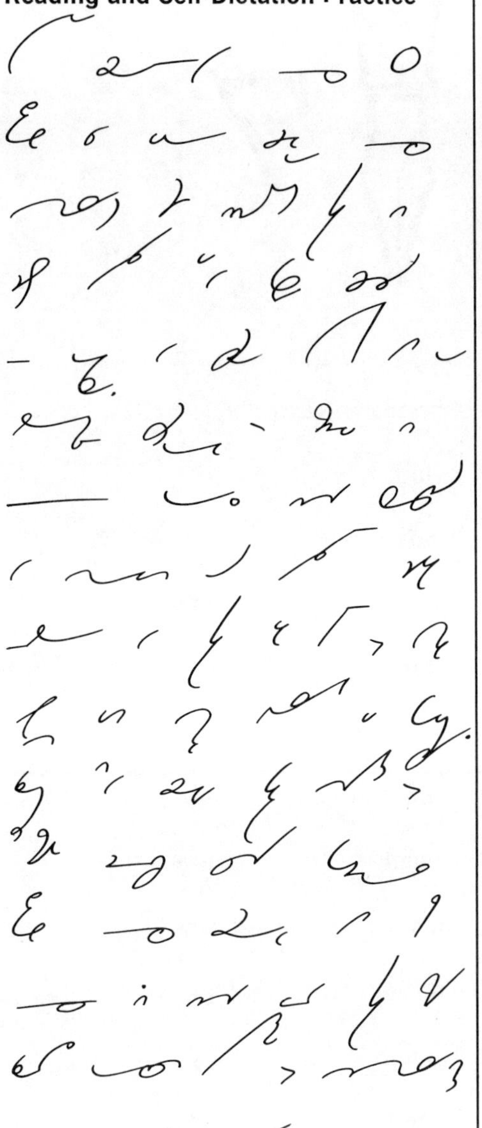

(114)

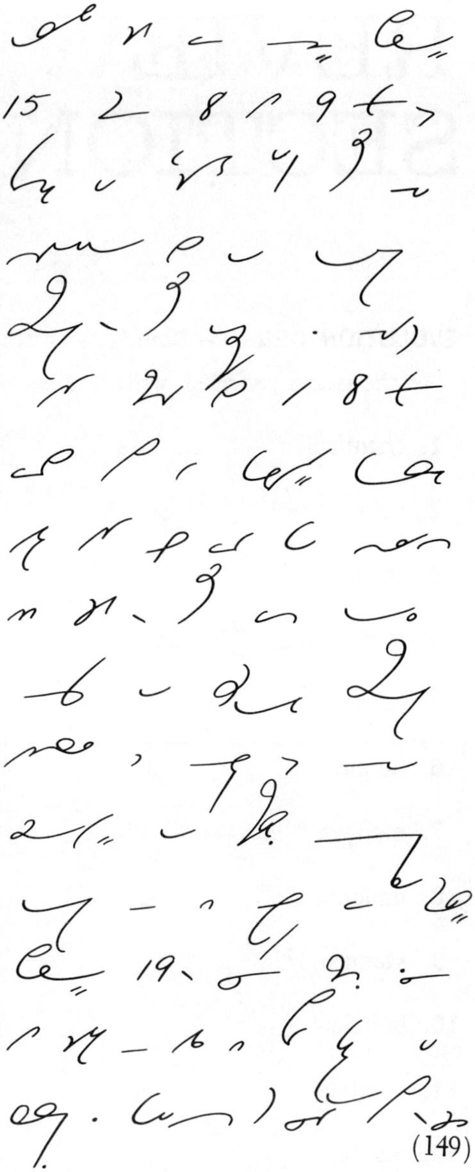

(149)

(37)

REVIEW SECTION 7

EVOLUTION DRILLS — Blends

In the spaces provided, write the correct shorthand forms.

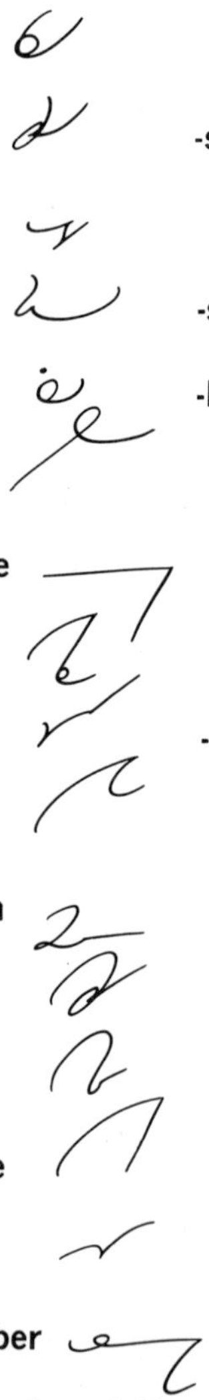

1. paint	-s	-ing	-r
2. find	-s	-ings	-r
3. resist	-s	-ing	-ed
4. fold	-s	-ing	-r
5. hard	-ly	-r	-ness
6. detail	-s	-ing	-ed
7. manage	-d	-ment	-ing
8. danger	-s	-ous	-ously
9. stand	-s	-ing	-ings
10. temper	-s	-ed	-ary
11. confirm	-s	-ation	-ed
12. divide	-s	-r	-d
13. devote	-s	-ing	-d
14. damage	-s	-ing	-d
15. contain	-s	-ing	-r
16. remember	-s	-ing	-ed

The key to these drills appears on page 39 of the Transcript.

Reading and Self-Dictation Practice

(92)

(96)

(71)

REVIEW SECTION 8

EVOLUTION DRILLS — Omission of Vowels

In the spaces provided, write the correct shorthand forms.

1. addition	-s	-al	-ally
2. renew	-s	-ing	-al
3. total	-s	-ing	-ed
4. come	in-	out-	be-
5. touch	-s	-ing	-ed
6. figure	-s	-ing	-d
7. event	-s	-ual	-ually
8. serious	-ly	previous	-ly
9. summarize	-d	-ing	-s
10. person	-s	-al	-ally
11. occur	-s	-ed	-ence
12. complimentar*y* → complimen*tary*	supplement-		element-
13. welcome	-s	-ing	-d
14. commission	-s	-ed	-ing
15. nation*al*	section-	ration-	fiction-
16. mak*er*	pack-	back-	stick-

The key to these drills appears on page 39 of the Transcript.

Reading and Self-Dictation Practice

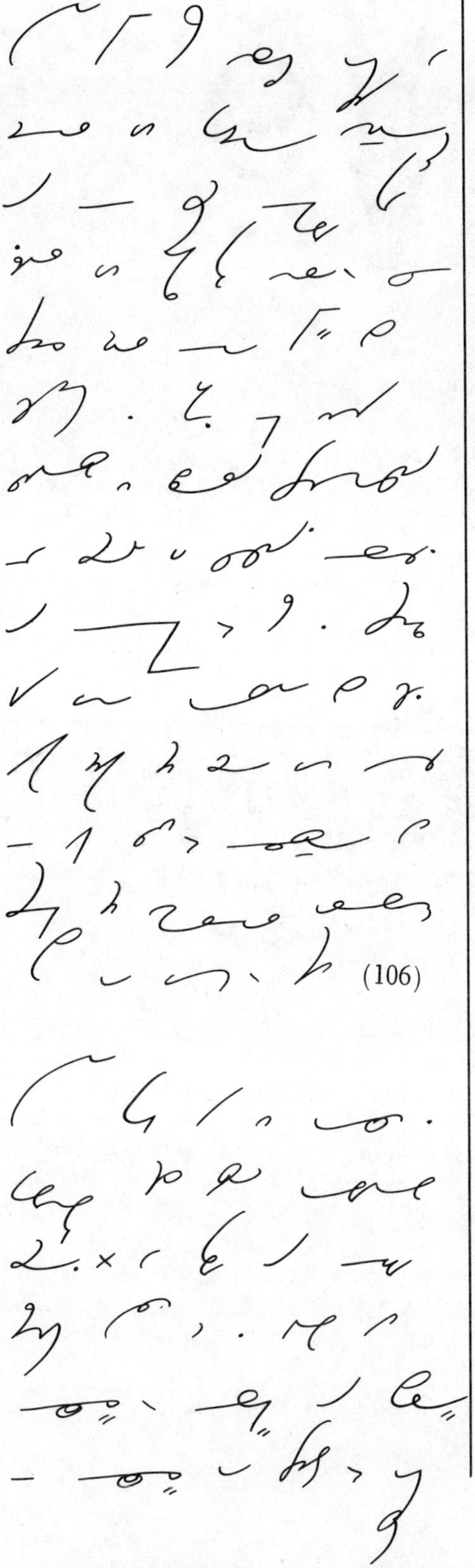

(106)

(96)

(78)

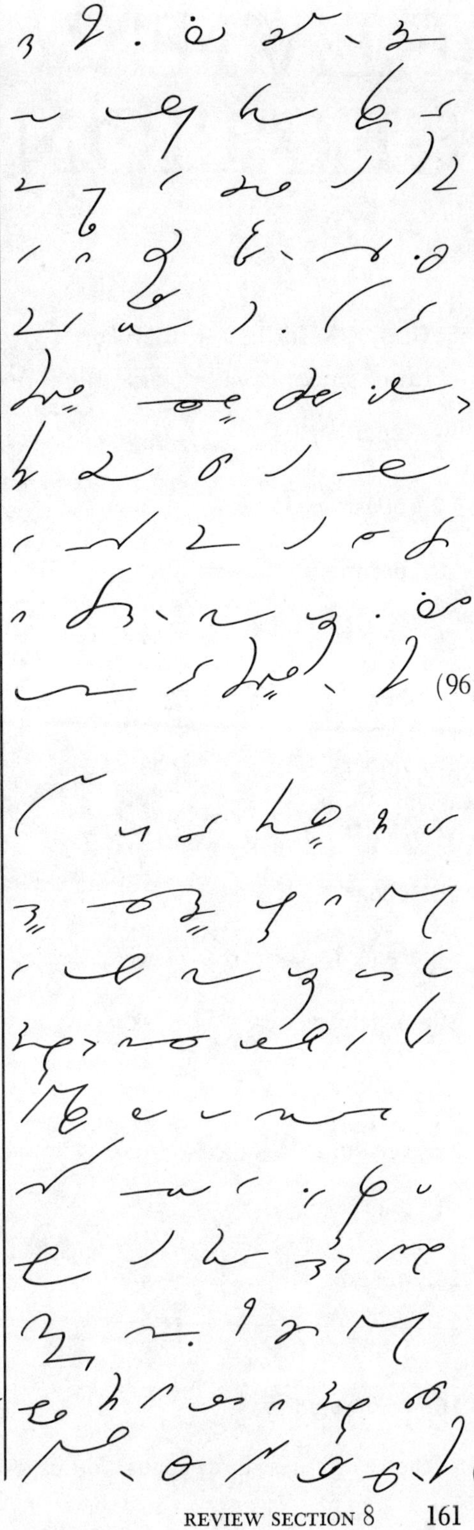

REVIEW SECTION 9

EVOLUTION DRILLS — Brief Forms

In the spaces provided, write the correct shorthand forms.

1. over	-come	-see	-paid
2. question	-s	-ble	-ed
3. progress	-s	-ed	-ive
4. satisfy	-s	-ing	-d
5. state	-s	-ing	-ment
6. under	-pay	-mine	-stand
7. request	-s	-ing	-ed
8. speak	-s	-ing	-r
9. regard	-s	-ed	-less
10. organize	-s	-ing	-ation
11. publish	-ed	-ing	-s
12. recognize	-s	-ing	-d
13. short	-r	-ly	-age
14. govern	-s	-r	-ment
15. object	-s	-ing	-ed
16. acknowledge	-s	-ing	-ment

The key to these drills appears on page 40 of the Transcript.

Reading and Self-Dictation Practice

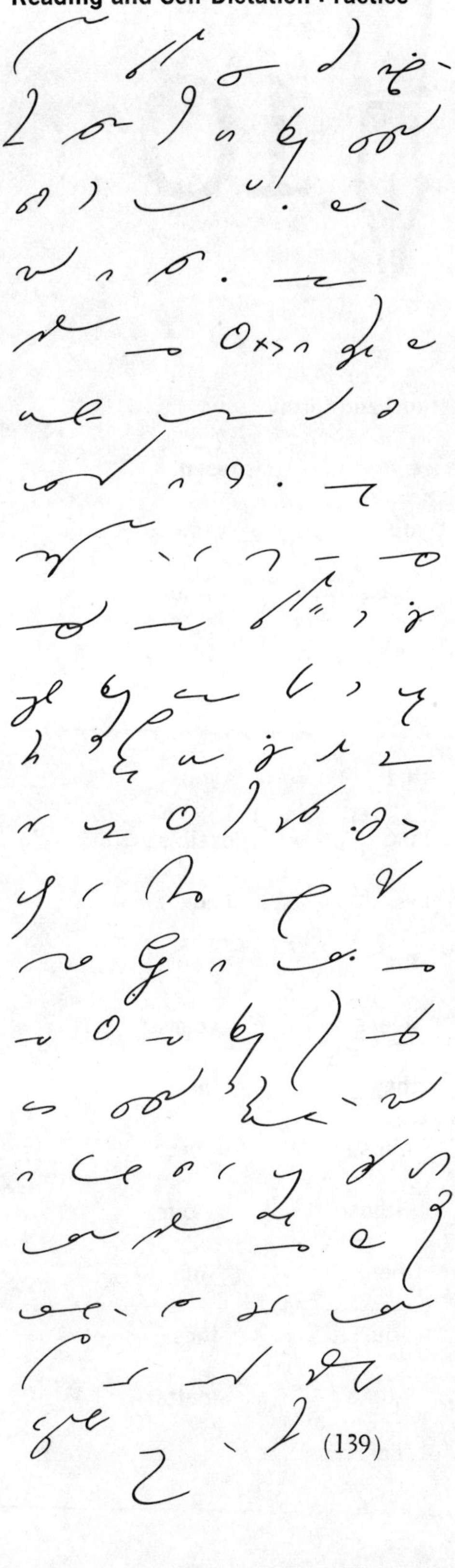

(139)

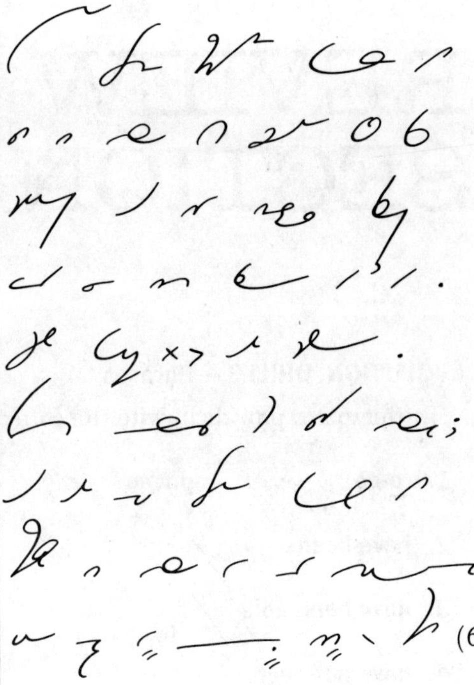

(64)

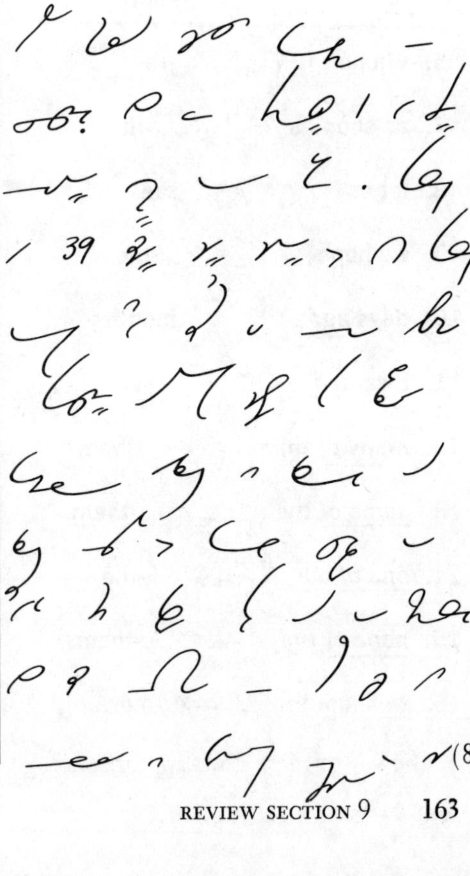

(80)

REVIEW SECTION 10

EVOLUTION DRILLS — Phrases

In the spaces provided, write the correct shorthand forms.

1. _to_ be  -put -have -present
2. have been  I- you- who-
3. have been able  I- you- who-
4. have not been  I- you- who-
5. _to_ me 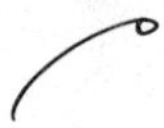 -know -make
6. I hope  -the -that -you
7. as soon as  -the -that -possible
8. let us  -see -have -know
9. we hope  -the -that -you
10. days _ago_  months- weeks- years-
11. I _wanted_  you- they- he-
12. _many of_ the  -them -those -these
13. _some of_ the  -them -those -our
14. _one of_ our  -the -them -our
15. _none of_ the  -them -our -these
16. _this_ month  -morning -time -matter

The key to these drills appears on page 40 of the Transcript.

Reading and Self-Dictation Practice

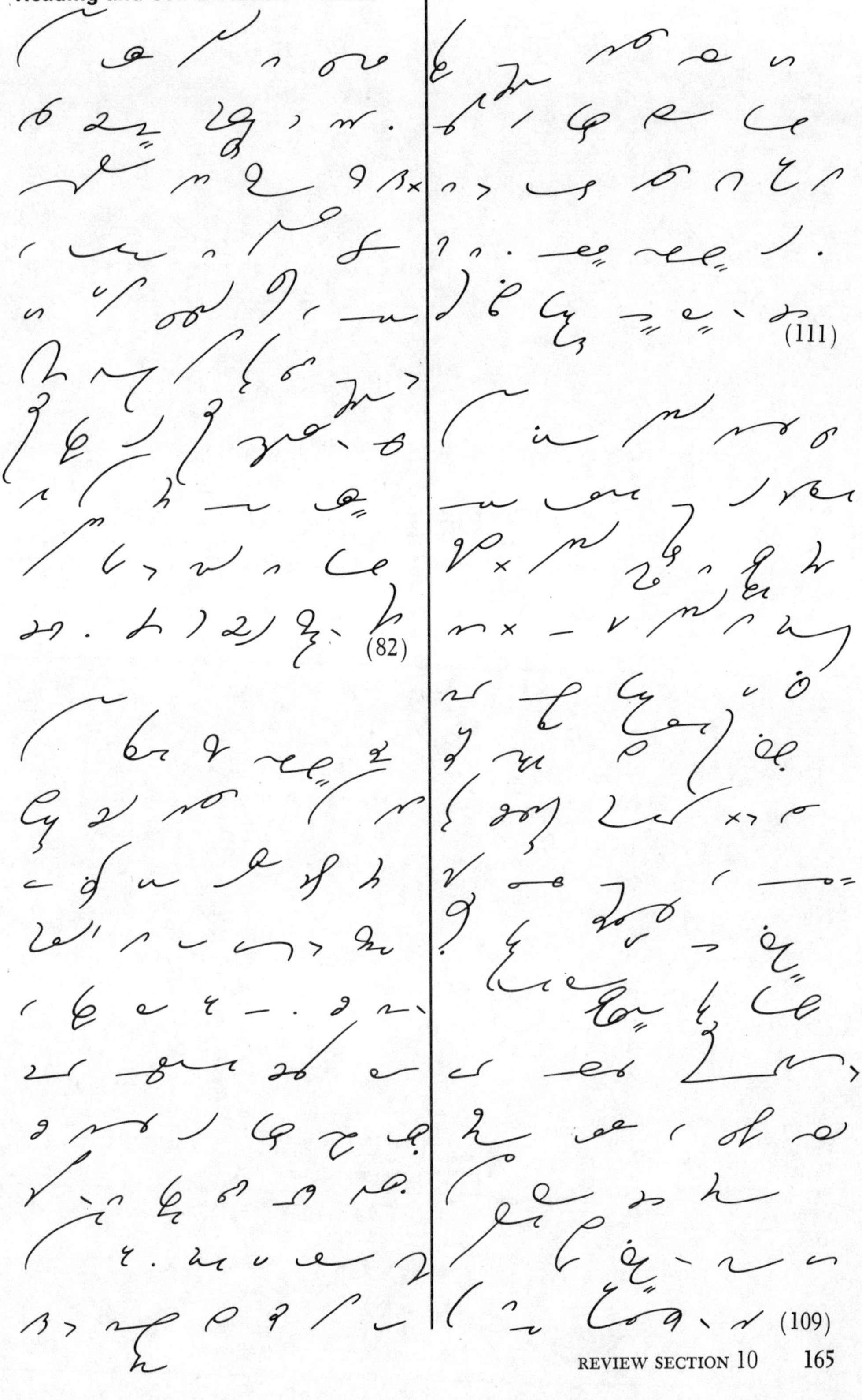

(82)

(111)

(109)

Appendix

States

The abbreviations in parentheses are those recommended by the Post Office Department.

Alabama (AL)
Alaska (AK)
Arizona (AZ)
Arkansas (AR)
California (CA)
Colorado (CO)
Connecticut (CT)
Delaware (DE)
Florida (FL)
Georgia (GA)
Hawaii (HI)
Idaho (ID)
Illinois (IL)
Indiana (IN)
Iowa (IA)
Kansas (KS)
Kentucky (KY)
Louisiana (LA)
Maine (ME)
Maryland (MD)
Massachusetts (MA)
Michigan (MI)
Minnesota (MN)
Mississippi (MS)
Missouri (MO)
Montana (MT)
Nebraska (NB)
Nevada (NV)
New Hampshire (NH)
New Jersey (NJ)
New Mexico (NM)
New York (NY)
North Carolina (NC)
North Dakota (ND)
Ohio (OH)
Oklahoma (OK)
Oregon (OR)
Pennsylvania (PA)
Rhode Island (RI)
South Carolina (SC)
South Dakota (SD)
Tennessee (TN)
Texas (TX)
Utah (UT)
Vermont (VT)
Virginia (VA)
Washington (WA)
West Virginia (WV)
Wisconsin (WI)
Wyoming (WY)

Principal Cities of the United States

Akron
Albany
Atlanta
Baltimore
Birmingham
Boston
Bridgeport
Buffalo
Cambridge
Camden
Canton
Charlotte
Chattanooga
Chicago
Cincinnati
Cleveland
Columbus
Dallas
Dayton
Denver
Des Moines
Detroit
Duluth

Elizabeth
Erie
Fall River
Flint
Fort Wayne
Fort Worth
Gary
Grand Rapids
Hartford
Houston
Indianapolis
Jacksonville
Jersey City
Kansas City
Knoxville
Long Beach
Los Angeles
Louisville
Lowell
Memphis
Miami
Milwaukee
Minneapolis

Nashville
Newark
New Bedford
New Haven
New Orleans
New York
Norfolk
Oakland
Oklahoma City
Omaha
Paterson
Peoria
Philadelphia
Pittsburgh
Portland
Providence
Reading
Richmond
Rochester
Sacramento
St. Louis
St. Paul
Salt Lake City

San Antonio	Spokane	Tulsa
San Diego	Springfield	Utica
San Francisco	Syracuse	Washington
Scranton	Tacoma	Wichita
Seattle	Tampa	Wilmington
Somerville	Toledo	Worcester
South Bend	Trenton	Yonkers

Common Geographical Abbreviations

America	England	Canada
American	English	Canadian
United States	Great Britain	Puerto Rico

Geographical Endings

In geographical endings, *-burg* is represented by *b; -ingham,* by a disjoined *m; -ington,* by a disjoined *ten* blend; *-ville,* by *v.*

-burg

-ingham

-ington

-ville

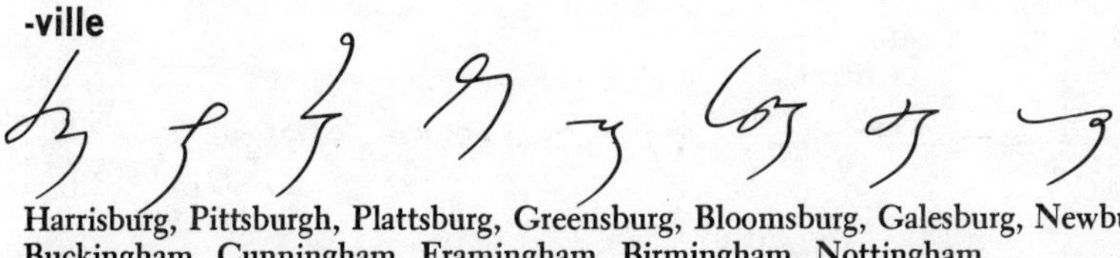

Harrisburg, Pittsburgh, Plattsburg, Greensburg, Bloomsburg, Galesburg, Newburgh.
Buckingham, Cunningham, Framingham, Birmingham, Nottingham.
Lexington, Washington, Wilmington, Burlington, Huntington.
Jacksonville, Nashville, Evansville, Danville, Knoxville, Brownsville, Zanesville, Louisville.

Index of Gregg Shorthand

In order to facilitate finding, this Index has been divided into six main sections – Alphabetic Characters, Brief Forms, General, Phrasing, Word Beginnings, Word Endings. The first figure refers to the section; the second refers to the paragraph.

INDEX OF BRIEF FORMS

The first figure refers to the section; the second refers to the paragraph.

Index to Material on Dictation Records

Record	Side	Band	Section	Para. No.	Speed
1	1	1	3	28	40
	1	2	4	35	
	2	1	5	38	
	2	2	5	40	
	2	3	5	42	
2	1	1	6	50	40
	1	2	7	55	
	2	1	8	63	
	2	2	9	66	
	2	3	10	77	
3	1	1	11	85	50
	1	2	12	94	
	1	3	13	100	
	2	1	14	114	
	2	2	15	117	
	2	3	15	117	
4	1	1	16	125	60
	1	2	16	131	
	1	3	17	137	
	2	1	18	143	
	2	2	19	157	
	2	3	20	161	
5	1	1	21	172	70
	1	2	22	175	
	1	3	22	178	
	2	1	23	183	
	2	2	24	193	
	2	3	25	203	
6	1	1	26	211	80
	1	2	26	214	
	1	3	27	219	
	1	4	27	221	
	2	1	28	226	
	2	2	28	231	
	2	3	29	234	
	2	4	30	247	

BRIEF FORMS OF GREGG SHORTHAND

IN ORDER OF PRESENTATION

The numbers refer to the sections of the text in which the brief forms are introduced

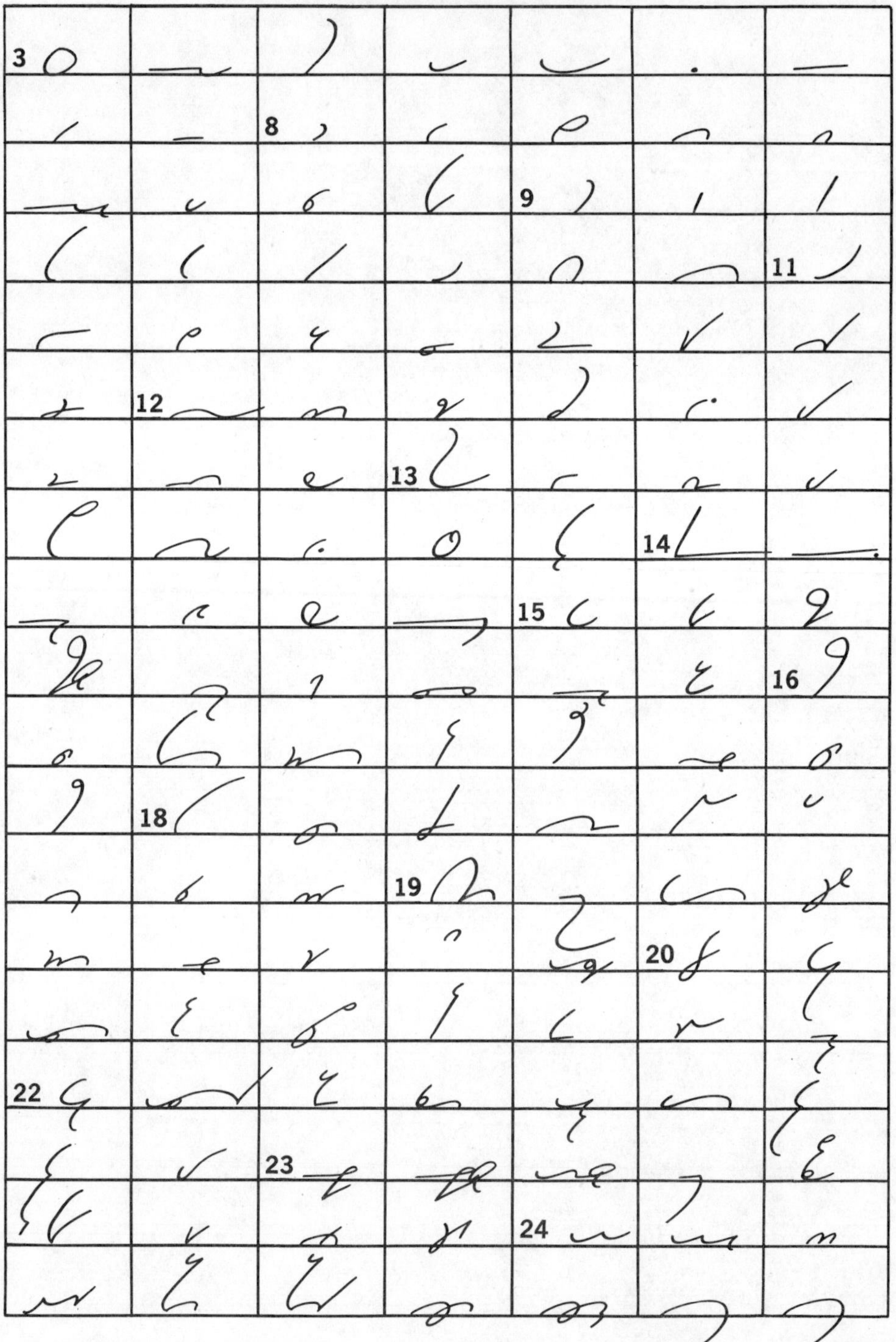